Run, It Might Be Somebody

Run, It Might Be Somebody

Ephraim Romesberg

Copyright © 2005 by Ephraim Romesberg.

Library of Congress Number: 2005907360
ISBN: Hardcover 1-59926-443-9
Softcover 1-59926-442-0

All rights reserved. No part of this book may be reproduced or transmitted in any form or by any means, electronic or mechanical, including photocopying, recording, or by any information storage and retrieval system, without permission in writing from the copyright owner.

This book was printed in the United States of America.

To order additional copies of this book, contact:
Xlibris Corporation
1-888-795-4274
www.Xlibris.com
Orders@Xlibris.com
29051

Contents

Part 1

Introduction 9

Chapter 1: Early Days on the Farm 13

Chapter 2: My Time in the Navy 101

Chapter 3: Hunting 121

Part 2

Introduction 139

Chapter 4: Married Man with Children Goes to College 141

Chapter 5: Living in Schenectady 149

Chapter 6: The Move to California 171

Chapter 7: Spain 175

Chapter 8: Vermont 189

Chapter 9: A Summer to Remember 195

Chapter 10: Limerick Station 205

Chapter 11: Back to San Jose 209

Chapter 12: Side Trip to Italy 211

Chapter 13: San Jose Finally Becomes Our Hometown 221

Chapter 14: Running 237

Part 1

Introduction

THE FIRST WORDS for this book were written in 1989 when I semiretired from General Electric's Nuclear Power Generation Division. I periodically wrote some notes since then but didn't get serious about putting them into some presentable form until more than fifteen years later. My initial intent then was to write about my experiences during my childhood days on the farm which I thought differed considerably from that of my children and grandchildren. I wanted them to know something about what it was like while growing up during the Depression on a small farm in the mountains of Pennsylvania. I completed that effort just last summer and the results have been included here in chapter 1 of part 1. Although chapter 1 of part 1 was all that I intended to write about when I first started, I got caught up in the effort and decided to add chapter 2, "My Time in the Navy," and chapter 3, "Hunting." I regarded the time period covered by the three chapters included in part 1 as the adolescent period of my life: My growing up years you might say.

In chapter 1, the childhood stories and anecdotes still remembered after more than half a century should not be taken as totally correct in every detail. They are based on my memory with a little help from a few of my brothers and sisters. Regardless, with the many changes that have taken place in the last fifty or more years, one could surely say that "things aren't like they used to be."

Changes that have taken place during my dad's lifetime and during my lifetime have been major. For example, my dad was born in 1878 in a log cabin. He grew up with only the bare necessities. Much like what we might picture the way Abe Lincoln grew up. Many changes had taken place by the time I was born in 1930 in the middle of the Great Depression. However, we still did not have running water in our house (except in the pantry where we had a hand pump and a sink), no bathrooms, no refrigerator, no radio or TV, no computers, no car, no telephone, no packaged food, very few if any supermarkets, no shopping malls, and no freeways or four-lane roads and no illegal drugs (except moonshine which my dad wouldn't allow in the house). Also we always had chores to do such as milking cows, feeding livestock, cleaning stables, helping in the kitchen, gardening, etc., so there was very little leisure time when compared to today. We had very few toys. We made up our own games which didn't require any equipment and sometimes didn't even have a name. We played kick the can, if we could find a can. At school we played prisoners base, mumbley peg, wassel hook, baseball with a multibladed pocket knife, softball with one mushy ball and one bat (no gloves), jump rope, hopscotch, marbles, and other untitled games which didn't require any equipment. We had snowball fights in the wintertime and we built small hiding places out of dead limbs and leaves in the spring and fall. We were poor but we didn't know it. We were taught to be thrifty. We wasted very little. Our mom used worn-out clothing to make throw rugs. Nothing, especially food, was ever wasted. Even the dish water, which contained some nutrients, was fed to the hogs. We were also taught to be responsible individuals by sharing the work and we were taught to respect, and even fear, authority. We never had time to get bored or get into trouble. Yes, on occasions we did get into trouble, but it was on a much lower scale than what is considered trouble today.

My time in the navy is also included in part 1 because my home was still officially the Pennsylvania farm until I left the navy and established residence in Connecticut.

Also included in part 1 are some of my hunting experiences many of which took place after I moved away from the farm. Those have been included because hunting was such an integral part of Pennsylvania life. Most of my hunting stories are presented in a humorous manner since I was never a very good hunter. Some readers may find this chapter of little interest, or perhaps worse, they may find it repulsive since hunting involves killing of animals. For those who are repulsed, please keep in mind that during the Depression, hunting provided a good portion of our diet, and helped to keep my family, as well as many others, off Roosevelt's Relief Program (now called Welfare). Aside from that, one could certainly argue that hunting as a sport (especially during the time period of this writing) would be far better than joining a gang or getting hooked on drugs.

After being discharged from the navy, Jean and I were married and we established residence in Connecticut, thus ending my life on the farm. Some of the remembered stories and anecdotes over the years since then have been included in the continuation of *Run, It Might Be Somebody* part 2. It spans over a half century and deals with life and the many successes and failures in raising a family while moving around the country in a rapidly changing world. It ends with the shy sickly boy now in his midseventies who can still finish a fifty-kilometer race even though his pace isn't what it used to be.

My three Wing grandchildren contributed to this document with sketches. Emily did the sketch of the two shy kids hiding in back of the straw stack on the cover page. Olivia did the nighttime grave scene in Uncle Milt's field included in the "Strange Stories" section and Graham did the sketch of me riding on our old horse Maude included in the "Farming without Modern Machines" section. My wife Jean and daughter Patricia provided editorial comments and suggestions.

Chapter 1

Early Days on the Farm
(1930-1948)

Location:

SHOWN ON THE following page is a photo taken sometime in the 1940s. It is the house where I was born. It looks bigger than it really is. It was, and is, located in Somerset County in southwestern Pennsylvania about sixty-five miles southeast of Pittsburgh in the upper reaches of the Appalachian mountain range. The nearest town of more than one thousand population is Somerset which is about twelve miles from the farm and today is located on the Pennsylvania turnpike. Flight 93, one of the September 11, 2001 hijacked planes, crashed near Somerset. Also, the rescue of the nine coal miners in 2002 took place only a few miles from Somerset. Other towns near by that might show up on a road map are Rockwood and Garrett. We went to high school in Rockwood. The farm was about midway in between these two towns. Getting more microscopic, the farm was between the two small mining towns of Wilson Creek (pronounced Crick) and Blackfield. These towns would usually not be found on road maps. Although they were once thriving little mining towns when I was a youngster, there is no longer any mining in either town. Only a few homes remain today in each. We went to grammar school in Wilson Creek.

The Old Homestead ~ 1940

The Old Romesberg Barn ~ 1916

The family reunion picture on the previous page is the only picture that I know of that shows the old barn pretty much as it was when I was born. My dad is in the back row just to the right of the tree in the background and he is holding my sister Luella. My mother is just to the left of the tree near the back and is holding my brother Merle. She is standing next to Mary Livingston Romesberg, my dad's mother. Other uncles and aunts and many close relatives and friends are there as well but as the years pass, fewer of them can be identified by name. The old barn was torn down in the fifties.

The Good Old Days:

Most of us probably look back to our childhood days as "The Good Old Days." And those typically were the days when times were really tough. How many times have you heard someone relate about the tough times when they were kids? What do you bet my kids will be telling their kids about how bad things were when they were young?

For sure, I heard a lot of stories about the "Good Old Days" and how tough things were. And I've told a few stories myself. But since I was the last of eleven kids, living conditions were better for me than they were for some of the older members of my family. In those pre-television, pre-radio, pre-electricity, pre-telephone, pre-cell phone, pre-indoor plumbing, pre-car, pre-plastic, pre-personal computers, pre-Velcro and pre-almost everything else that was either for pleasure or convenience, life was different. Sometimes I believe that in total, it might have been better. It was, in most ways, less complicated. In the following paragraphs, I've tried to recall some of the stories that I either heard, or lived myself. Some of them come from older brothers and sisters, or from my mother, or from my own dim memory. I can't vouch for the accuracy of them all but at this point in time, does it really matter. Besides, the picture that I try to paint is for the most part fairly accurate.

Family Members:

My Dad

His name was Ephraim (just like mine). Most people called him Eph. His family called him Pop or Pap. He was the eighth of twelve children of Levi and Mary Ann Livingston Romesberg. He was born on May 27, 1878, in a log cabin, which was located across the road from my uncle Milt's house which was just a stones throw from where

I was born. He died March 25, 1964. His father, Levi, was born October 31, 1840, and died March 20, 1889. When Levi died, he left a wife and twelve kids, including Pop who was only twelve, with no money, no income, and virtually no food. Pop had to quit school to help support the family. As a result, he never went past third grade. The photo below was taken about 1900.

Pop and Uncle Alex ~ 1900

He grew up, lived all his life, and died all in the same area where he was born. The log cabin was long gone by the time that I came along but another house was built near the log cabin and also near the house where I was born. My sister Luella remembers that when she was only about ten years old, a new cellar was dug and a new foundation built and the original house (not the log cabin) was moved onto the new foundation. We're not sure why it was moved. Merle changed the roof line and added more space in the attic. The result was the house shown earlier where I was born. It is still there today although no one in the family owns it or lives in it.

He eventually took over the home place, which according to my brother Floyd consisted of about 325 acres total, with about a hundred tillable.

Also, according to Floyd, Levi, who was a heavy drinker, had originally owned about 450 acres but sold off over a hundred acres probably due to a cash flow problem. Levi had seen value in land ownership primarily for use in farming and for the timber that could be sold off. There were others, such as a local coal baron named Zimmerman, who knew that the real value in the land lay hidden beneath the surface. When Pop took over ownership of the land, the treasure that lay beneath the surface had already been sold off. It appears that Zimmerman, perhaps by means of some seemingly shady deals, had acquired the coal rights for a pittance and had then sold them to the Somerset Coal Company in 1902, for $120,000 which at today's dollar value would amount to about $10,000,000. This information is based on recent research by my brother Floyd and our nephew Merle. Could it be that our grandfather had sold the farm coal rights for a few bottles of whiskey? Perhaps Pop knew this but never spoke of it. But one thing is for sure, Pop never drank. He saw what it did to his dad, so he never allowed alcohol in the house, except a small amount for medical reasons. In the meantime, Zimmerman was one of the richest men in Somerset County. To this day, you can still visit the Zimmerman mansion that sits atop a hill in Somerset.

During my lifetime, the necessary means of support for our family came from raising our own fruit and vegetables and meat (beef, pork, chickens) plus selling cream, milk and some butter, eggs, timber, and doing some outside work such as cutting brush for the electric company. Hunting game also provided a significant portion of the meat (i.e., deer, squirrels, rabbits, pheasants, and ground hogs)

Floyd says that Pop once told him that an abundant population of squirrels provided an additional meat supply during an especially hard winter during the Great Depression. During that winter, the squirrel population was especially high due to an abundant supply of acorns in the surrounding woods. The acorns were more abundant than usual due to climactic conditions that year. Pop may have regarded this as manna from heaven.

He was an active parent in grammar school activities. He often came to the one room schoolhouse to visit and to talk to the students. He was active in the Lutheran church and in politics and he was a regular writer of articles for local newspapers. He served as local fire warden and constable for many years. Mom would often tell stories about times when he was called he would leave his team of horses standing in the middle of the field to go fight a fire or attend to some other emergency. Some one of the boys or a neighbor would have to go retrieve the horses and bring them back to the barn.

Mom and Pop ~ 1960

I mentioned in the last paragraph that Pop was active in the Lutheran church. Someone told me that he read the bible more than thirty times during his life time. All of his kids, including me, at least started out as Lutherans. Many people during my lifetime assumed, or thought, by reason of my name, that I was Jewish. Later in life, I had acquaintances for as many as twenty years who assumed that I was Jewish. I was often a bit embarrassed for inadvertently deceiving them. When I was hired by Henry Stone at GE in Schenectady he took time to explain to me during my first day on the job the location of the Jewish synagogues and other related activities. I never told him that I wasn't Jewish but I am sure he found out soon enough. I have to confess that I never quite knew who I really was or what I really believed. I was born in Pennsylvania in the midst of the Amish people to Protestant parents, was given a Jewish name, was taught Sunday school in a Lutheran church, and later became a Catholic when I met and married Jean.

During his life, Pop worked at many jobs in addition to cutting timber and farming to support his large family. He worked at a spoke factory before I was born. They made spokes for wagon wheels. The factory was located deep in the woods adjacent to our farm. I went to the location as a small boy but there was nothing of it left. He also cut cordwood to be used for firewood. He cut ties and props for the coal mines. When I was in school I still remember him cutting brush along the power lines for the electric company. He also served as fire warden and constable and game warden at various times. Before he had a family, he played cornet in the Wilson Creek band.

He was fifty-two years old when I was born. He was fourteen years older than my mother was. I only remember one grandparent and that was my mother's father, George Swearman. All the other three had died before I was born. He seemed more like a grandfather to me. My brother, Wilbur, was more like a dad to me. Or you might say that I had several dads and several mothers since my sisters were always trying to baby me and spoil me. There are many good memories that I still have of my dad and I talk about some of those later.

My Mom

Her name was Mayme Susan Swearman (Bockus) Romesberg. Swearman was her maiden name and Bockus was her name after her first marriage before she met and married my dad. She was born September 23, 1892. She died October 26, 1965. She lived her early life in Summit Mills, Pennsylvania, in a small house on the hill in a picturesque area pretty much surrounded by Amish farmers. Her father was a coal miner. His name was George Swearman, and he was born August 30, 1861, and died October 23, 1938. He was the only grand parent that I ever knew personally and I only knew him for eight years. George was first married to Annie Fair and they had a baby but both wife and baby died in 1887. George married the second time in 1889 to Missouri Belle Tressler and they had thirteen children, three boys and ten girls. George worked most of his life in the coal mines. He had black lung disease when he died. In those days, there was no union so the miners had virtually no rights. Pay was very poor and there was no social security, no pension, no sick pay, no benefits, and no protection of any kind.

When my mother was very young, her father got sick and could not work. There was no money to buy food and she described periods when the only thing to eat in the house was bread and molasses. At that time, her three brothers had to go to work in the mines in place of their dad when the youngest was only eleven. During the winter months, they never saw the light of day except on Sunday. They left for work in the dark and came home in the dark. They had a short half-hour lunch break, which was spent inside the mine. They left a double set of tracks in the snow when they went to work. One set was their own footsteps; the other was the lunch bucket dragging in the snow.

Mom and Baby Mary ~ 1913

Mom completed grade school through the eighth grade but did not go to high school which in those days wasn't considered that important especially for women. When she was seventeen years old she married Frank Bockus. One year later, Frank was killed while working on the railroad. She was left with a small baby girl named Mary (see photo on previous page which was taken around 1913). The railroad paid her $100 total compensation for his death. She had to go to work as a domestic for an Amish family. Later she went to work for my grandmother, Mary Livingston Romesberg on Pop's farm. That's how she met and married Pop. In the meantime, her small baby Mary (my half sister) was raised by her deceased husband's family. In the coming years she and Pop had a total of ten kids. I was the last. When they saw me, they named me Ephraim Jr. after Pop. Years later, I asked why he waited until the fifth boy to use his name. He said that I looked like him. I never bought that. No baby looks like anyone at birth. The real reason, I believe, was as follows: As each son was born ahead of me, he wanted to use the name Ephraim but Mom objected because I don't think she liked the name. This happened after each of my four brothers was born. Finally they got to me and she agreed to name me Ephraim on one condition. No more kids. And so it was. I got the name Ephraim, and became the youngest (and last) of eleven children.

Siblings

This family photo on following page was taken in 1948. Back row from left to right is Merle, E. Jay, Paul, Floyd, and Wilbur. Front row is Helen, Elaine, Mary, Mom, Pop, Luella, and Betty.

So just for the record, this is a list of my siblings. Except for Mary, we were all born and grew up in that same little farm house shown earlier:

Mary Cathryn Bockus Ringer, born August 3, 1912, died of cancer April 25, 1986.

Elsie Luella Romesberg Ogle, born August 31, 1914.

Merle Elwood Romesberg, born November 19, 1915, died January 27, 2004, of congestive heart failure.

Wilbur George Romesberg, born July 28, 1917, died of Parkinson's disease May 10, 2000.

Della Jane Romesberg, born March 4, 1919, died of pneumonia and typhoid fever October 10, 1925, at age six.

Helen Devore Romesberg Forsythe born January 6, 1921, died of congestive heart failure May 1, 2000.

Paul Emerson Romesberg, born November 13, 1922.
Betty Louise Romesberg Clarke born December 2, 1923.
Lois Elaine Romesberg Johnson born March 11, 1925, died of Alzheimer's disease August 25, 2005.
Floyd Eugene Romesberg, born January 31, 1927.
Ephraim Jay Romesberg, born November 25, 1930.

Eph and Mayme Romesberg family ~ 1948

Mary

Mary was the oldest of my siblings. She was actually a half sister. Her father, my mother's first husband, was killed while working for the railroad when she was just a baby. She was raised by her father's parents so she did not live with the rest of the siblings. She was married and had a baby boy just seventeen days before I was born. She and my mother were pregnant at the same time. She had Bobby on November 8, 1930, and Mom had me on November 25, 1930. I got to know her quite well as I got older because

Bobby and I were pretty close. She lived near by and Bobby and I spent a lot of time together on the farm especially during the summer. We also went to high school together but not grammar school. They had another son named Bill. I never really knew Bill that well. He was a lot younger than Bobby. They had a daughter named Jean. But I was really closest to Bobby. His name comes up more later.

Mary ~ 1927

Luella

Luella was still at home when I was born but left to marry Woodrow Romesberg shortly after I was born. She says that when I was born she was embarrassed at school because Mom was having so many babies. She lived close by when I was small, and she had two beautiful little girls named Peggy and Joann. When Peggy was born, they took me to see her and I said in my baby speak, "Wally has a Wat." That was my way of saying, "Luella has a rat." Sorry Peggy, I really didn't mean that in a bad way. Woodrow died when I was only about three years old and left her with two little girls and very little money. The grandparents on both sides helped to take care of her and her girls. Later, she married John Ogle and they had a son named Johnny. They moved to Boswell and sometime later they moved to Erie. Peggy, Joann and Johnny were my good friends when we were small. Johnny and I spent a lot of time together on the farm but later in life, we didn't see much of each other. I saw Johnny in 1952 on a trip through Erie. But then he went off to college and then to a job away from home, and our paths didn't cross again until I went to Alaska in 2000, forty-eight years later.

Luella ~ 1932

Merle

Merle set a good example for the rest of the boys in the family. I saw him as a brother who could do just about anything. He was very handy around the house and the farm. He made some changes to the old house when I was very small. I remember he was always building or fixing something. He built a new spring house when he was still pretty young, maybe only about twenty or so. I sometimes served as his handy man when I was small. In 1942, he went into the army for a couple of years. When he came out, he married Dorothy Schafer and they moved into the Bittner place (a farm nearby). With Dorothy's help, he became a very successful dairy farmer. They had two sons and a daughter. His son, Merle Junior took over the farm when Merle retired. His son Larry currently works for his daughter Nancy who, along with her husband, owns and operates a number of BP gas stations.

Merle ~ 1945

Wilbur

Wilbur was like a dad to me. When I was small, he and my dog Bingo shared a bedroom. Luella tells a lot of stories about Wilbur. Some of those are covered later. He married Sue Enis who was an only child. As a result she and he inherited the old Simon Enos farm which was located about three miles on the other side of Rockwood. The farm had a sugar camp which Wilbur still operated when I was small and when I was in high school. Farming for Wilbur was hard, especially during the maple sugar season. Wilbur and Sue had four kids, two boys and two girls. His oldest son, George, died in about 1960 in a farm accident, and his wife died of cancer some years after that. His son, Wayne, and daughter, Shirley, live in the Rockwood area. His daughter, Sue, lives in Baltimore. He eventually sold the farm and moved into Rockwood. He had a hard life on the farm.

Wilbur ~ 1960

Della

This is one of the very few pictures in existence of Della. Actually, it is the only one that I ever remember seeing. I don't know when it was taken but I think she was at least five years old. She died when she was six years old and that was before I was born. She was named after Pop's sister (my aunt) Della. She is buried next to Mom and Pop and Uncle Alex in the Hauger Cemetery between Rockwood and Wilson Creek. There is a small lamb on her headstone. I remember seeing a small black purse that had belonged to her. I saw my mom sitting quietly in her bedroom one time just looking at the purse. During most of her short life, Della had eczema on her arms and legs. There was no known remedy to stop the itching at that time. It has been suggested in recent years that the problem may have been a form of allergy.

Della ~ 1924

Helen

As a kid, I don't remember a lot about Helen. I do remember that she had a steel guitar that she was learning to play. Pap played a cornet and he would sometimes corner her so they could play a duet. Helen would look for an escape route when she saw him coming. When I was still small, and sometime before the war, she went off to school to become a nurse. She later lived in Washington DC with her husband, Johnny Forsythe. They had two daughters named Judy and Patricia. In 1952, Johnny was killed in a car accident when he swerved to avoid hitting a dog, and Helen, just like Luella's situation earlier, was left with two small children. She later moved back to Somerset and was about to marry her friend Frank when he was killed in a coal mining accident. During this time period, she had an excellent reputation as a nurse while working at the state hospital. At one point she started a day care center for young children but it didn't work for her. It was an idea before it's time in Somerset. Judy later moved to Washington State and Helen and Patricia followed. While there, Patricia died (at age forty) and Helen and Judy had a falling out so Helen moved back to Somerset to an assisted living place. She had been bipolar all of her life and later suffered from congestive heart disease and dementia. Misfortune seemed to follow her throughout her life.

Helen

Paul

Next comes Paul. He was the biggest, the tallest, member of the family. I guess he was the only one that was over six feet. He spent a short period of time in the army during WWII and then came home and took over the home place. During my high school years, I spent a lot of time working on the farm with Paul. At that time Merle and Wilbur had moved away and Floyd was in college. We laughed a lot while working on the farm. Paul was always singing silly songs while we worked. Songs that he made up. I can still remember him singing the words, "Old Mandy Nider, she drank so much cider, she peed all over the floor." And he gave me the name Icky Blicky Tarpan Butch Petty Brown Skunkfat Lardy. The silly nonsense broke up the monotony of the work we sometimes had to do. He married Violet Schafer (Dorothy's sister) and they stayed at the old homestead to take over the farm. Violet was a kick. She was more fun then a barrel of monkeys. They had a whole bunch of kids and they named them Jimmy, Johnny, Joey, Jeffrey, Janie, Joy, and Janis. I hope I didn't miss any. After I left home to join the navy, Paul eventually decided that farming, especially on a small farm, wasn't his thing. He had always wanted to be a minister. So he followed his calling and he became a minister.

Paul ~ 1945

Betty

I think that I was closer to my sisters than my brothers when I was small. I think especially Betty because I always went crying to her if I was hurt or needed something. I know one time before I was old enough to go to school, I followed the other kids. When they got to school, there I was. Betty had to carry me all the way home while I bawled and screamed the whole way. Sometime after high school she went to Erie and lived with Luella. At one point, Betty had a boyfriend and his name was Speedy Bittner. He was a pilot of small planes and I can recall times when he would fly over our house and do a wing dip as his way of saying "Hi." One day he went swimming in a local river and he drowned. I know Betty was pretty broken up at the time. Later, she went to school in Philadelphia and became a dental hygienist. She married Ken Clarke who had a PhD in Chemistry and worked for DuPont Chemical Company. They lived for a few years in Wilmington, Delaware. They had two kids, Tiffany and Kevin. They later moved to Switzerland for a temporary assignment. They eventually made that a permanent assignment and they still live to this day (2005) in Geneva, Switzerland, with a summer home in Morgans which is in the foothills of the Alps. Tiffany became a pediatrician and lives in Pennsylvania. Kevin lives near his parents in Switzerland.

Betty

Elaine

As I grew older, I guess I was closest to Elaine. She was most like our mother. Elaine had a talent for singing and playing the piano. But unfortunately she was never able to break away from the farm and develop it. She had planned to go to Pittsburgh after high school and pursue a career in music. But unfortunately, her graduation from high school came at a time when she was needed at home. Our mother was not well at this time and she had to stay and become, in essence, the new mother. She had to sacrifice her own interest for the family. I didn't appreciate that then but I do now. I remember one Christmas when Mom was in the hospital and it was just Elaine, Paul, and Pop and I. We didn't really give each other presents. We realized Christmas Eve that we should give something for Elaine. The best we could do was to wrap a $5 bill up and put it on the tree. That was our present to Elaine. Elaine later married Wilbur Johnson, and they lived in Casselman, which is a small town near Rockwood. They had two kids, Ken and Sheryl. Ken became a lawyer and set up an office in Rockwood, and Sheryl married Roger Harbaugh and lives nearby. Wilbur died in 1981 and Elaine moved to Rockwood and lived in an apartment. She still played the piano and sang. She would often sing at weddings. I visited her often over the years and she would always cook special food that she knew I liked. She was very much like our mother.

Elaine

Floyd

Floyd was three years ahead of me in high school. He was an excellent student and basketball player and was a hard act for me to follow especially since I wasn't really very motivated at that point in my life. He finished high school and then went on to college at Penn State. To pay for his college, he cut timber off the farm and sold it to the coal mining company for use in the mines. His little brother, me, helped some as well. He did well in college and then went on to graduate school in Cincinnati, Ohio. He eventually got his PhD in chemical engineering and went to work for Dow Chemical. He was instrumental in developing various plastics, and in particular he was closely involved with the development of the well known saran wrap that we all use on a daily basis. Floyd now lives in Ohio on a 107-acre farm with his wife Shirley. He still holds on to many of the old farm ways. He raises his own vegetables and berries and essentially all of their meat comes from hunting, primarily deer. His son Floyd Eric, who almost made a career out of going to college, lives in southern California where he is doing research work which I believe will ultimately contribute to finding a cure for cancer and AIDS. Floyd's two daughters, Beverly and Cindy, are both married, and live in Ohio.

Floyd

Junior/E.Jay/Barkey/Spike/Eph/Ephraim

I was the last of the litter of eleven. Since I was the baby in the family, I think that my mother and my sisters tended to spoil me. I can still remember Betty and Elaine giving me a bath in a wash tub. I have been told that when I got into trouble or had a problem, I usually went crying to Betty. She must have been a softy. In later years, I became closer to Elaine because Betty moved away while I was still in high school.

During my life, I have been known by many names. Prior to high school, I was called Junior. During high school and even now when with the Romesberg family, I am E.Jay. At the end of high school and in the navy and college, and to people in Connecticut, I am known as Spike. At GE, where I worked for over thirty years, I am Eph. In California and in the running world, I am Ephraim. So I may from time to time in this story, use one of the above names when referring to myself. Aside, from those names, I was also called Barkey, and some other silly names, by my brothers. Merle gave me the name Barkey. The name was somewhat appropriate for two reasons. First, I coughed a lot due to hay fever and asthma and they claimed that I sounded like a dog barking especially in the middle of the night when I awoke with an asthma attack. Also, I had very dry skin as a little kid, and still do, so that my skin, according to my brothers, looked like the bark of a tree.

Junior/E. Jay/etc.

I left home to join the navy just a few days after high school. After five years in the navy, I married Jean Whitehill from Norwich, Connecticut and immediately entered college at the University of Connecticut School of Engineering. After college, I worked for General Electric in the nuclear power generating business until about 1990. I am now retired and we live in San Jose, California near our four kids Gary, Tom, Tricia and Laura and seven grandkids.

Here is another picture that I value because I think that it is the first picture of me ever taken. I must be about three years old at the time. It was taken around 1933. It may also be the first picture ever taken of Floyd.

Also shown in the picture is Helen, holding Peggy and next to her is Elaine, then Lois Weimer, and Betty. Floyd is in front of Betty and to his right is one of the Weimer girls. The little guy in front looking down is Junior (that's me). Between Floyd and Junior is Sonny Weimer. He and I were in grade school together. He must have been a couple of years older than me. The house in the background is our summer house which was used in the summer for canning vegetables. It was later moved and turned into a brooder house. The brooder house caught fire and burned down while I was in the navy. More on that later. The story of the fire and the aftermath is one of those stories that Paul's wife Violet loves to tell.

Junior w/siblings & Weimer Kids ~ 1933

Heritage:

Except for my grandmother Mary Livingston, whose ancestors were predominately Scottish, my ancestors on both my mother's side and my father's side came from Germany. Pop still spoke Pennsylvania Dutch, which is considered Low German. When we were kids, I think he would speak Dutch when he didn't want us to know what he said. He and Uncle Alex or Uncle Milt would speak Dutch when they got together. My older brothers and sisters learned some of it but I never really learned any, to speak of. My wife Jean and I, as well as my brothers and sisters, still have sauerkraut and pork on New Year's. Other than that, I don't think we have any special customs relating to our German heritage.

The immigration of our ancestors from Germany started in the early 1700s. The decision to leave Germany and come to America grew out of the concern for the conditions that were created by the thirty-year war, which left Germany devastated. Additionally, the incentives to come to a better life in Pennsylvania promoted by William Penn provided additional reasons to make the big move.

Farm Life/Hard Work, Sacrifice, and Fun too:

My three older brothers never completed high school. Merle and Wilbur started but quit during the fall harvest. Wilbur relates that he had no clothes fit for high school. Mom went to the attic and brought down an old pair of Pop's band pants. She removed the white stripes, which ran down the side of the legs, and Wilbur spent several hours removing the pieces of white thread to improve the looks. He also had no decent shoes. He remembered resoling his shoes himself using roofing nails to attach the soles. He clinched the nails on the inside, but was unable to do it properly. When he walked the four miles plus to school the nails started to wear away at the skin on the bottom of his feet. Besides all that, there was work to do at home. Maintaining the farm, doing the daily chores and cutting timber to supplement the family income required their help. This all took place during the Depression and they also had to go to work outside the farm part time to help pay for food and other necessities. But probably more important than anything else, it was fall, and the leaves were falling and soon it would be hunting season. More on hunting later but to young boys in Pennsylvania, hunting season was a strong draw, much stronger than high school. Who needed high school anyway? So after only a month or two, they both in turn quit school and continued to work on the farm. Paul, seeing the example his two older brothers set, never started.

Merle tells of walking ten miles to work, getting paid ten cents per hour, and then walking ten miles home. Money was so hard to come by that he once carried twenty-five cents in his pocket for a full week when the carnival was in town. Each night he went there but didn't have the heart to spend it. He saved it and probably eventually gave it to our mom to help pay for necessities.

There was an incident that is still vivid in my mind that took place when I was not yet in school. A neighbor was having trouble controlling a horse and Merle came to his aid. Somehow a hook on the horse's collar caught Merle in the middle finger of his right hand. I remember a lot of blood and the eventual loss of his middle finger at the second knuckle.

Before I was born, Helen lost the little finger on her right hand in a hazelnut-shucking event. She and Wilbur were removing the husks from hazelnuts. Wilbur was using a hatchet to separate the husks from the nuts. Helen reached in the working area to pick up nuts just as the hatchet was coming down. Years later, she described riding with Pop to Rockwood, over four miles away, to Dr. Speicher's office in a horse drawn buggy with rags wrapped around the wound. Wilbur was so afraid that Pop would kill him for chopping off his little sister's finger that he hid out in the woods the rest of day and on into the night to give Pop time to calm down.

Wilbur had a knack for doing weird things. Luella tells of the time he stuffed pebbles in his ears and Dr. Speicher had to make another house call to remove them. One other time he threw the works from a clock up in the air and it came down and hit him on the head between the eyes. He told Mom that Luella did it. When I was little I remember he had a pipe, don't know where he got it, but he used it to try smoking corn silk. That wasn't so bad but then he tried smoking coffee grounds, which proved to be worse than the corn silk.

Paul & Floyd ~ 1933

Here is a picture of Paul and Floyd taken during the Depression. Looks like Paul had outgrown his pants. I don't know what Floyd was wearing on his head. Looks like goggles. In those days we had to get a lot of wear out of a pair of pants. Mom probably took those pants that Paul was wearing and put patches on the knees. Paul once explained to me how to get more miles out of a pair of socks. He said that when you wore a big hole in the heel you should wear the sock upside down. That is, put the heel with the hole in it at the top of your foot until you wear another hole in the sock on the opposite side of the first hole. At that point you put the pair of socks in the bag for Mom to either darn or throw in the ragbag. Or if you really wanted to get more wear out of them, you could rotate them 90 degrees in one direction and then 90 degrees in the other direction until all the holes met each other and the sock ended up in two parts. Then you could throw the pieces in the rag bag.

During my early years on the farm, we traded eggs at our uncle Milt's store for groceries. We would carry the eggs in a basket down the path through the woods and come back with certain groceries and other necessities not available from the farm. There was no money involved. Just eggs.

One time Floyd got a dozen oranges and ate six of them on the way home. He told Mom that Milt only had six. On another occasion, he opened a large can of fruit in the fruit cellar but couldn't finish all of it so he got me to help. The idea was to completely empty the jar and then wash it and put it with the other empties to hide the evidence.

According to other members of the family, Floyd also got his arm caught in the washing machine wringer. I have heard jokes of other female body parts getting caught in the wringer but Floyd is the only person I know of that caught his arm in the wringer. I don't know how he managed to do that but it caused a fuse to blow and loss of power until Luella brought some new fuses home from Rockwood.

Speaking of fuses blowing, I do know that if spares weren't available, sometimes a penny was substituted for the blown fuse.

Except for Merle, Wilbur and Paul, all the rest of us kids went to high school. It was four and a half miles from our house to the school and the primary means of getting there was to walk. The worst part of the walk, was the several mile stretch called the Baker Flat. It was cold and windy in the wintertime and for some reason, the girls in the family never wore anything on their legs. I remember walking down the Flat behind Floyd who served as a windbreaker. He was my big brother my freshman year and he took good care of me. Sometimes we rode a bike; sometimes we got a ride with somebody. But many times, we walked all the way. Floyd describes a wild bike ride down the curvy Rockwood hill with Elaine riding on the frame. The brakes burned out and they had to lean hard to make the curves. They coasted a long way into town but they made it without crashing. When I was a senior, we finally got school bus service.

My Entry into This World:

Shortly before I was born, my brother Wilbur tells of going with our dad to the barn to hitch up old Babe to the buggy. He was to accompany Pop to take the buggy to Summit Mills to pick up Aunt Minnie to bring her back to our house. The trip was about seven miles each way. Aunt Minnie would stay with Mom until sometime after I was born. Sometime after Aunt Minnie arrived, Wilbur was mowing brush along one of our fields when one of my sisters came to him with the news of my entry into this world. He mowed around a small oak tree and proclaimed it as my tree. He explained this to me later when I was old enough to understand. The tree grew into a large and stately oak and I always made it a point to visit that tree on my trips home. I pointed it out to my kids when I brought them back to the farm for visits. During the times when I went there alone, they would ask me if I saw my tree. And I would tell them, yes, I saw my tree. There came a day in the mid-1980s when I went to see my tree and it was gone. It had been cut down to make access for truckers or perhaps for a driveway for a new house. But even after the tree was gone, I would still visit the place and would always be heard to say, "This is the place where my tree once stood."

My healthy entry into this world was considered by some to have beaten the odds. It seems that my mother had fallen down the stairs shortly before I was born. Some thought that I might be adversely affected. But obviously I wasn't. Although some might feel otherwise, I turned out reasonably normal.

The country was in the middle of the Great Depression when I was born. We were poor but we always had plenty to eat. Most of our food came from the farm or from the woods in the form of deer, squirrels, rabbits, pheasants, or groundhogs. I think that we got some new clothes before school and those would generally be expected to last until the following year. To save money, Mom would make some of our clothing and she patched pants and shirts and even socks where practical. She also saved rags and used them for making rugs.

Sex Education:

There wasn't any. Neither of our parents ever told us about sex. I think that we were told that babies came from trees. But growing up on a farm with animals made it pretty easy to eventually figure it out.

Superstitions:

My parents grew up at a time when there were fewer doctors and less medicine. So of necessity, there were more home remedies and home methods used to cure injuries and illnesses. Pop, as did most people at that time, gathered various roots for making tea for medicinal purposes. Perhaps best when taken with a little Moonshine or Jack Daniels. Another thing that Pop did which was also a mystery to me, and which is now pretty much completely lost, was a "faith healing" method that was known as Pow Wow. I guess the way it worked was he simply performed a little ceremony, or said some words, over the injury and it was felt that there was some curing power in the process. I have been told that when I was small and before I learned to walk, I crawled over the big register above our furnace and burned my hands and knees. It was said that he performed his Pow Wow ritual over me and I immediately stopped crying. There were many other examples of that same ritual being performed during my early days. I believe that he stopped performing about the time that Dr. Speicher became more available to make house calls.

Also on the subject of superstitions, many Pennsylvanians used hex signs over their doorways. I am not sure if we did or not. I think that it was mostly the Amish that used them. The idea was to keep away evil and help insure only good things would enter the household.

We always drank a lot of milk—well we lived on a farm where we had cows so what would you expect? We also ate a fair amount of fish. These were usually pretty small fish and were ones that Pop or some of his kids caught in local ponds or streams and Mom cleaned and fried. But as a rule, we never had fish and milk in the same meal. Mom felt that we would get sick if we had both at the same time. It apparently had something to do with too much calcium being leached out of the milk when taken with fish.

At the time it might have sounded like just another superstition, but Merle's wife Dorothy refused to use aluminum pots and pans from the very beginning. She said that they were not healthy. Many years later, we learned that there is a high probability that they may be a causal factor in Alzheimer's disease. Perhaps she was way ahead of her time.

Life without Electricity:

We got electricity in the old country farmhouse about the time I was born. Just before that we had carbide lights in the house. That was before my time so I don't know much about that system. I do know that it involved a tank, which contained carbide, outside the house. When I say we had electricity in our house that means we had at most one light bulb in each room and I don't remember any outlets. We probably had one for the refrigerator and that's about it. Before the refrigerator, we had an icebox. In those days ice was cut from ponds and kept in an ice house insulated in saw dust. But actually, we used the springhouse to keep things cold but there was no way to keep anything frozen. One vivid memory regarding electric lights in our house: we always had to turn out the light if we were the last one to leave the room. If we didn't, Pop would yell at us for wasting money. In Pennsylvania talk, we would say, "Be sure to outen the light."

Before electricity, food was preserved by canning and in the case of meat, by smoking. We had a smokehouse for curing ham, bacon, and sausage. A small stove was used in the smokehouse and wood, still containing sap, was used to make the smoke. One time I was supposed to hang a bunch of meat on the hooks up high and then make a good "smoky" fire. I got the order backward and made the fire first. Then when it was smoking really well, I hung up the meat. That was a bad decision. I shed a lot of tears by the time I got all the meat hung up in a very smoky atmosphere.

Because canning involved a lot of cooking in the summer time, we had a summerhouse for the express purpose of canning food for the winter. The idea was to keep the heat out of the house during the hot summer days. The summerhouse contained a cooking stove and lots of space to prepare and store the ingredients and the jars used for canning. Since we used jars, it seems that canning should have been called jarring. Our summerhouse was later converted to a brooder house, which burned down when I was in the navy. I talk about that in more detail later. One time a weasel broke into the chicken house and killed about three dozen laying hens. Mom cleaned, cooked and canned them (or jarred them). We didn't usually can chicken. If we wanted chicken for dinner we just went out to the coop, grabbed a chicken and chopped off the head. Rather than let the meat from three dozen chickens go to waste in this case, she canned them and nothing was lost except the loss of part of our egg supply.

We stored apples by burying them in the fall for use during the winter. A spot in the garden was cleared and a layer of straw followed by a layer of apples was put down. After that, the layering would continue until all apples to be stored were used. The top of the layering was then covered with earth or sometimes manure which was used to help generate a little heat so the apples wouldn't freeze. Probably a half-dozen layers were put down depending on how big an area was used for each layer. In the wintertime, we would go to the garden with a bucket and after brushing off the snow we would retrieve a bucket of apples and take them into the kitchen by the coal burning kitchen stove. My memory tells me that those were the best apples I ever had. We did wash off the straw and any manure that may have come into contact with them. Well, sometimes we skipped the washing and just wiped the apple off on the front of our shirt. Usually they were a little soft and I reckon they were quite close to the point where they would start to rot. I can recall eating a half dozen or more while I sat by the stove with my feet on the open oven door. This was a simple pleasure for sure, especially on a wintry evening with the cold wind howling outside the kitchen window.

We also dried certain foods so they could be stored through the winter. I know we dried beans, and to some extent we dried apples as well. We used some of the apples to make cider and applesauce. We also had a dark place in the cellar that was designed especially for keeping potatoes. Sauerkraut was the method for keeping cabbage over the winter.

We had a neighbor who stored apples in a barrel. When he picked apples to eat, he always picked the ones that were soft and starting to rot so that other apples would not be affected. He claimed that all winter long he ate partially rotten apples because the rotting process was always one batch of apples ahead of him.

Pennsylvania Speak:

In Pennsylvania, we had funny ways of saying some things. Such as "throw the cow over the fence some hay, onced." Some times we would ask our mom what she was making and she would say "woonanauz." When you wanted someone to turn out the light, we would say "outen the light." When we ate dinner, we were "fressing." We called calves "hommies" and baby chickens "peep pees" and little pigs were called "wootsies." Eggs were called "gockies." When I first courted Jean, my wife, I called her my little wootsy and I told her that it was an endearing word. When you didn't feel well, you were "grexing." When you were really sick and you were vomiting, you were "kutzing." When you were surprised you would say "I tu leva" which meant oh my goodness. When you were a little annoyed you would say "Jimses Pats." And if you were clumsy, you were "dopick." "Mox Nix" meant it didn't matter. By the way, I have no idea how to spell these words because Webster didn't put them in his dictionary nor can you find them in a German/English dictionary. There were other words and expressions but I have forgotten them.

We had the habit of ending statements with "onced." It was a way of ending a sentence, like saying: "that's my final answer, period." We would say things like: "Do me a favor, onced." Or "I have to go milk the cows, onced." I think I have heard other people in other areas do something similar. Like later in life when Ernie Karner and I went moose hunting in Newfoundland, we had two guides that would end statements with the word "boy." It was said in a very sharp way. For example, one guide would say to the other, "We better get going, boy." Or, "I think we should go to the other side of the lake, boy." Another example that Laura and I have used ever since we saw the movie "Sling Blade" is to use a grunt at the end of a statement. The main character in that particular movie would end each statement with an "uh huh." The "uh huh" was done in a very guttural way. For a long time after seeing that movie. Laura and I would end statements with "uh huh" until we annoyed Jean so much we though it best to quit.

In Pennsylvania, before I was born, when a young man was courting a young lady, he was allowed to stay overnight. I am told that they were allowed to sleep in the same bed provided the bed was rigged such that a sheet was between them. I think that they called that "bundling. The reason for allowing this was due to the long distance that would often exist between the two parties involved. This practice always brings up some interesting wise cracks and questions.

Farming without Modern Machines:

Before I was born, and actually after I was born as well but to a lesser extent, a large percentage of the working time spent by the farmer went toward clearing the land to make it tillable. This included removal of rocks, brush, and trees including the stumps. A lot of this was done with the hand saw, ax, and of course fire. But one implement that I thought was interesting was the stump puller. I only ever saw this implement in operation once and that was when my family moved our summer house from near the road to the back of the house. I don't know why they moved it other than the fact that it was sitting very close to the road. Maybe the highway folks wanted it moved. Anyway, this is how a stump puller worked, according to the expert, me, who never really saw one work. But trust me; I couldn't be that far off. The central part of the device, the part that provided the mechanical advantage in pulling a stump was a capstan. It was basically a drum with a strong steel cable wrapped around it. The capstan was anchored to something that was more rigid than the stump that was to be removed. A large tree usually served this purpose. A strong steel cable was then anchored to the stump to be removed and the other end of the cable would be attached to the drum portion of the capstan. The idea was to turn the capstan, which was anchored to a tree, and as it turned it would wind the cable, which was attached to the stump, on to the drum and in so doing would pull out the stump. Horses were used to turn the drum. This was done by attaching a heavy piece of timber to the drum like a big handle or crank. A team of horses was then hitched to the tongue and they would walk in a circle to wind up the cable. As they walked in a circle, they had to step over the cable that was hooked to the stump as well as the anchor cable that was hooked to the big tree. During one such operation, my uncle Ralph was driving the team when something went wrong. Apparently, a break occurred in the connection between the team and the beam which was hooked to the drum. The large amount of energy tied up in the cable caused the beam to swing back at very high speed. The beam hit Uncle Ralph's leg with such force, it cut off his leg below the knee. Ralph's wife Hattie took him immediately to the hospital before he bled to death. Ralph used a wooden leg the rest of his life.

    I remember being sick a lot as a kid. I had hay fever and asthma. Mom used to prop me up at night with several pillows and put smelly stuff on my chest to help me breath. I remember having nightmares at times because I had trouble breathing. When I was a little older, twelve or so, there was a time period when I remember making regular trips to Dr. Musser in Somerset to get an allergy shot. They had first given me allergy tests to determine what I was allergic to. In a word, I was allergic to farm dusts. The allergy treatments apparently worked because eventually my hay fever and asthma problems went away. But until the allergy treatments took effect, they went easy on me with the farm work. When I was about six years old I drove the old model T truck while my older brothers loaded hay or grain on the back. Of course, I was so small someone else had to jump on to start and stop it. Actually all that I was doing was steering. When I got a little bigger, I drove a little Allis Chalmers tractor. I spent a lot of hours cultivating corn. As it turns out, that was the last job I did before going off to the navy.

Barkey on Tractor—1943

Merle and Wilbur worked on the farm like men when they were still boys. They handled a team of horses when they were as young as ten. The two of them together worked to remove rocks and stumps to make the land farmable. They would dig a hole around a large rock and then they would use a long pole, which I think they called a crow's foot, as a lever to raise the rock up using their own weight. They would get the rock up enough to get a chain under it and then pull the rock out with the horses. They used the same procedure with large stumps.

Somebody once wanted to know what we grew on our farm. Wilbur's response to that question was "mostly rocks." It seems like every year new rocks seemed to show up after the fields were plowed and harrowed. We were always picking up rocks off the field and hauling them to piles or fences along the edge of the fields. Merle gave our farm the name "Stony Acres Farm." It was definitely appropriate. The name still shows on the spring house that he built below the old homestead.

Until about the time I left to join the navy, we farmed pretty much the old fashioned way. We did have a mowing machine to mow the hay. When it dried, we raked it into windrows using a horse or small tractor and a buck rake. I remember a time when I was riding the buck rake while Paul was driving the tractor. I think that he was driving in high gear and moving pretty fast on a sharp turn where the field met the woods when the rake came unhitched from the tractor. The tongue of the rake hit the ground and the rake stopped instantly. I went flying into the brambles of the woods. It's a wonder we didn't get hurt more than we did.

Speaking of getting hurt, Merle was driving the team of horses home with a load of hay from the field over at the Long farm one summer day when a little mishap occurred. As we were leaving the field to get on the dirt road, the wheels hit a rough spot, which caused the whole load to shake from left to right. I was on the load at the rear with our cousin Dwight Romesberg who was supposed to hold me so I wouldn't fall off. The load shook so much that we both fell off and Dwight fell on top of me. As a result of the fall, I ended up with a broken arm. Merle carried me home while Dwight brought the team and the load of hay behind. He brought me in to Mom and told her that Junior broke his arm. So she called the doctor (we must have had a phone at that time) and he came out. He gave me ether and set my arm and put a splint on it. When Elaine came home from school she smelled the ether and fainted.

But I digress. Back to the old-fashioned way of making hay. After the mowing, drying, and raking, pitch forks powered by muscles were used to load the hay onto a wagon or old truck bed and then it was hauled to the barn, or hay shed, and muscled up into the hay loft. At the Bittner farm, more on this later, there was a forklift to help lift the hay up into the hayloft. One person, usually Paul, would stick the fork into the hay on top of the wagon and tractor or horse power was used to lift the hay. We would use a rope, or cable, hooked on the tractor drawbar on one end of the rope and to a pulley system on the other end of the rope. My job was to drive the tractor from up close to a point away from the barn which would be the distance required to lift the bundle of hay hanging on to the fork lift up to the rafters. At this point Paul would trip the hook and the hay would fall off the forklift into the hayloft. It was a lot better than doing it by pitchfork. And it was a good job for me since I stayed pretty clear of the dust which gave me hay fever and it gave me a chance to drive the Allis Chalmers.

Until I joined the navy, we still cut corn with a sickle and set it up to dry in shocks. Later on a nice crisp fall day, we would take the shocks and drag them to a spot in the field, which I will call the husking spot. There you would lay the corn stalks across your legs and remove the cornhusks from each of the corncobs with the aid of a corn husker. I still have two of the huskers in our spare bedroom. The husker was made of leather with a metal rounded point which would allow you to rip half, more or less, of the husk off the ear and then with the other hand you could peel off the other half and break the cob at the base and throw the ear on the pile all in one motion. Floyd claims that he could do an ear in one second. Maybe so, but it takes time to set up, and then after you do all the corn stalks in one shock, you need to go get another shock. I remember husking corn with Pap on a beautiful fall day and he bet me that he could husk corn faster than I could pick it up. I took him up on his bet and I lost. But he tricked me. He would throw each ear in a different direction so that I had to run between ears. At the end of the day, we would have all the corn loaded in a wagon with a few pumpkins thrown in for effect, we would ride home seated on the wagon seat behind a team of horses and the corn would be unloaded in the corn cribs and the pumpkins would go primarily for the pigs. Of course some of the pumpkins would go for canning for pumpkin pie.

Graham's sketch of Barkey on our old horse Maude

    This is me on our horse Maude as drawn by my grandson Graham Wing. Until I was about 13 or so, we always had a team of big workhorses. The two horses I remember best were a mare named Maude and a male named Barney. Barney was a nervous type. He would stand in his stall and rock back and forth. Wilbur or Merle told me that was because he had lived in a barn with chickens. The horses were used to do the work that tractors would later do, such as plowing the fields, harrowing after plowing, pulling a seed planter, cultivating corn and other row crops, pulling the mowing machine to cut hay, pulling a hay rake, hauling things, and dragging logs in the woods. I remember riding on the back of the lead horse, probably Maude, while dragging logs. Also, I remember riding on a horse being used singly to walk between the rows pulling a cultivator. Pop would be walking in the back of the cultivator and holding the handles. The horse didn't really need much in the way of guidance. The team was used for plowing a field and the horses would follow the furrow. My slight fear of horses probably resulted from my being so small and they were so large. Sometimes when my bigger brothers were not available, I had to lead both horses, one on each hand, to the water trough. I was always scared. Once one of the horses, and I think it was Barney, put his foot down on top of mine while standing at the trough. It was muddy and my foot was pushed down into the mud. I had to just stand there until he was done drinking so he would move and I could get my foot free.

There is one other memory that I have of horses on our farm. Horses dying. I think that Pop was always buying horses that were not what you might call the best. He couldn't afford the best. Wilbur once said that he recalled a four-year period when a number of horses died. It seems that we always had horses that my mom referred to as Old Plugs that were ready for the glue factory you might say. I have a vivid memory of men coming to our barn and dragging out a dead horse and loading it onto a truck. I was told that it was being taken to the glue factory. This particular dead horse was the only one that I could remember but I know there were others. So the mere mention that a horse might be ready for the glue factory was a way of bargaining with the horse. You could threaten a horse by saying "shape up horse, or you'll end up in the glue factory."

As I recall, about the time I left for the navy, Paul had taken over the farm and between he and Merle, they started to become mechanized. Before long, I saw hay balers, combines, new and bigger tractors, and things that I didn't even recognize. I always claimed that I was so good when I was helping with the farm work that when I left they had to buy a lot of new machinery just to replace me.

Shy, Sickly, and a Little Spoiled:

On the subject of being sick a lot (I spoke of that earlier), Luella tells the story about the time she came home from school on a cold wintry day and I was sitting by the kitchen coal stove wrapped in blankets with a cup of hot chocolate and smelling like an open jar of Vicks vapor-rub. When she inquired about me, Mom told her in a sad tone that Junior (that would be me) was sick. And as she said that I snuggled down a bit further in the blankets in total comfort. It was a cold day out and this surely beat going to school and doing outside chores. Mom spoiled me and so did my sisters.

I was a very shy kid when I was little. So were the rest of my siblings. One time, Floyd and I were out near the barn and we saw a car coming up the road. Since cars very seldom came by our place, this was something special. Floyd saw the car coming and he yells out, "Run, it might be somebody!" So we ran and hid behind the straw stack until the car passed and was out of sight. Thus, the source of *Run, It Might Be Somebody* as the title of this book.

The significance of this later event might need a little further explanation. Apparently, we were so shy, or so embarrassed at our own appearance, that we felt that anyone who could afford to drive a car was in a class above us and that we should not presume that this person would want to see us. More precisely, we should not clutter the scenery by being part of it. I think that this idea *Run, It Might Be Somebody* tells volumes about us living on this little farm out in the country. I think that we grew up thinking that we were just plain country folks that didn't quite fit into the high society of the city folks. In my case, I think that I grew up believing that certain doors were closed to me. For example, I was firmly convinced as a youngster that I could never be a medical doctor. I am not sure that I wanted to go that direction anyway but I would never have considered starting. Eventually I think we became more confident about our self image and didn't run if a stranger drove up the road. Or did we? Maybe we did, and maybe sometimes we still do.

In another case, I remember a woman from the city came by one day in a big car and asked Wilbur if she could take a picture of him feeding the pigs. Wilbur and I thought that was a pretty big deal to have some fancy lady in a big new car wanting to take his picture. Of course she probably wanted a picture for the collection showing how the other half lived.

Paying the Doctor Bills:

We didn't have any medical coverage in those days. I have often wondered how Pop paid the doctor for the many office visits and for the many house calls. I think that some times the doctor got paid off with chickens or other farm produce when there wasn't enough cash available. For sure, the doctor did get paid one way or another. The costs in those days weren't as high as it is today because the cost to administer medical coverage programs or the high cost of legal litigation did not exist. The system did work and those who needed medical coverage did get the help they needed at least to the extent that it was available.

Cats and Dogs:

We always kept a lot of cats on the farm. They kept the mice population down. Maybe the rats too but even with a lot of cats we still had lots of mice and rats. One time, I was leading the horses to the watering trough and one of the cats got squished by a horses hoof. Later I told Mom that Barney squished a cat and we only had seventeen left. Mom used to feed the cats cows milk straight from the cows. They liked that. The milk was still warm. Occasionally, my mom would also squirt milk at visiting grandkids straight from the cow's tit while she was milking. I know Joann still remembers getting squirted that way. And when it happened, my mom would look innocent as though she didn't know where it came from.

When I was very small, barely old enough to remember anything, I do believe we had hunting dogs. They were used for hunting raccoon and groundhogs and probably squirrels and rabbits as well. They were kept chained up by a small dog house. I think that Merle and Wilbur and probably Woodrow Romesberg would use them for hunting. They were not what I would consider pets.

One day when I was about ten years old, Wilbur brought home a little rat terrier just for me. I gave him the name Bingo thinking that it was very original. Later I found out that Bingo was probably the number one name for a dog. Bingo was a house dog. He slept with me for years. He would be up on a chair or couch to look out the window when I came home from school. He was a pretty good watch dog whether we wanted a watch dog or not. When someone came by the house, he would run and bark and make a general nuisance out of himself. He had long toenails and when he ran through the kitchen toward the back door, he made this loud clicking sound. In the summer, the screen door almost always had a hole in it so he could run straight through it. When someone came by the house, he would take off from where ever he was and he could go from zero to about twenty miles/hour in about one second. One day, Mom asked me to patch the screen door to keep the flies from coming in. I used a piece of screen and some very fine wire, or string to "sew" the patch over the hole. It took me quite a while to fix it. I'm sure it was a pretty crude job but it was the best I could do. When I was done, I sat down on the wood box to admire my work. Just about that time, someone came by the house. Bingo had good ears and he came running as he always did. I could hear the toenails clicking on the kitchen linoleum as he came around the corner into the back room heading for the back door. Not knowing that I had just covered the hole, he hit the patch at full speed. The door flew open, Bingo bounced in one direction and the patch in another. My patch job was ripped off in an instant.

There were times in the winter when it was so cold, even my bed apparently wasn't warm enough for Bingo. On at least one occasion, he found a warmer place, the kitchen oven. Sometimes, Mom would leave the oven door open at night. On one such occasion when it was cold, Bingo crawled into the oven to sleep. In the morning Paul came down and closed the oven door and started to make a fire. Bingo woke up and made a ruckus so Paul heard him and opened the oven door to let him out otherwise we would have had a hot dog.

Although he was a house dog, he did have free reign outside the house. He would often go away from the farm but would always come back and would he home when I came home from school. One day, I came home from school and Bingo wasn't there. We later found his cold dead body near a house in Wilson Creek. Paul had very harsh words for the man who lived in the house because we were certain that the man had shot Bingo. He claimed that he was bothered by a pack of wild dogs. After Bingo was gone, I went home and built a wooden wheelbarrow. Why did I do that, I don't know. I just had to do something.

After Bingo, there was Rex. Rex was a very useful farm dog. I would ride my bicycle to the bars where the cows went in and out of the pasture. I would lower the bars and tell Rex to go get them. Rex would go down into the woods or fields and round up the cows and bring them out to the bars. Actually it was a pretty easy job because usually the cows were ready to come home to be milked and to be fed grain or whatever was on the menu. Rex and I worked well together. Rex was also a very good squirrel dog. He was not a rabbit dog. A good rabbit dog will get on the trail of a rabbit and will make noise (barking) and follow the trail and bring the rabbit around in a circle permitting the dogs master to shoot the rabbit. Rex would not do that. As a squirrel dog, he would see a squirrel in the distance and run fast toward the squirrel and chase the squirrel up a tree. This would usually be a tree that was not a den tree. The den tree would allow the squirrel to get away. But by chasing the squirrel up a tree without any place to hide, the hunter could get a shot before the squirrel traveled across tree tops to get into a hole. Also, a squirrel will often hide on the side of the tree or tree limb away from the hunter. But if the hunter, I for example, just stood still, Rex would go around the backside and force the squirrel to come over on the side of the hunter. Then we could have squirrel potpie for supper.

There was also Jumbo. I don't really know what he was good for. Probably for rabbits, but Jumbo didn't really express any interest in hunting. He was just there as a good friend. He was mellow.

We had other dogs, such as Pepper and Oscar. But they came along at a time when I was probably occupied by other matters. Like going off to seek my fortune.

One-Room Schoolhouse:

Wilson Creek School House

Like my brothers and sisters before me, I went to a small schoolhouse in Wilson Creek where grades one through eight were taught in the same room. It was a short walk from our house on a dirt road through the woods. As I look back on it, I think it was a good system. Not only were you learning while the teacher was teaching your grade, you were hearing what the other grades were learning. In the one room there was a coal burning stove at one end of the room near the first graders. The eighth graders were at the other end of the room furthermost from the stove. It was almost an incentive to flunk. This photo was taken in the 1960s long after the building was used as a school. There were two rooms but during my eight years there, only one room was used and that is the room shown on the right. The building was being used for storage when this photo was taken. It burned down shortly thereafter.

During the winter months, a boy would be selected from the upper grades to come to school early and start a fire in the big old coal burning stove. Usually there would be some fire left from the day before. When it was my turn to do it the teacher told me that the key to unlock the outside door would be above the door on top of the doorframe. He said to be sure to remove my glove before reaching for it. That was good advice which I never forgot. Doesn't sound all that important but with the glove on, it would be easy to knock the key off and lose it in the snow, which I think had happened earlier.

We had a teacher named B. B. Moore. I never knew what the *B*s stood for. During hunting season he would bring a twelve-gauge shotgun to school and stand it in the corner. When school was over, and I wouldn't be surprised if he didn't dismiss us early sometimes, he would go squirrel hunting on the way home.

My first grade teacher was named Miss Schmucher. She was my favorite teacher. I never saw her again after I left first grade. Elaine saw her one time in the late nineties. She was living in Florida and was visiting relatives here. She told Elaine a very interesting story. When she was teaching at Wilson Creek, she was actually a married woman and her name was no longer Miss Schmucher. She could not have gotten the job if it was known that she was married. During the Depression, giving a job to a married woman while married men were unemployed was felt to be unfair.

We had a teacher named Robert Reese for a year or two. I remember his car. I can't forget it. One day, I was bringing the cows home from the Long place with the help of my dog Rex when he happened to be driving by. I had the bad habit of throwing small rocks at a cow if it tried to turn into a field or any place where it wasn't supposed to be. Actually that was Rex's job but I often assisted him. As it so happened, one of the cows was poking her nose between the rails, which were used as a gate at the opening to a field. I threw the small rock to discourage her and the rock hit the rail at just the right angle so that the rock bounced back and hit and broke the head light on Mr. Reese's car. I felt awful. I was literally sick over it and I don't think that I told anyone. He knew that it was an accident and he told me not to worry. However, I did feel responsible for breaking his headlight so I looked through our shed and found another headlight from some other old car and gave it to him. But it didn't match and he later found another one somewhere else. But I never forgot that and I never forgave myself for such a stupid act. He later became one of my teachers in high school. He was at my forty-five-year reunion and I asked him if he remembered the broken light incident and he said that he didn't. Finally I felt better knowing that he hadn't hated me all these years for breaking his headlight.

During those early days in that one room schoolhouse, teachers would often find a place to live nearby on a temporary basis. They would also visit the homes of students and have a chat and maybe a cup of tea with the parents (usually the mother). I remember sitting quietly in the parlor while they talked, mostly about little Junior, and little Junior, that would be me, would be embarrassed.

During recess we played softball and other games such as marbles and prisoner's base. The softball field was set up in such a way that a long fly ball could knock out windows in the schoolhouse. The softball that we used was very soft so I guess we were actually playing mush ball. I remember one year I took the softball home and repacked it. I started out with a gourd and then wrapped strings around it until it fit snug within the cover. Then I laced the cover probably with a little help from my mother. The school budget didn't cover a new ball.

Other recess activities included building forts and playhouses in the woods. Rocks were moved to make indentations in the ground and then dead trees and limbs were stacked over the top of the indentation to form walls with space left for an entry way. Leaves and other wooded material were placed on top to form a roof. Many recesses were spent building and expanding these structures.

In the wintertime, we would have snowball battles between two groups where each group was fortified behind walls made out of snow. Each group would have a large store of snowballs before the battle would begin. After a fresh fallen snow, we would also make a large circle in the snow and we played a game where some of us went into the middle and threw snowballs at others on the circular track. Those in the outside circle would have to change places when they got hit. In the spring kids, usually boys would find young birch branches and chew the bark which was like chewing gum.

Once during class time the teacher suggested that we play a game with initials to see what they spelled. He started with Shirley Pritts. "Shirley, what's your middle name?" he asked. "Ann," she responded. "Shirley Ann Pritts, that spells SAP." Everybody laughs. "How about you Floyd, what's your middle name?" "Eugene," Floyd responded. "Floyd Eugene Romesberg," that spells FER." Slight response, but that wasn't as good as SAP. "Okay, let's try another one. Paul Steel, what's your middle name?" "Ivory," Paul replied. The teacher hesitated for a second or two and then says, "Let's play another game."

We got into a lot of scraps during recess. I think that a lot of the times the teacher promoted, or encouraged it. At least, the teacher didn't discourage it. I believe it was a positive factor in growing up. It may have been a way of letting off steam. I can remember getting into a lot of fights with Bill Pourbaugh. and I would end up with a lot of scratches from his long fingernails. As a result, I gave him the nickname of "Wildcat." The last I heard, he was still alive and was still called Wildcat.

In those days teachers were allowed to swat or spank kids. That may sound surprising to anyone in my grandkids' generation. Wilbur told a story that even I find hard to believe but he swore it was true. There was a one-armed teacher at Wilson Creek before I had reached first grade level. He sometimes spanked boys (never girls) who got out of hand. Since he had only one arm it was hard for him to hold the boy and spank him at the same time. So he accomplished this by placing the boy halfway out the window, then he would close the window down on the boys back to hold him in place and then he would proceed to spank him with his one available hand.

Floyd also tells about a teacher using a switch on a boy while I was in school but I must have missed it. I was probably out sick when it happened. Here's the story and it is perhaps as bad, or worse, than the one armed teacher story above.

It was common practice for teachers to keep a switch above the door. I do remember that part but I never saw the switch being used. Floyd did. The switch was cut from a long thin branch. If used as a switch, it would act very much like a whip. That's why they called it whipping. On this occasion, Floyd's good friend Bill Shaw must have done something to displease the teacher so he took down the switch and then took Bill outside and proceeded to give him a whipping on his bare backside. The whipping actually drew blood according to Floyd. When it was over, he put the switch back and poor Bill suffered through the rest of the day with what must have been a very painful backside. Floyd remembers that later that evening Bill Shaw's mother Mrs. Keeler (don't ask why the different last name) came to our house and had a short private conversation with our pop who at this particular time was the constable of the local township where we were located. The next morning while school was in session, Pop came down through the woods to the schoolhouse and after a short private conversation with the teacher outside the schoolhouse door, the teacher came inside and removed the switch from above the door and handed it to Pop. Floyd says that he watched Pop walk back up the path toward our home and as he did, he took the switch and broke it in two pieces over his leg and then threw it off to the side.

I believe that this action taken by our dad most likely ended forever the harsh treatment, at least at our little school, that teachers were allowed to use to control students. What he did was a good thing but he might be surprised to see how far the pendulum has swung in the other direction if he could visit schools today.

There were two brothers who went to school while I was there and they were known as Butts and Beans Pritts. Supposedly, Butts got his name from smoking cigarette butts and Beans got his name apparently from eating a lot of beans. I don't remember their real names. I do remember that they never dressed very warm in the wintertime. I was impressed with their apparent ability to stay warm with just a tee shirt and a light jacket. I lost track of them after school except briefly after the local soldiers came home from World War 2 and Butts was one of them. He had been in the army and had spent time on the battlefield. I asked him if he had ever shot anyone and he said he had. I wondered what it was like to shoot another person. He said that it was like shooting deer.

Sometimes the teacher would have individuals get up in front of the room, which of course contained all eight grades, and sing a song. Sonny Weimer and I sang a duet, we sang "Billy Boy."

It went something like this:

> "Oh where have you been, Billy Boy, Billy Boy, oh where have you been, Charming Billy?
> I have been to seek a wife, she's the joy of my life, she's a young thing and cannot leave her mother.
>
> How old is she, Billy Boy, Billy Boy, How old is she, Charming Billy? She's three times six, four times seven, twenty-eight and eleven; she's a young thing and cannot leave her mother.
>
> Can she bake a cherry pie, Billy Boy, Billy Boy; can she bake a cherry pie Charming Billy? She can bake a cherry pie, quick as a cat can blink her eye; she's a young thing and cannot leave her mother."

Other kids sang some more or less ordinary songs but I remember two songs that were a little bit different. First Bill Shaw got up and sang a song about a horse:

> "First verse:
> Oh the horse ran around with his feet on the ground, the horse ran around with his feet on the ground—the horse ran around with his feet on the ground, the horse ran around with his feet on the ground."

Second verse:
Oh the horse ran around with his feet on the ground, the horse ran around with his feet on the ground—the horse ran around with his feet on the ground, the horse ran around with his feet on the ground.

Third verse:
Oh the horse ran"—Teacher interrupts at this point and tells Bill to sit down.

Then at some later time, Bob Keeler, who was quite big for a grammar school student, got up and his song, sung to the same tune as bill Shaw's song above, and this is more or less how it went:

"Oh I stuck my head in an old skunk's hole; I stuck my head in an old skunk's hole.
Oh I stuck my head in an old skunks hole; I stuck my head in an old skunks hole.

The little skunk said you better take it out, you better take it out, you better take it out.
The little skunk said you better take it out, you better take it out, you better take it out.

But I didn't take it out, I didn't take it out, I didn't take it out.
So I didn't take it out, I didn't take it out, I didn't take it out.

Pssst, I removed it."—Teacher also had Bob sit down while he tried to suppress a snicker.

There was a time when Floyd and I were in grammar school when a local newspaper carried a running picture story of Treasure Island. Bill Shaw had access to this newspaper and he would cut out the picture section from each issue and bring them to school for Floyd and me. We would both anxiously await each episode from Bill. We got the entire condensed version of Treasure Island presented with words and pictures that way. Somehow, I think I enjoyed that story presented in that manner better than seeing it presented as a movie many years later. To this day, Treasure Island is still one of my favorite stories.

There were only three kids in my eighth grade class when I graduated from Wilson Creek School. They were Glen Judy, Sonny Weimer and me. There were only about thirty in all of the eight grades.

We did our own window washing as this photo shows. Sonny Weimer is doing the washing and I am the one giving directions and holding the ladder.

Washing School House Windows

Bobsled:

During my grammar school years, I remember we had a really neat bobsled. It was home made and I don't know who made it but it was a fine piece of work. It consisted of a board, or plank, about five or more feet long and a foot wide. At the rear was a frame attached to the board that was formed to hold two runners about one foot long. At the front were similar runners except it was attached to the plank with a bolt so that you could turn the front runners with handles that extended to the sides. It worked well as a sled for kids or for hauling things. I can remember taking it over past Wilson Creek to the Kendall's hill when there was snow on the ground and we would sled down the hill. A bunch of us would get on the sled at one time. At the bottom of the hill, we would take a sharp left turn and see if anyone could hang on, which was usually nobody. We would upset and roll down the hill in the snow. I think on some occasions we would go there at night.

Our bobsledding ended one day when Floyd came to me all worried because Merle was looking for the sled to haul something and he couldn't find it. So I asked Floyd why he couldn't find it and he told me that he had sold it to Bill Shaw for a quarter. Holy cow! a quarter, what a deal. I don't recall what Merle's reaction was. But Bill Shaw got a good deal. And we couldn't go bobsledding anymore but I think we had out grown that activity at that time anyway.

Model T Truck:

My brother Merle bought an old Model T truck in the mid-1930s for less than $10. He drove it home in the dark down the old Dinky track from Matt Romesberg's place and I, along with all of the other brothers, were with him. Floyd and Paul sat on each of the front fenders with lanterns since there were no lights or if there were they didn't work. I stood upon the truck bed in back of Merle the driver. Wilbur was in the other front seat. We moved at no more than five to ten miles an hour. It was a major event. It was the most exciting event of my life up to that point. It was the first vehicle that we had on the farm.

My big brothers found a lot of things to haul with the old truck on the farm. They even allowed me to drive it when I was still pretty small. I can remember seeing the truck backed into the barn for off loading hay with the back end of the bed on the ground and the front wheels lifted completely off the ground with the front end pointed toward the sky like a teeter totter.

Dinky Track:

You may need some explanation on just what is a dinky track. When the little town of Blackfield was still a coal mining town, coal was brought out of the mines and transported about four miles give or take a few on small tracks powered by small steam engines. The steam engines were called dinkies. The tracks were called dinky tracks. Coal was loaded on little cars and the dinkies would haul the loaded cars on the dinky track about four miles to the B&O railroad tracks between Rockwood and Garrett where they were loaded for shipment to Pittsburgh. After the mines in Blackfield shut down, in the 1930s, the tracks were torn up and the roadbed was used for horse drawn wagons and later for cars. Today it is used mostly by people like me who are visiting and want to take a ride, walk or run down nostalgia lane.

The Stolen Calf:

The incident of the stolen calf was a lesson in kindness and forgiveness. It happened in the early thirties and I only vaguely remember what happened. Floyd recently refreshed my memory. One of our calves was stolen. This was during the Depression, so losing a calf that would grow into a source of beef was considered a pretty big loss. There was a hole cut in the fence and there were tire tracks as evidence to help determine who did it. With the help of local police, the guilty individuals were found. They were having dinner and the stolen calf was the main course. Pop realized when he saw the individuals involved that they probably needed it worse than we did so he refused to press charges. I came to believe that this act of kindness was a trademark of our dad. It fits right in with his policy of spontaneously inviting people, including strangers, to stay for a meal.

The Old Saw Mill:

In the thirties and forties we had a sawmill in the woods below the house. It was located close to our little Sugar Camp. Merle was the chief operator. I think that he set it up in the first place. Other brothers helped by rolling logs into place on the carriage and carrying away slabs and stacking the lumber. I helped with minor tasks where I couldn't get hurt or cause too much trouble. The logs for use in the mill came from our woods. The lumber was used for building various structures on the farm.

Also, when Merle built a new house when he got married, all the necessary lumber except for the trim came from the mill.

During this same time period, when I was between about five and twelve years old, I was the "fetch it" kid. Merle was the handy man who could do just about anything. He was a stone mason, carpenter, plumber, mechanic, taxidermist, and an all-around fix it kind of person. I was the one who would get a wrench or find the crow bar, or whatever. But I was learning "how to" in most cases.

Maple Sugar Camp:

Up until the early or midforties we had a little maple sugar camp in the woods below our house located beside the sawmill. It was a small camp, as camps go, and was just for our own use. We probably only got a couple of gallons of maple syrup per season. It was a little wooden structure with one side open. In front of the open side was a large iron kettle. A fire would be built under the kettle and the sap from the sugar maple trees would be poured by hand into the kettle. We would tap the trees nearby (some of them not so near) and carry the sap in buckets to a storage barrel in the shack for storage until it was put in the iron kettle and boiled down for syrup. It took about twenty gallons of sap to get a gallon of syrup. One time, Betty carried two big buckets both filled with sap, and just as she got near the camp, she fell and spilled both of them.

Floyd and I stopped by the camp on our way to school one day to stoke the fire under the kettle which contained concentrated sap which had already been boiled down to a point where it would soon be syrup. It was understood that Paul was going to go down right away and oversee the process. He forgot and as a result the kettle boiled dry and the syrup was burned.

Indoor Bathroom:

When I was about twelve or so, Mom had a birthday party of sorts for me, Paul and Merle whose birthdays were all in November. A lot of the Wilson Creek kids were there including Shirley Pritts, who was someone special to me at the time. We had just recently had indoor plumbing installed at our house and I couldn't wait to show it off. So when Shirley asked to use the bathroom, I was delighted to point her upstairs. My mom made sure that nothing ever got started between us by reminding me that Shirley was my cousin.

Big Family in Small House:

Before indoor plumbing, we had an outhouse just like most everybody in the country did in those days. It was really exciting to go there in the wintertime when the temperature was below freezing. And it was a long way from the house. I remember going there one time in the night and it was cold so I ran as fast as I could. There was an old cherry tree stump below the house near the springhouse. I hit that stump with my foot and suddenly my body became airborne. I went straight out over the stump and landed in the snow on the other side.

People who have never had the opportunity to grow up in a small house with a large family without indoor plumbing might wonder how in the world you survived. Where did everyone sleep? How did you take a bath? Where did you go to the bathroom? Good questions. I'll try to tell you how it was when I was a boy. But first, I should tell you what it was like before I was born. Here is how Luella described it.

There were only six rooms in the house when Luella was little. The kitchen, sitting room and Gramma's bedroom were downstairs. Uncle Alex's bedroom was at the top of the stairs. He was pretty lucky, he had his own room. Mom, Pop, and five kids, slept in the middle bedroom in two large beds. In the end bedroom, two teachers who boarded with the family for three years and a hired girl slept in one bed. There was no bathroom.

The house had been enlarged by the time I came along at which time there were six bedrooms. They were all small. One bedroom, at the top of the stairs which I guess was Uncle Alex's bedroom earlier, would become a bathroom later when I was twelve. Another bedroom was more like a hall since it led to the attic. As I write this now, I wonder why we didn't use the attic as a bedroom as my brother Paul and his wife Violet did later when they raised their family there. But when I was born, there were Mom and Pop, Merle, Wilbur, Paul, Floyd, Luella, Helen, Betty, and Elaine and I. Before me and to some extent also after I was born, there were always a few boarders in the house besides the family members already mentioned. To this day, I am not sure where everyone slept but here is my best guess. Mom and Pop in one room along with the baby. Baby is defined as the youngest one in most cases or one younger than about two years. Helen, I think was in the small bedroom which later became the bathroom. Luella, Betty and Elaine shared another room. They slept three in a row and at times when there was another in the room, the fourth person slept at the foot of the bed. Paul and Merle shared another room. Wilbur and I, when I was a bit bigger and left my parents room, shared a room and Floyd had the small hall-like room to himself. Now what about the boarders? Kids doubled up I guess when there were boarders unless some of the boys were living elsewhere. For example, Wilbur worked for our aunt Sadie and uncle Homer Boger on his farm and Paul worked for Aunt Ada and Uncle Ray Sechler at Summit Mills and the time frame for that was sometime in the thirties. They each earned $21 per month by the way. That opened some space at our house for boarders. It is not clear to me where they slept. But the exact details don't really matter. The main point was that there was always about ten or more people sleeping in a relatively small space upstairs without running water or a bathroom. I told you earlier I was going to tell you about how they managed without these conveniences. Do I have to?

Well I'm sure you have all heard of bedchambers. We called them pots or sometimes piss pots. They looked like white buckets with a rounded top. One could sit on these with a bare bottom without leaving a ridge mark on the bare skin. Of course they also had a lid. According to my recollection, these were used primarily by the girls. There were rumors that in some cases the boys used the open windows if they had to pee. I don't think that was the case especially in the wintertime because the yellow snow would have been a dead giveaway. But I can't be too sure it didn't happen. I know Paul after eating too much watermelon, used the window on one occasion to throw up. But in an emergency at night, the outhouse was a possibility and I know that I had to use that choice more than once. Of course if it was simply a matter of taking a whiz, a short walk outside the back door was perfectly okay. Otherwise, it was a long walk or jog depending on how urgent the trip was to the outhouse.

Regarding the bedchamber, I have heard the story many times about a small mishap, which occurred one time when Betty and Elaine were in the process of emptying the contents. For unknown reasons, they sat the pot down at the top of the stairs while they went on to something else. One of the other house inhabitants, probably one of the boys, accidentally kicked the pot and it went tumbling down the stairs spilling the contents along the way. Mom had a fit. She said to them, "I knew that would happen as soon as you sat it down." Later when we talked and actually laughed about it, Floyd would always ask Mom if she knew it was going to spill, why didn't she insist that they move it before it got spilled.

On the subject of boarders Paul tells the story of one boarder who was using the soap dish by the sink in the pantry as a drinking cup. I imagine that the water must have tasted strange considering the fact that we used Mom's home made soap which used lye as one of the ingredients. This source of water was located in the pantry off the kitchen. We had a sink and a hand pump and until I was twelve this was the only source of water in the house.

During those years, the mattresses on the kid's beds were big "ticks," made the size of a regular mattress and filled with straw. Every spring and fall, Mom would empty them and fill them with fresh straw. No wonder I had hay fever.

During the Depression years, I remember one of the Schroyer boys would come to our place occasionally to buy straw which they used for their mattresses (ticks in those days). Pap told me to charge a dime per bag. One time I filled a sack for one of the boys in the dead of winter. He had old rags wrapped around his feet in place of boots and his old gloves were full of holes. I told him to keep the dime.

Extra Plates For Dinner:

Whenever someone came by the house near mealtime, Pop would invite them to stay and eat. I remember times when I came downstairs for breakfast and there would be a stranger at the table. I think I regarded that as normal. These were hard times and probably those people were out of work.

Some of Luella's Memories:

Luella claims that you haven't lived until you ran barefoot through a cow pasture in the early morning when the dew is still on the grass and you then feel the warmth of a fresh cowpatty ooze up between your toes.

Luella remembers that she and Merle peddled milk in gallon buckets in Wilson Creek in their bare feet. She also told about Uncle Joe taking them in his two-seated Ford to visit aunts and uncles in Summit Mills where Mom's family lived. Sometimes they went on Saturday in the horse and buggy and stayed overnight when they visited Gramma and Grandpa Swearman. She and Merle rode in the back in the luggage carrier.

Luella also described house cleaning every year. The beds were all torn apart, the room was emptied and everything scrubbed with Mom's home made lye soap. They dunked the bed slats in a bucket of water, first one end and then the other. They even washed the bed springs. Also, every Saturday morning, one of her jobs was to take the cooking kettles to the ash pile and scour the bottoms with ashes. She said that Mom would scold her if she didn't clean the ears of the cooking pots.

She often remembers sadly when Babe, a favorite horse, fell and broke his leg. Pap cried when he had to shoot it.

This is how she described our sister Della's death on October 10, 1925. She died at the age of six due to typhoid fever and pneumonia. Mom burned sulfur in a dish in every room to fumigate the house. She burned the big sticks of O-Boy gum friends had bought for Della. During much of her short life, Della had eczema all over her body, mostly on her hands and arms. She scratched until it bled. Mom made long white muslin sleeves and tied them on her arms. The night before she died the potbelly stove in the sitting room wailed, and Pop cried when the Confluence Hospital called and said they feared that she would not live. They brought the little casket in the front door and put it in Gramma's little bedroom. It was a very gloomy, snowy day. Teddy, the dog, walked around so sad with his head between his legs. People brought food to our house and a big can of store bought peaches. Luella was eleven years old when Della died.

Everyone had their special place at the dinner table. All the kids—or most of them if we fit—lined up on a long bench against the wall. Pop was at one end and Mom sat where she could be up and down to replenish things as necessary. There was always room for Uncle Alex at one end and unexpected company would squeeze in someplace. Nobody was allowed to start eating until everyone was at the table and Pop was finished with the blessing which to the kids seemed way too long.

Milking Cows:

From the time when I was little (about five years old), I helped with the milking. At that time, I think that this usually was the job for my mom and Betty. The boys helped too but I think that they were often late returning from the fields or woods so they were not always there. I being the youngest and being considered somewhat sickly was usually there and was available for milking and for other work around the house. Later during World War 2, there weren't very many helpers left at home, and at that time we had cows to milk at the home place as well as the old Bittner farm which was about 1.5 miles away. This became especially hard when I was still in high school and Floyd was in college. Mable Hay lived near the Bittner place, and she boarded her cow with ours and as payment, she would help with the milking. I think there must have been times when she did most of the milking herself. One time in the middle of winter when the weather was especially bad, Paul was late coming home from the Bittner place and Mom got worried that he might be stuck in the snow so she sent Floyd to look for him. She got even more worried later when neither of them came home. In the meantime, I was hiding in the corner hoping they would show up before she decided to send me.

The Bittner place was a farm that was purchased by Uncle Alex and given to my brothers and me (five boys) with the understanding that at some future date one of the boys would buy out the other four and would then move onto the farm. One additional proviso was that whoever took the farm would also take Uncle Alex in his old age (Uncle Alex had never married). Later when Merle came home from the army, he bought us out and took over the farm, which he eventually turned into a very prosperous dairy farm. I realized later in life that this was another case of the boys being given preferential treatment over the girls. In effect, each of the boys in my family was given 20 percent interest in a farm. The girls weren't given anything.

When Merle and Dorothy took over the farm they had a lot of work to do. The old farm house was in really bad shape. They lived in it anyway until they built a new one. Also, the barn needed a lot of work. But Merle was good at this sort of thing and eventually they had a new house and a more modern barn. When they first moved in, there was a large hole in the field below the house. Mr. Bittner, the previous owner, had a dream that there was a treasure buried in the field under a large oak tree. So he commenced digging with pick and shovel and he dug until he died. At some point, he had found a key and he took that to be a positive sign and he dug all the harder. But no treasure was ever found. Pap took on the job of filling the hole and he did it with pick and shovel and a wheel barrow. It took him months but he eventually completed the job.

But getting back to milking cows. We used a three-legged stool to sit on and we always did the milking from the right side of the cow with our head against the cows flank. Some cows were kickers and most all cows would slap you with their tails once or twice during each milking and more during the fly season, which was almost all the time. The tail slapping on the side of the head would sting and if it was wet and/or dirty, that was even worse. The milk bucket was held between the feet. When finished with one cow, we would pour the milk into a five gallon milk can. When Mom was milking she would be ready to spray any grandkid in the face with milk straight from the cow's tit if they happened to come near. Actually, she didn't limit her targets to just grandkids. I know she got me a few times. She would also get a cat now and then. She was really good at it. I've seen her take a cow's tit and pull it off to the side and catch a kid right in the face with a stream of warm milk at a good five yards or more. And the kid who got hit wouldn't even know where it came from. She would have that totally innocent look about her when she did it. I would have put money on her as the best and fastest, and sneakiest, cow tit slinger in the county, maybe the state. When all the cows were milked, we would make the long walk, with the five-gallon can of milk, to the cellar of the house where the cream would be separated from the milk using a cream separator. The separation process utilized centrifugal force to do the separation. We usually sold the cream. We also made butter, butter milk, and schmear case (Pennsylvania cottage cheese).

Rats:

It seems like we always had rats in our barn or other out buildings. That's why we kept so many cats. At times, we had as many as twenty or even more. There was a period during the war when I rigged a flashlight to a .22 rifle and would go out at night to the barn where we stored hay and fodder and would shoot rats through the cracks in between the barn boards. After doing this a number of times, the rats left. However they moved to under the chicken coop. After that I tried shooting them from an apple tree near the coop. I also set a trap in a small pen behind the coop. When I went to check the trap, a rat jumped up in front of my face and it scared me half to death. I retreated so fast that my head hit the doorframe on the way out. The rat was caught in the trap and was just trying to get away from me. I have disliked rats ever since. Now my grandchildren have pet rats. Also, at the time of this writing, researchers have determined that if the right buttons are provided, rats could be trained to fly an airplane. Are they kidding me?

World War 2:

This picture on the next page was taken when Merle was in the army. It must have been around 1943. From left to right are Merle, Floyd, Paul, E. Jay, and Wilbur in the background on a bike.

World War 2 had a big effect on my life, as it did on everyone else. Before the war, I remember hanging over the workbench watching Merle doing his taxidermy work. He had become a taxidermist by completing a correspondence course. He could mount deer heads and other animals. Shortly after the attack on Pearl Harbor, he was drafted into the army. During the war years, I looked forward to the day when he would come back and resume where he left off. But of course, those days never returned. I had grown up more, and of course he came back to his own new life with his new wife Dorothy. They settled down on the old Bittner place. I guess the war years served as a break point for me between being a boy to becoming a man.

Junior and Brothers (Wilbur on Bike)

During the war years, we had rationing. I came home from Uncle Milt's store one time and forgot to take the ration stamps out of my pocket before going to the barn. As a result, I fed the stamps to the cows. I remember my parents had to go through a major bureaucratic snarl in order to get them replaced.

My First Love:

Most of the time during my high school days, I walked or rode a bicycle. When I would go to see Doris Jean Tedrow, which was almost eight miles from home, I either rode the bike or walked. I spent most of the time getting there and getting back so that the actual time spent there was pretty short. When I came home from the navy on a weekend pass, I went to visit her one time and her mother allowed me to stay over and sleep on the living room couch. During the night, I had to get up and use the outhouse and in the process, I somehow locked my self out. I had to pound on the door and Doris Jean had to come down and let me in. Sometime later when I came home and went to see her, Bink Carpenter was there to see her also. And so ended our relationship. I was only planning to be in the navy for five years and I couldn't understand why she couldn't wait. She was my first real true love not counting Shirley Pritts and she didn't really count.

Doris Jean and I actually went together, so to speak, for about two or three years, counting the navy time when we hardly ever saw each other and she was probably seeing Bink on the side. One time she and I went fishing in a creek near where she lived. I carried a can of worms and when we got to the fishing hole, the can was empty. I was carrying the can upside down. I must have really been in love.

When I saw Bink Carpenter at her place, I went home and never went back until forty years later. While I was visiting Elaine one time in the eighties, I went for a morning run and went from Rockwood toward the old Tedrow farm to see if I could find it. It had been about forty years since I had been there. I could remember the barn below the road and the house sitting back well off the road on the other side. But when I got to where I thought the farm should be, I couldn't find anything that resembled the place. I finally found the barn foundation, but no barn. I could never find the house. It was completely gone.

Castrating Hogs and Delivering Baby Animals:

We always had a bunch of hogs on the farm and Pop would always castrate the males. When he did this, he would have one or two of us kids hold them. I remember Floyd and I trying to anticipate when he would be doing it so that we could be someplace else. It never worked.

There was a time when we had a big sow pig that was very late on delivering her brood. Something was wrong and she couldn't push them out. Since I was small at the time and had small hands and arms he got me to try to hand deliver them. So I reached in and could feel a baby pig but it was too slippery to pull out. He told me to keep trying. I tried to hold on to the nose or jaw or anything that I could get a good grip on but I finally realized that I could do it if I pulled on the lower jaw. I told him that if I pull on the lower jaw I thought that the lower jaw would break. He said to do it because he believed the baby pigs were already dead and the sow would die if we didn't get them out. So I delivered thirteen baby pigs all dead and many of them with broken jaws. Shortly after, the old sow was up and about seemingly none the worse for her ordeal. However, that was her last litter of pigs. She became the main act at the butchering that fall.

I had a similar experience with a baby calf that was coming out backward. Pop had me reach in and turn the calf around. That case worked out better than the pig incident. Some experience for a twelve-year-old.

On the subject of Pop being a lay vet, when a cow got into the fresh clover and got all bloated, he had to relieve the gas or the cow would die. He once showed me how to do it. He took a knife, and in the appropriate place on the cow's stomach, somewhat toward the back as I recall, he punctured the cow's stomach to let the gas out. Within a few minutes, the cow was up and about almost like nothing had happened. I never had the opportunity to see if I could do the same.

I got a new work jacket for Christmas one time and the hogs shredded it into pieces. While cleaning the pen, I had hung it on a peg while I went to the barn for some straw for bedding and while I was gone one of the pigs must have gotten up on her hind legs and got it and chewed it into pieces for bedding. They couldn't wait for me to bring the straw. I never forgot that because I felt very guilty for not taking better care of something so important.

Why Did Uncle Milt Limp:

My uncle Milt had this terrible limp. His one leg was much shorter than the other. From the time I first remember him until he died after I left home to seek my fortune, he limped. When he moved around his store to fill an order, he had this very pronounced limp. When I was little I just took it as a fact; that's the way Uncle Milt walks. But I guess at some point, I asked the question: why does Uncle Milt limp. Well, the simple answer was that he got hurt in a coal mining accident. After his accident, he found something better. He became Owner, Manager, and Operator of a small country store in Wilson Creek. The best description I could give regarding the type of store is the country store you might expect to see if you watched *Little House on the Prairie*. It's the store where we kids would deliver a basket of fresh eggs in exchange for various necessary supplies.

My Nephew and Buddy Bobby Ringer:

I call him Bobby in this writing even though he isn't really Bobby anymore.

I always thought it was strange that I had a nephew older than myself. My sister Mary got married young, as they did in those days. She had a baby, named him Robert Franklin Ringer, on November 8, 1930. I was born on November 25 of the same year.

Here on the next page is a photo of Bobby, me and Peggy. My three sisters in the back are from left to right Betty, Helen, and Elaine.

Bobby and I went to high school together. He sometimes called me Uncle. Other kids thought it was strange too that an uncle and his nephew would be in the same classes. Bobby was more into sports during those years than I was. He played basketball and I played in the band and sang in the chorus. I tried basketball but between band, chorus and farm chores, I didn't really have time to practice.

Junior, Peggy, Bobby and my 3 sisters

Bobby worked on the farm during the summers of our high school years. We called him either Bobby or Pinto. He goes by Bob now but for this writing, since I am writing about the past, I will continue to refer to him as Bobby.

One time, Bobby and I tried to chew tobacco. We both got sick. I think we probably swallowed some of the tobacco juice. We were probably influenced into trying it by the big painted signs that were on many of the barns at that time. The signs read "Chew Mailpouch Tobacco, Treat Yourself to the Best." Some treat all right. We vowed that we would never chew tobacco again. I have noticed as recently as 2003 that those signs still can be seen on old barns in Pennsylvania.

On the farm, Bobby and I had pet calves. His was named Jack Jack, and mine was Boopy Doo.

Bobby worked on the farm a lot during the summers. I don't think that he ever got paid anything for it. Of course I didn't either but I was a more direct part of the family. During one summer after Merle came home from the army we spent a lot of time helping him remodel his barn. We worked as his assistants. During one stretch, we became cement mixers. We used a big shallow wooden box to mix the cement. We would put the cement and water in the box and mix it with garden hoes. Sometimes we would get it too sloppy and sometimes it would be too dry and Merle would growl us. We were high school kids on summer vacation and it was during our goofy years. We fooled around a lot so Merle had to be pretty patient with us. But it was a good life for us and I think that we learned a lot and had fun at the same time.

Developing a Strong Respect for the Law:

This story involves Peggy and me when I was about six and Peggy was about four. I don't think Peggy remembers the story but I remember it very well. It took place in Boswell which was a small coal mining town near Somerset and about twelve miles from my home. That's where Luella and John moved after they got married. Sometimes when they came to visit us at the old homestead, they would take me back with them for a few days. Peggy and I were close in age and we played together, mostly outside, and we weren't limited to the yard. One time we were sitting on the curb and were innocently throwing small rocks into the road (street). They were very small stones and I would say they had to be pretty harmless. While sitting there I must have heard or sensed something to my side so I turned my head and the first thing I saw was a very big black leather boot. Actually, there were two boots and above the boots was this giant of a man dressed in a black leather-looking uniform and waving a billy club in his hand. His face was very stern and he had a very mean look about him. I knew he must be a policeman because I had heard of such people and had probably seen pictures of one. But I had never really seen one. I was very scared. I knew right away that we had done something wrong and that we were in big trouble. Well, he pounded the billy club in his hand a few times, and in a stern voice told us that we should not be throwing rocks into the road and to pick them up.

That was my first run-in with the law and I never forgot it. It taught me to respect the man in uniform, the policeman. I wonder sometimes if the current generation has the same respect for the law. More often then not, when a crime is committed, it is the policeman who is often considered the bad guy. We are told that we must have compassion and understanding for the criminal because the criminal is a victim too.

Snowed In:

In the modern world, when someone is snowed in by a big snow storm for a day or two, you would think it was a catastrophe. We rely so heavily on being able to go places on a daily basis, such as the grocery store, that if for some reason we are unable to do so, it becomes a major crisis. Not so when we were kids on the farm. There were no snow plows so that when we got a snow storm and the wind blew the roads shut, which was pretty much every winter, they stayed that way until the snow melted or somebody removed the snow with a shovel. At least that's the way it was in the thirties. Sometimes our dad would use a horse pulling a log to make a path to the schoolhouse. There was no need to go anyplace anyway since we had pretty much all we needed at home. Sometimes a horse drawn sleigh was used which would turn a slight inconvenience into a fun event for the kids.

The Shirley Temple Girls on the Slate Dump:

Wilson Creek had a large slate dump near the entrance to the mine. Slate is black like coal. If you play in it, you will look like a coal miner. When coal was brought out of the mine, the slate was separated from the coal and was dumped on a pile which, over the years, became a small mountain which is what it was when I was young. Kids loved to slide down the side. We used a board, or a piece of card board, or sometimes we just used the seat of our pants. The grade was such that you would reach a pretty good speed by the time you reached the bottom. It was not what you would call a clean activity but it was fun. Perhaps more so because we did in fact get dirty. We usually did this activity with appropriate dress such as our dark colored farm work clothes. On one occasion however, Betty and Elaine couldn't resist the temptation of the slide while dressed in their Shirley Temple dresses. I don't remember the reaction from Mom but I am pretty sure that the Shirley Temple girls got a scolding but I would also bet that it was a scolding with a smile. I'm sure that our mom, if able, would have wanted to join them on the slide.

Working with Pop:

Pop was a hard worker and always believed in a day's work for a day's pay. He had very little respect for middlemen (those people who took a cut but didn't actually produce a product). I think that in his mind, salesmen, lawyers, realtors, advertiser and promoters for example were pretty much excess baggage. He believed that one should not spend energy or money on that which wasn't bread, as he would say. He would also never hire a person who smoked. He didn't want cigarettes around the place for fear of fires and also, anyone who smoked wasn't working when he was lighting a cigarette.

During the summer vacation from school I often worked with Pop in the hot summer sun hoeing and pulling weeds from long rows of corn. When we would get to the end of the row, it seemed like a natural time and place to take a rest. And we would, but Pap would have me picking rocks from the field while we rested.

During the Depression, I remember on several occasions going with him with buckets along the railroad tracks to pick up coal for home use. During those same years, we would trade props for use in the coal mine for coal. The props were cut from oak trees in our woods to a length of thirty-two inches, which was the height of the coal vein at Wilson Creek. We would haul the props down the hill to the mine in a horse drawn wagon. I can remember sitting beside Pap on the old wagon seat and sometimes he had me use the brake and it scared the daylights out of me because I was so little I could hardly handle it. The brake consisted of leather covered pads that were pulled against the back wheels by means of a lever beside the wagon seat. It was all I could do to apply enough force to be effective going down the hill and I was always afraid of not doing it well enough and the wagon would go out of control.

At the Wilson Creek coal mine, we would unload the props, get credit, and in exchange we drove away with a load of coal. There was no need to use the brakes on the way home but I worried about the horses being strong enough to get up the hill.

I still have that wagon seat at my home in California. It sits in front of the house in the entry area beside the front door. It is one of my favorite things that I have from the farm.

Every year we went to the Elijah Hoover place to pick huckleberries. When I was very small, I remember going there in a horse drawn buggy. I can remember Pap scolding us for eating and not picking. I was always afraid of running into rattlesnakes. We also picked blackberries and elder berries which were used to make jellies. In the fall, we picked hickory nuts, hazelnuts, and butternuts which we stored for the winter like the squirrels do.

Pap had a pocket watch which he had bought in 1900. It was one of those really good watches like the railroad engineers and conductors used. He carried the watch in his watch pocket and he had it attached to a small chain which was attached at the other end to his belt, or belt buckle. A familiar sight would be to see him standing in the middle of the field, or where ever he was, pulling the watch out of his pocket, opening the metal cover, and checking the time to make sure he would be home in time for supper. Throughout his life, he did this maneuver of taking out his watch many times. Shortly before he died Floyd and I were visiting with him and we noticed that with both of his hands, he was pulling what appeared to us to be an imaginary chain out of his watch pocket. He was using both hands. He did not have his watch with him at the time. He would alternately pull with one hand and then the other. He was just quietly and calmly trying to pull his watch from his pocket. After doing this for some time, he handed me the stack of imaginary chain that had accumulated in his lap. I took it of course even though it was imaginary.

My Mother Hardly Ever Rested:

If the men on the farm worked hard during those early days on the farm, then for sure the women probably worked even harder. Mom prepared three big meals every day, washed and ironed clothes (also dried them outside on a clothes line), planted and tended a large garden, milked cows, separated the cream from the milk, churned butter, patched clothing, made rugs out of old rags, cleaned house, scrubbed floors, washed windows, washed kids, helped with farm chores when the men didn't get back from working in the fields on time, and anything else that needed to be done in the care and feeding of ten kids and husband. And she still had time to grow some of the prettiest flowers in the area. And she, women in general at that time, acted very unselfish. Women rarely, if ever, sat down through a complete meal. She usually didn't eat with the large group. Instead she took care of the family, and especially the men. It was only after the men were fed that she sat down herself. It was often said, that Pop would starve beside a loaf of bread if he didn't have Mom to slice a piece for him.

Mom had a great sense of humor. She liked to joke and play tricks. One time I was hanging over the big pan watching her mixing bread dough. I was probably about five at the time. She grabbed my head and lovingly shoved my face down into the dough. She also liked to tell jokes. Such as the one about the train coming into the town of Dunkate. There was an outhouse by the tracks as the train came into town. When the train conductor yelled out the name of the town as the train entered, Kate who was in the outhouse at the time responded with "Yes, all but wiping."

Luella reminded me that Pop always went to bed early and Mom preferred to stay up later. She liked to relax and talk especially with my sisters. They would tell each other jokes some of which were a tad risqué especially when Mary and Luella came to the house. Pop probably was never aware of the kind of jokes they told. I was because sometimes I would listen from around the corner.

Mom also liked to sing while she was cooking or working around the house. A few of the songs that I can remember her singing were: "If I had the wings of an Angel, over these prison walls I would fly," or "It was sad when that great ship went down" (referring to the Titanic), or another one about Floyd Collins who was trapped and eventually died in a cave.

I think she also sang the Coal Miners song: "It's dark as a dungeon and damp as the dew, where dangers are double and pleasures are few, where the rain never falls and the sun doesn't shine, It's dark as the dungeon, way down in the mines." She used one verse of "Abide with Me" as a timer for poaching eggs.

When either Floyd or I was a baby and was still nursing, she couldn't remember which one; she put apple butter on her nipple and got a major complaint from whichever one of us that it was. Floyd claims that he was the one but I am not completely sure. Floyd also managed to get his arm caught in the washing machine ringer while Mom was washing clothes.

Some years later, when I was about thirteen, give or take a few years, Mom fell down the stairs again. This time she broke her false teeth and cut the inside of her mouth and was bleeding a lot. It was a Saturday night and Pop and I were the only ones home. The doctor came and stitched the inside of her mouth. He came to our house so often, he certainly didn't need directions. He had me helping by holding her mouth open. Pop growled because my sister Elaine who was out on a date was not there to help. At the time, I couldn't understand why he was so angry.

On the subject of growling, I think that he sometimes verbally abused Mom and my sisters. He did not treat the women in the family as well as he treated the men. I think that farm men in that time period always wanted boy babies so they would grow to be helpers on the farm. So they had a natural inclination toward favoring the boys. I never noticed that until I got a little older. The incident when Mom fell down the stairs and Pap was angry at Elaine for not being there was an example. He could have been angry at one of the boys for not being there but he was only angry at Elaine. It was a Saturday night and Elaine was out on a date.

As I grew older at some point I became aware that all was not well with my mother. She was becoming increasingly depressed and eventually she had a nervous breakdown. I believe that the hard life that she had along with the apparent lack of outward affection from Pop were contributing causes.

My sister Elaine always reminded me of Mom. When I would go to her house for visits later when I had moved away from home, she would always treat me like my mother did. When she served a meal, she would be up and down during the meal taking care of her guest and barely taking time to eat herself.

Strange Stories:

Olivia's Sketch of Night Time Grave Scene

We didn't have television in those days so story telling was a more common form of entertainment. And I seem to recall that a lot of ghost stories were common. As a result, I remember being afraid of the dark. One time I walked my cousin Lynn Romesberg home to his house up near Blackfield. It was getting dark and I was afraid to come home alone so he had to walk back home with me and then go home again. Another time, Floyd, Paul, Clyde McClintock and I listened to a program called *The Shadow Knows* and after it was over, Clyde was afraid to go home by himself. Paul claimed he couldn't walk him home because he had to get up early in the morning. Floyd had some other flimsy excuse as well so they both went off to bed. I tried to talk Clyde into staying at our house but they had no phone at his house so his mother would worry. So I had to walk Clyde home myself. The return home, about a half mile, had to be one of the scariest times in my life. I had to pass by the field where on certain nights a dreaded light would often appear above the grave of a condemned man. (See the sketch on preceding page by my granddaughter Olivia Wing depicting the grave at night with the hoot owl keeping watch.) Would the light appear this night and if it did, could I live through it or would it scare me to death?

The story, actually true, started some years before I was born. I am told that the first man to be hung in Somerset County was buried at the edge of one of Uncle Milt's fields. We farmed the field for Milt and every year when it was plowed, we would move the headstone, which was just a flat field stone actually, to allow the plow to go by and then we would put the stone back. Eventually the stone was never put back so the exact location of the grave was lost. From the road that passed our house, people would oft times see a light that appeared to come out of the grave and hover for a period and then go back down into the ground. It was said that the light was the ghost of the hanged man returning to haunt those who were responsible for his hanging. Perhaps he was also a bit annoyed that we didn't even put back the headstone.

So being scared already by the radio story, I was petrified that the light would appear. I started to regret that I was partly responsible for failure to put back the head stone and I swore it I got home alive that I would go find the field stone and place it where it belonged. Fortunately the light didn't appear that night. If it had I think that I might have died of fright. When I got home, I went straight to bed and covered my head. In the light of day I was no longer scared so I never did put back the stone.

So what was the light? Many people did see it and I am pretty sure that I did as well. So if the light was real, what was it? Floyd thinks that he has the answer. Here's his story: There was a path through the woods beyond the field where the light would appear. If someone walked this path they would be visible from the road as they passed through the edge of the field and then into the woods. Also, the path would drop a few feet as it went away from the field. Anyone traveling that path at night would be carrying a lantern (flashlights were scarce at that time). So from the road, the lantern would appear to come up from the ground as the person came out of the woods near the road, would appear for awhile as the traveler crossed the field, and would then appear to be returning to the ground as the light disappeared into the woods on the other side of the field. Personally, I don't believe Floyd's explanation. I think that it was the ghost of the hanged man looking for the farmers who took away his headstone and failed to put it back. That's my story and I'm sticking to it.

My sisters Betty and Elaine often stayed up late at night doing homework at the kitchen table. One time when they were all alone studying late in the evening, when the house was quiet and dark, they heard a strange noise in the clothes closet. They had no idea what it could be and they started to imagine that something strange was happening. So they approached the closet door armed with broom sticks and with much caution prepared for the worst. They slowly opened the door expecting perhaps a wild animal or a rat to jump out at them. Or maybe it was a ghost. But it turned out to be only me and my dog Bingo asleep on top of shoes that we kept in a big wooden box in the closet.

There is another strange story that I still remember but the origin is no longer clear to me. It may be related to some thing that I heard during those scary tales we often heard on the radio or from listening to Pop and others during one of their story telling episodes. Perhaps it was something that I heard before bedtime which became a nightmare during one of my asthmatic attacks. Here's the story as I remember it. It may sound a lot like one of Ripley's Believe it or Not stories. I'll tell it to you as I remember it and you can BELIEVE IT . . . OR NOT.

The story took place in and around Blackfield early in the 1900s. Blackfield in those days was a regular little town of several hundred people. There was a schoolhouse, which was still there when I was a boy, but at that time there was also a grocery store, a pool hall, and a bowling alley. According to the story, there was an old woman who lived in a small cabin in the woods outside of town. There was no actual road leading into the place and the cabin was sitting among the trees and underbrush such that it was difficult to find unless you knew where to look. The old woman came into town almost daily to work at whatever work she could find to obtain enough money to buy food and whatever else she needed. There was a rumor that a strange man also lived in the cabin but was rarely ever seen outside. Several young boys in town at that time became curious to find out more about the strange man so they decided to investigate to see what they could learn. So one summer day, they followed the woman to the cabin, keeping at some distance from her so they would not be seen. After they discovered the cabin location, they began to stake out the place to see if they could see the stranger when he came out. They figured he had to come out sometime. They noticed right off that there was a spring and an outhouse near the cabin and they figured he most likely would need to use both on a daily basis. Concealed in the brush, they waited. They hadn't waited long until they saw what they had hoped for. The stranger came out and first headed for the outhouse. What was strange about him was that even though it was hot weather, he wore a loose-fitting hood over his head. From a distance, he appeared to be unshaven and not very clean. After the outhouse, he went to the spring to fill a water bucket that he had brought with him. At the spring, he filled the bucket and then commenced to remove his hood, presumably to wash or take his morning bath, if you will. When he removed his hood, the three boys hiding in the brush nearby almost lost their composure. They looked briefly and then turned and ran back to town as fast as they could. What they had seen was far beyond anything that they could have ever imagined. When they had regained their composure, they agreed that they would never tell anyone what they had seen.

Under the hood, unbelievably was a large growth that extended from the man's neck at shoulder height that resembled a grotesque head of a man. Although deformed, it appeared from their vantage point to have eyes, ears, nose and mouth. It was, I decided many years later, the man's conjoined twin. The man shared his body with his twin's head.

Shortly after the boy's discovery, the cabin in the woods mysteriously caught fire and burned completely down. The old woman and the strange man were burned beyond recognition.

Was this story true? Or was it just a bad nightmare?

Pranks:

Wilbur and Walter Snyder were twins and they were regular little pranksters. Here are a few examples of their pranks.

They got their brother Bob to help them with this one. Their prank took place on the road leading out of Wilson Creek where the road crosses a bridge and the train tracks. The tracks were used by the coal miners to haul the coal from Wilson Creek to the main line in Rockwood. Sometimes the coal cars at Wilson Creek would sit across the road and block traffic. Since there was such little traffic at that time, hardly anyone cared about the road being blocked. If you were on foot, you could walk around the cars with no problem. But a team of horses pulling a wagon, or a car, which was rare, would have a problem. So one day when the coal cars were sitting across the road, one of the Snyder twins goes up to the man at the coal cars and tells him to move the cars so he can get his team across the tracks. The coal man wanted to know where his team was. The Snyder twin says the team is just around the corner. The coal man asked him if he could wait awhile but the Snyder twin said no, he was in a hurry to get his team and load across as soon as possible. So, even though it required a lot of effort on the coal mans part, he moved the cars. So the Snyder twin goes back and he and his twin teamed up like a team of horses and hitched themselves to a little wagon loaded with a small amount of hay. Bob then walked behind the wagon with pretend reins and the three of them came across the tracks with the twins playing the part of the horses pulling their little toy wagon load of hay. I guess the prank was so good that the coal man who went to a lot of trouble to move the coal cars couldn't do anything but laugh.

The Snyder family lived right next to the Hauger Cemetery for some time and this provided a natural setting for the twin's prankish nature. They would lie in wait for some non suspecting walker to come by in the dark and then they would jump out from behind a tombstone dressed in white sheets pretending that they were ghosts coming back from the dead.

There were other pranks that they pulled that were a little more drastic but for the most parts, their antics were pretty harmless. At least they weren't on drugs nor did they physically harm anyone.

Butchering:

Butchering a pig was a big event which took place generally once a year. It started out with a big fire being built under a large iron kettle. One of my brothers used a .22 to shoot the pig in the head and then the throat was slit to eliminate most of the blood. When I was fourteen, Merle told me that I was big enough to do the shooting. I took the .22 rifle and shot it right between the eyes. I wasn't very thrilled about doing it and I never did it again. After the pig was dead and the throat cut, it was hoisted up with a block and tackle and then the hair was removed with scrapers and hot water. Most of the meat, the hams, the shoulders, the side meat, and the bacon were sugar cured and then smoked in the smoke house which was done over a period of time. The smoked meat was then buried in the granary in the oats bin for safe storage until it was used. Some of the meat was canned and some of it was cooked in the big iron kettle to be ground for the pudding meat. The hog intestines were cleaned and scraped and then filled with sausage meat to make the sausage.

Butchering day was a fun day and Luella and John and their three kids would come. Also Uncle Alex was always there too. Floyd remembers that Uncle Joel would also come and he remembers that he would have a bottle of whiskey in his pocket. As usual, there was plenty of food. One of the products that resulted from the boiling down process was lard and what remained we called cracklings. The cracklings were like candy for us kids. I think here in California today, more than sixty years later, you can still buy cracklings at the flea market. They call them something else.

Picking Potatoes:

Bobby Ringer and I went to a neighbor's farm one day during our summer break from High School to pick potatoes. We got paid eight cents per bushel. We each picked over a hundred bushels so we were paid over $8.00 each. That was good money for us at that time. I remember when I got to one hundred bushels I picked another eleven bushels just to get change over and above the eight bills I was anticipating. I wanted to have some loose change so that we could stop at Tony Bertinio's to buy some ice cream on the way home and still have the $8.00 to take home.

Threshing:

Every year in the fall there was a day when neighbors would come to our farm to join forces with our family to thresh oats and wheat. This was one of the most exciting days for me during the whole summer and I would have trouble sleeping the night before. The day would start with the sound of the big coal fired one-cylinder steam driven tractor with big steel wheels slowly chugging up the dirt road pulling a threshing machine. "Chugga, chugga, chugga" was the sound that it made. The steam driven tractor would then be lined up so that a belt drive could be hooked up to drive the threshing machine. Neighbors, with wagons drawn by horses, would show up and the work of hauling the sheaves of grain from the fields to be loaded into the threshing machine would begin. Each wagon in turn would load sheaves into the machine and out would come straw, which was blown into a big straw stack, and the grain, which was separated from the straw, would come out into wooden crates. I usually worked at the grain end of the machine and would help to carry the grain into the granary. I stayed away from the blowing straw because of my marked propensity toward getting hay fever.

While all this was going on, my mother and sisters and other neighbor ladies would be preparing a big dinner which would be fit for a king. At lunch time, the men would stop on the way into the house at wash basins with soap and towels that were set out for them to wash up. They would wash their hands up to the elbows and their faces and that's about it. The rest of their body and clothes would remain pretty dusty. They would all make the traditional noise that men make by blowing air out through their mouth and nose while splashing water on their face. They would then sit down to the feast while all the women would stand by to refill any dish that was emptied and to cut more homemade bread if necessary. After all the men were fed, then the ladies would take their turn at the table.

This practice was going on when I was born and continued pretty much up until I left home to join the navy. However, the horses were replaced by tractors and the big steam driven tractor with steel wheels was replaced by a more modern tractor with an internal combustion engine and rubber tires while I was still in high school. Also, about the time I left home, the threshing machine was about to be mothballed in place of combines which did all the grain separation from the straw in the field as the grain was being cut. So the days of the large gathering to separate the grain from the straw, or threshing, were gone forever.

When I think about how my life was as a kid on the farm, I feel sorry for anyone who had his or her start in the city. My kids grew up in the city but we tried to teach them some of the values that we learned as country kids.

Elmer Pritts and His Sunday Afternoon Drive:

My brother Merle told this story. It took place in the area near Rockwood, Pennsylvania, sometime in the 1920s or early 30s. This was back in the days before Eisenhower and the interstate highways. It was before freeways and even before asphalt and cement roads. It was back in the days when horses were still used for transportation and for hauling things. At that time there were very few cars and no hard top roads at all. Just dirt roads and when it rained, they became mud roads and the few cars that did exist would cut deep ruts through the mud. To minimize the depth of the ruts, wooden planks were often laid end to end to cover the ruts. One such road in the vicinity of Rockwood is still called the Plank Road even though planks haven't been used for over sixty-five years.

Elmer was one of the fortunate few at that time to own a car. So Elmer, dressed in his best Sunday suit, picked up his lady friend on a Sunday afternoon for a drive in the country. Well, it had to be in the country since that's the only thing that existed at that time in that part of Pennsylvania. Unfortunately, while cruising along at about ten miles per hour on one of those dirt and mud roads, his wheels got into some pretty deep ruts causing the bottom of the car to drag across some rocks. Fearing the worst, Elmer stopped the car and got out to inspect the damage. His suspicions were confirmed when he spotted a small but steady stream of gasoline coming from a small hole in the bottom of the gas tank. He knew he had to act fast, since there were no gas stations nearby, and even if there were, it was Sunday and they would be closed. And there was no towing service available to come pick him up. But he had to do something quick to avoid losing all of his gas. So while lying there in the mud, part way under his car, and in his best suit with his finger over the hole in the gas tank, Elmer somehow managed, with his one free hand, to find a piece of wood, take his pocket knife from his pants pocket, open the blade, whittle a plug to the correct size, and insert the plug in the hole to stop the leak. Having done all that, Elmer got out from under the car, brushed himself off, got back in the car, and continued his Sunday afternoon drive with his lady friend.

Little Sirecho:

Bob Lutman, who is a good friend from my days with GE, had a lot of funny stories about his youth. One that I remember took place just after World War 2. He was only about three years old at the time and someone had given him a little guitar. He just loved that guitar and played it all the time. About that same time, the GIs was coming home from the war and some of them brought with them a wife from overseas. And many of those wives were Filipinos. So one of the frequently heard song verses at that time had the words "Oh She's My Filipino Baby." So little Bobby had his own version of that song that he sang while he played his little guitar and it went something like this: "Oh the pig that had no babies." And of course when he sang it that way his grandparents and parents laughed and encouraged him so he would do it more. Well, kids don't always get things quite right the first time. Sometimes it takes time to learn. Here's a case that took about fifty-five years.

When I was about five years old, there was a song that went something like this: "Little Sirecho how do you do, Hello . . . hello, Hello . . . hello. Won't you come over and play with me. You're a nice little fellow I can tell by your voice, but you're always so far away. Hello . . . hello, Hello . . . hello. But you're always so far away." The first and third hello above were loud, the second and fourth were softer and more distant.

Now I remember this song as a kid and it was one of those tunes that stuck with me throughout my life. From time to time even up to now, and I'm seventy-four, I would find myself mentally singing that tune. But that's not the story. Here's the story. All those years, up until I was nearly sixty years old, I thought this was a song about a little guy named Sirecho. Well, that's what the song says. "Little Sirecho, won't you come over and play with me, you're a nice little fellow I can tell by your voice but you're always so far away." But one day while running, that old tune was going through my head when all of a sudden, out of the blue, it hit me. There was no little guy named Sirecho. There was only an echo. It was little Sir Echo. It took me almost fifty-five years to figure that out. Well, like I said, some things take time.

The Blind Preacher:

Edward Keib stood by the back door of our old farmhouse on a Sunday afternoon after a morning of first preaching the gospel at one of the nearby churches then followed by a big Sunday dinner at our house. He sensed something happening up by the shed so he calls out in a condemning sounding voice, "Junior, are you climbing that rope again." He was right, I was climbing the rope so I answered "yes, I am." He then added in a firm voice, "This is the Lord's Day, it was meant to be a day of rest, so stop climbing the rope." This was a rope that we kids used for fun and exercise. It seemed odd to me that doing so on any day, including Sunday, could be considered by anyone as being a bad thing. I didn't understand his insistence that I stop just because it was Sunday. I did stop however but after all these years, I still remember it.

Edward Keib was a blind preacher who, along with his mother, stayed at our house for a two-week period while he spent time spreading the gospel in our area. They called this two week-period a revival if my memory serves me right. I was about eight years old at the time. This was at a time when our family consisted of ten people. The reader might wonder about the sleeping arrangements. I checked with Luella and she remembers that Mom and Pop gave up their bed and both Edward and his mother slept in the same bed in Mom and Pop's room. Mom and Pop moved into one of the beds normally occupied by one or two of the girls. The girls tripled or quadrupled up in one bed. Or some of them slept on the floor. Luella remembers Mom saying how happy she was to get them out of the house and get her own bed back. She also remembers that Pop was always inviting people to stay even though we really didn't have the proper accommodations. Inviting someone for a meal, which he very often did, but inviting them to stay overnight in a full house was another story.

Edward was a young man probably no older than twenty-five at the time. His mother served as his eyes since he was totally blind. This brings up another memory that involved me. Remember, we didn't have indoor plumbing so the Reverend needed a guide to go to the outhouse which was located down near the pig pen. I had the task of showing him the way on his very first trip there and then explaining to him the necessary detailed procedures required for him to do what he needed to do. Why me, I wondered. I was only eight years old. Of course, it was probably felt that the task would be best performed by a male since the Reverend Keib was a male. I guess his mother could have helped him but since she was also unfamiliar with our arrangement, she was probably not the best suited for the job either. I think that it should have been a job for one of my brothers or my dad, since it was his idea to keep him and his mother at our place during the two-week revival period, but they all had made themselves unavailable. So I had to do it.

When we got to the outhouse, I explained to him that it was a two-holer and that he could use either one. He asked about toilet paper and I had to tell him that there wasn't any. Actually it would be years later when we first used toilet paper after we had installed indoor plumbing. I had to explain to him that he had just two choices. I guided his hand to the Sear Roebuck catalog as the first and probably the best choice. I explained that he could just tear off whatever he felt he needed. He didn't seem to be too enthralled with that choice so he asked about the other. I guided his hand to the box containing the other choice. He looked confused and then asked "what are these?" "They are dried corn cobs," I said. He thought about it for a moment and then decided on the Sears Roebuck catalog.

When we finally got an indoor toilet some four years or so later, Mom asked Pop to pick up some toilet paper on his next trip to town. Being somewhat slow to adapt to the modern ways and being somewhat thrifty, when he came home he had bought just one roll. We still had about eight people in the house at that time. I can still hear Mom laughing and asking Pop how long he thought that should last.

Floyd's Good Christmas:

Floyd wrote this some years ago. It is one of my favorite Christmas stories. I have read it to my family at our Christmas dinner. With his permission, I am including it here as he wrote it:

"The wind blew gently as millions of big snowflakes seemed to be racing to get to the ground first. My cheeks and nose felt gently cold as flakes hit me and seemed to tell me I was in the way, keeping them from hitting the ground and building up a layer for the big logging sled which the horses pulled to bring the big logs to the sawmill. Maybe Santa needed the snow on the ground, too, so his reindeer could pull his sleigh easier. I kept walking and making tracks in the fresh snow as I approached Wilson Creek, where there were more spruce trees. My eyes searched back and forth as each little tree was beginning to bend with the load of new fresh snow building up on the tender branches. Finally, I saw one I liked. I walked around it several times. I finally shook off the snow, and then walked around it again. Then I cut it down with the little saw. I started back home following my tracks that were already disappearing with fresh snow. I knew the way to our big white farmhouse, and I wondered if Mom would approve of my choice. This was the first year I went for the tree myself. I kept counting the days until Christmas—five more and then it would be Christmas morning. This was Saturday, December 20, 1935. I was eight years old.

"This Saturday afternoon, I helped Mom with the usual chores. I caught three roosters and cut off their heads, and Mom dunked them in boiling water so we could pluck off the feathers. Tomorrow would be our usual big Sunday chicken dinner with mashed potatoes and gravy. My sister Luella and Wood came with beautiful little Peggy, who was less than two years old.

"Then came Monday—three more days until Christmas. It stopped snowing on Sunday. The snow was about a foot deep except in the road. It was drifted shut in some places three to four feet deep. This was the day Mom and Pop went to Somerset with Matt and Lil to buy presents. Mom and Pop walked the mile out to the highway through the deep snow, and there the four of them crowded into Matt's little pickup truck. They got back well after dusk. I was already fast asleep. When I got up the next morning and came to the kitchen, Mom was sitting at the table drinking a cup of coffee. The oatmeal was ready for me. She said 'Eat a big bowl, it's cold outside.' Then she said she and Pop came home well after dark and each had a big bundle of presents and she was afraid she dropped someone's present as they plodded through the deep snow in the darkness. So she asked me to follow their tracks all the way back to the highway and to look carefully to make sure someone's present wasn't dropped and then one of the ten kids wouldn't have a present. So I did. Right from the porch door I started. I stepped in Mom and Pop's footprints in the snow, making sure I hit every one, and I looked carefully to both sides to see if a gift was dropped. I went past the summer house, the chicken house, through the oats field to the woods, past the pine trees to the road, then a field, an orchard, Harrison Pritt's house, then his barn, the big woods and the ball diamond, the Long farm, the spring along the road, and finally the highway where they got out of the truck. I stepped in all their footprints and looked to both sides—all the way there and back. I rushed into the kitchen, 'Mom, you didn't drop a single gift.'

"Christmas morning came and we went to the tree early, the tree I cut and dragged the long way home. There was my present. As I opened it, I thought of Mom and Pop's trip-they walked the one mile through the deep snow and then rode twelve miles in the cold truck to Somerset, then through the deep snow and darkness. They hung onto each child's gift, making sure none got dropped. My gift was a book—*Black Beauty*. I looked at the picture of the beautiful horse on the cover of the book. I knew I would treasure the gift. Not because of what it cost, but because of the love and care of Mom and Pop. How they walked through the darkness in the deep snow, each carrying a bundle of gifts and each making sure none was dropped so each of us ten kids would have a present Christmas morning."

The Lord's Prayer:

I went to Bible school at the Blackfield church when I was pretty small. I had to learn the Lord's Prayer and one day Floyd was helping me. I remember we were walking up the road between Uncle Milt's place and the church and here's how I remember the teaching process went: I would recite the prayer words until I got stuck and Floyd would help me out. I got all the way down to the part that goes "Give us this day our daily bread" and I couldn't remember it. So Floyd would give me a jump start with "Give us"—and then I followed with "Give us this day" but once again I was stuck. So Floyd says "Our daily" and I repeat, "Our daily . . ." I was stuck again. So Floyd says, "What do we have to eat every day?" So my eyes lit up and I said, "Give us this day, our daily potatoes."

Neighbors:

Living on a farm we didn't have many close neighbors. Uncle Milt and Aunt Emma lived about the length of a football field south of us in the direction of Blackfield. West of us about a quarter of a mile was the home of Harrison and Mammy Pritts. When I was between about five and ten years old one of my favorite things to do was to go to their house and sit at their table with a tin cup of black coffee while Harrison smoked his pipe and told stories about the old west. I loved the smell of his pipe. He kept the tobacco in a tin can and he used slices of apples to keep it moist. I'm sure that his stories were somewhat embellished but I couldn't get enough of them. One time, I was there so long that Mom had the other kids looking for me. That's when they discovered that Mammy was giving me black coffee in a tin cup. I was only about five years old at the time. I can still remember the look of their place. They had a well out front with a wooden bucket and a rope and crank used to pull the water up from the well. In their kitchen, they had a cuckoo clock.

I seldom went to Uncle Milt's house. I am not sure why but it seems the atmosphere there was less friendly than at Harrison's and Mammy's place. I do remember that they had a very nice home, a cut above most of the country homes at that time. Older brothers, especially Wilbur and Merle, made regular visits to their house before I was born. They would go there with Pap every Saturday night to listen to the radio. They especially liked to hear Amos and Andy. Some years later, when I was just six or so, Bob Ringer (that's my sister Mary's husband) brought us a big Atwater-Kent radio and Merle set it up in our living room. It was one of those big floor models. Would be a valuable antique today. To all of us, it was like a miracle. Now it was possible for us to hear the news, baseball games, boxing matches, mystery programs, *Fibber Magee and Molly*, *Amos and Andy*, *The Lone Ranger*, and many other programs. Floyd and I could even move it close to a window, turn the volume up loud, and listen to the Pittsburgh Pirates baseball game while we worked in the truck patch near the house. I guess that wasn't such a good thing for Mom's nerves.

About a mile south of our house was the town of Blackfield, if you can call it a town. It had been a thriving coal mining town before I was born but by the time I first went there, the coal mining had ended. A school remained there until the late 1930s but there were at most about 1 dozen or so houses. I also remember that in some places in and around the town there was smoke coming out of the ground. I was told that the coal under the ground was burning. And it seems that this continued for some years before it stopped.

When the coal mining dried up, unemployment in Blackfield went up close to 100 percent. I don't really know if that's true but it always seemed to me to be that way. One of the well-known inhabitants in all the years that I knew him from the midthirties until after WWII didn't have a real job. He and his wife could be seen driving past our house in their old jalopy several times a week on their way to Welly's Bar for a drink or two and then to bring home a six-pack or so. They didn't have to work because of President Roosevelt's Relief Program, or if not that program, some other program which provided him a monthly check without working. Actually, I think Pop and later Paul offered him work but he refused because he would lose his government check. Since he had lots of free time, he had a whole bunch of kids. I have heard this but don't know if it is true for certain, one of his kids had a kid. I don't want to think about who the father was. Some of his kids grew up to rely on the government for support just as he himself did. I often thought, as did Pop I'm sure, that he should have never been put on relief at the start. He would have found work, or help from people like Pop, and he probably wouldn't have had so many kids in poverty. He, and his family, would have been better off.

Another infamous family in Blackfield was the Kelly family. My recollection of the Kelly brothers was that they were somewhat reckless and daring. One time Matt and his brother were down by our barn and one brother held a corncob in his hand while the other brother shot it out with a .22 rifle. Merle gave them a lecture and told them never to do that again. Another incident years later suggests the seriousness of their situation. Some one of the family came down to our house with the urgent news that Matt had shot himself and needed immediate help. Merle and Floyd dropped whatever they were doing and went off to do what they could in the old Dodge panel truck. They found Matt with a bullet hole in his side. He had rigged a shot gun up with a string attached to the trigger. When he pulled the string, it moved the gun so it wasn't a direct hit. Floyd and Merle carried him to the back of the pickup and drove him off to Somerset. Floyd held him in the back of the truck and he relates that Matt must have only weighed about eighty-five pounds. The wound was covered with blood and leaves. I can't say that they rushed him to the hospital because Merle was not what you would call a fast driver, but they got Matt to the hospital in time. Matt survived and I guess he lived many more years. I would like to think that his life straightened out after that but I'm afraid it didn't. Some years later when I was in high school, I was coming home from band practice and as I was passing by Welly's Bar, there was some big commotion going on. There were a bunch of cars and I think at least one police car. As I passed by the bar they were carrying a body out. I learned later that a man was killed and Matt was involved in the incident.

There were other more upright citizens living in Blackfield but I never really knew very many of them. Some of my cousins lived near Blackfield and they were good people. My cousin Gook stayed up at the Matt Romesberg place when she visited in the area. I never knew her real name until Luella told me recently that it was Grace. We always called her Gook. They were all good people but the problem with Gook was when she came to our house she would give me a big hug and kiss and run her fingers through my hair and rave about how cute I was. I was so embarrassed. Sometimes when I knew she was coming I would try to hide but she would find me.

My sister Luella was first married to Woodrow and they lived near Blackfield. Peggy and Joann were born there. Woodrow died when Joann was still very small. She later married John Ogle and they moved to Boswell. But Peggy and Joann came to our house often. We posed for a picture on one of their visits. I'm the one in the middle.

Junior and Ogle Kids and chickens ~ 1939

I was more familiar with Wilson Creek which was about one half mile north of our farm. My uncle Alex who never married lived there. The story has been told that he had a lady friend and they were about to be married but she died. He never courted another. He worked in the coal mines when he was young. He would come to our house about once a week for a good meal. I think that he went to the homes of his other brothers sometimes as well. When he came to our house, he had the habit of sitting in the rocking chair with his hands linked behind his head and he would hum. Yes, he would just hum. He didn't talk very much. When Pop would come in from his work, they would talk in Pennsylvania Dutch. When supper was ready, Mom would say, "Come on, Alex," and he would come to the table. One time, for reasons I can't remember, I was at his house and he gave me lunch. We had a sandwich made with homemade bread, butter and onions, and with a little salt. I still like an onion sandwich made the same way. When Merle took over the Bittner farm he fulfilled his part of the deal with Alex. He took Alex in his declining years as part of his household until Alex died. It was common in those days that the family members took care of the old instead of sending them to a nursing home.

There were probably about twenty houses in Wilson Creek when I went to grammar school. Albert Kusch was one of my good buddies also lived there. He later joined the navy with Bobby Ringer and me. He read a lot of books and had the reputation for being very bright. Shirley Pritts also lived in Wilson Creek. She was about my age and I always thought that she was the prettiest girl in the Wilson Creek School.

During my eight years in grammar school in Wilson Creek, I always regarded Sonny Weimer as my best buddy. He also lived in Wilson Creek. He never went to high school. The last time that I saw him was just before Bobby Ringer and Al Kusch and I went off to join the navy. He was fixing the roof on his parent's house at the time. I told him that we were joining the navy and suggested that he come with us. He said no. Shortly after that he was drafted into the army and was sent to Korea. He never made it back alive.

Frankie and Louie Omerzo lived in a company house by the Wilson Creek coalmine. Louie was about my age so I knew him best. He served in the army in Korea and was one of our decorated heroes.

Jesse Albright was another Blackfield neighbor. He loved to hunt so much, that when he died, his wife had him buried with his guns.

There were other neighbors but generally not within easy walking distance. But we all had one thing pretty much in common. None of us had much money (except perhaps the Zimmerman family). But I don't think that mattered very much.

Grandparents, Aunts and Uncles:

It is not my intent to get into the family tree very much. It's way too complicated. The book titled *Romesberg Family History*, or more precisely *The Romesberg-Remsberg-Ramsperger-Riemensperger Genealogy*, compiled 1984 by the Romesberg Historical Committee provides a pretty good summary of the Romesberg history back to Germany and from there back to Switzerland in the early 1600s. Also, a book titled *Biographical Review and Genealogy of Frederick Swearman and His Descendants* compiled 1974 by David Hay covers the family history on my mother's side.

Here is a photo of my paternal grandparents Levi and Mary Ann Livingston Romesberg. The photo was taken before 1889, which was the year he died. Mary Ann lived for another forty years after Levi died. Those were the hard years that I spoke of earlier when Pop had to quit school at the age of twelve to help keep food on the table for the large family.

On the following page is a photo of my maternal grandparents George and Missouri Belle Swearman. My mom is also in the picture in the back row next to Missouri Belle. The photo and description beneath the photo was taken from the *Biographical Review and Genealogy of Frederick Swearman and his Descendants* by David Hay.

Here are the names of my aunts and uncles. On Pop's side, there were one dozen total. Ten grew to adulthood. On my mother's side, there were a baker's dozen. Eleven lived to be adults.

The following lists the twelve siblings on the Romesberg side:

Barbara Ellen	2/17/1865-3/12/1902
Joel	4/28/1867-8/6/1938
Emma	5/19/1869-10/27/1908
Alexander	5/13/1871-5/6/1958
Hiram (Davey)	3/2/1871-1924
Levi	8/31/1873-10/14/1877
Nettie	4/2/1877-4/18/1877
Ephraim	5/27/1878-3/25/1964
Milton	3/14/1881-8/4/1963
Joseph	5/4/1883-6/23/1968
Ralph	12/13/1885-6/8/1969
Della	9/10/1888-1/6/1984

Likewise, here are the 13 siblings on the Swearman side:

Frederick Swearman	4/6/1890-8/24/1924
Katie Francis	5/27/1891-7/9/1967
Mayme Susan	9/23/1892-10/26/1965
Minnie	1/28/1894-2/25/1953
Robert	4/17/1895-?
Nellie	3/8/1897-3/9/1897
Myrtle	4/6/1898-9/3/1898
Sadie	3/18/1900-?
Bertha	11/6/1901-11/1/1966
George	4/15/1903-?
Ruth	3/11/1909-?
Ada	6/21/1910-?
Grace	12/13/1912-11/29/1972

Just a few notes on some of my memories of aunts and uncles that were still living after I was born:

Aunt Della and her husband Scott Snyder lived about fifteen miles from our house. They came to our house quite often on Sunday and they would bring the Sunday papers with the funnies. I liked to read about the Katzenjammer kids, Maggie and Jiggs, Andy Gump, Smokey Stover, and others that I have forgotten. Aunt Della always brought us something. Della was a very sweet lady. Sometimes we kids would go to her house in Acosta, Pennsylvania, (another coal mining town) and stay overnight.

I have written about Uncle Alex who lived in Wilson Creek and came to our house every week. Also, Uncle Milt was the one uncle who owned and operated the store in Wilson Creek. Uncle Ralph was the one who lost his leg to the stump puller.

Uncle Joel (pronounced Yoel) seems to have followed in the footsteps of our grandfather Levi. He liked his whiskey. He also played poker with some of his friends. On one of those poker nights in an old shack down by the railroad tracks in Rockwood, a fight broke out during the game. Perhaps someone was cheating. When the fight was over, one of the players lay dead due to a heavy blow to the head. Uncle Joel was found guilty of manslaughter and had to spend time in prison.

I never knew Uncle Hiram who had died at age fifty-one in 1924 some six years or more before I was born. Mom once told me that he had gotten a piece of steel in one of his eyes. It may have come from using a large sledge hammer to drive a metal wedge. From my own experience, I have seen the metal on wedges get all bent over around the top and sometimes pieces of the metal would fly off when the wedge was struck. Perhaps this is what happened to Hiram. In those days, they didn't know how to deal with eyes like today. It was very painful and the metal worked its way deeper into the eye. He would sit in pain for days in the cold dark cellar to avoid sunlight. The ordeal eventually caused his death.

Uncle Joe lived just the other side of Wilson Creek. I didn't know Joe very well but I know that he was a good man. I think that I knew his son Clarke better. Seems to me, I may be wrong on this one, that I was introduced to Clarke's wife's little sister as a potential girl friend when I was still in school. I received the photo of the old barn included on page 1 from Clarke's son Clarke Jr.

On my mother's side, there were more uncles and aunts. Most memorable for me was Uncle Rob. He was in the army and spent months in a trench in Europe during the Second World War. He may have been exposed to poison gas, I'm not sure. When he came home, I never heard him talk about the war. He was a kind and gentle man. When he was just 11.5 years old his school teacher signed a working certificate so he could go to work in the coal mines with his brother Fred. Eventually all three brothers, Fred, Robert, and George, had to work in the mines because their dad could not work due to rheumatic fever and probably miners asthma and/or black lung.

My mom's sisters all lived about ten miles away and we would see them often mostly at their homes. We always had a big meal. During each summer there would be a Swearman reunion which was a special treat for us kids. All of the living aunts and uncles on my mother's side would be there with their spouses and kids. It was a big group and a lot of fun for everyone. We always played games especially softball during those events. My brother Paul was a power hitter and one time he hit a long drive to left field beyond the limits of the playing area. The ball landed among the parked cars and broke one of the car windows. Would you believe that it was his own car that he hit? I always believed that the Swearman family members were all very kind and gentle people.

High School Days:

Having been through high school during my teens followed by a tour of duty in the navy, I think I have concluded that all boys (well maybe some boys) should skip the normal high school and should be sent straight to military school. When a young man is going through puberty, it is a difficult time to be learning anything. I don't feel that I learned much in high school. I did get a lot out of playing in the band and singing in the chorus, but the normal classroom stuff, I was not ready to really learn. I needed time to grow up and get motivated. Later when I finished five years in the navy, and then went on to college, I was a different person. I was motivated.

The high school that I attended was the same one that Floyd and my sisters before me had attended. It was in Rockwood and consisted of one main building and one separate building which was used primarily as the music hall and auditorium. It was a small school, there were only thirty-five in my graduating class. We didn't have school buses then and it was over four miles each way. And as we describe it to our kids now, we point out that it was uphill both ways and always cold and windy. Actually, bus service started my senior year. So I only had to endure three years of getting to school by walking, hitchhiking, or by bicycle.

My sister Mary Ringer, and her son (my nephew) Bobby, lived in Rockwood during the time that we went to high school. Bobby and I spent a lot of time together except he played basketball and I played in the band. Sometimes I would stay over at his house depending on what was going on and if I wasn't needed at home on the farm.

In the wintertime it could get pretty bad walking down the Baker flat between our place and Rockwood. I always felt sorry for my sisters before me because they had to walk most of the time. It wasn't so bad for me because I was usually able to get a ride with someone or ride the bike. But there were times when we, usually Al Kusch and I, had to walk the whole distance.

We had to read Macbeth for Literature class and for me it was like pulling teeth. I finished reading it finally but somehow the book got left out in the rain and got ruined. The teacher demanded that I pay for the book. I think it was something like one dollar. I claimed that it wasn't my fault. So I took up a collection and collected the amount due in pennies and gave them to the teacher. She was not happy with me.

One time several of us were in the pool hall shooting pool and were consequently late for band practice. Our teacher, who was an ex-marine, got angry and suspended all those who were late except me. He knew that I lived far away and was often late for a good reason. I didn't confess to being in the pool hall. The real truth was, I only stopped by on the way to practice to see who was there and then like the rest, lost track of the time.

A man named Walt lived near the high school building. He had a crow named, oddly enough, Jim. On days when it was warm enough to open the window, Jim would sit on the window sill and talk to us. He would say things like "where's Walt" or "I'm going down south." He would also laugh at us. He would say "Haw, Haw, Haw" instead of "Caw, Caw, Caw" like other crows.

Ridgerunners ~ 1948

This photo shows the four of us known at that time as the ridge runners. From left to right are Glenn Baer, EJay Romesberg, Al Kusch, and Bob Ringer. This picture was taken in Rockwood in about 1948 when we were all seniors. By golly, I think I still have that shirt that I was wearing.

My biggest satisfaction in high school came from playing in the band and singing in the chorus. We were a very small school but we still had a very large band and chorus. There was a very high percentage of participation. There also seemed to be a lot of community support. We went to nearby towns to participate in many musical events during the summer months as well as during the school year.

We also had a brass sextet consisting of three trumpets and three trombones. I played one of the trombones. We would often play at churches and other community gatherings. There was a time when I was late to a scheduled performance at one of the churches in Rockwood and as a result our time slot had to be postponed to a later period. Our leader, Mr. Illar, gave a lengthy explanation as to why I was so often late at such events. He explained how I had to milk the cows, slop the hogs, feed the chickens and then walk four miles uphill from the farm to the church. What he said was true in general but quite exaggerated. I can still remember the very last time the sextet performed. It was at the Grange Hall on New Year's Eve and for our very last piece, we played "Auld Lang Syne." The very last note for me in that piece was a low b flat. I don't think that I ever hit a low b flat before or after but I hit it then. For me, it was like scoring the winning touchdown in the big high school playoff game. I felt like I retired from the sextet a winner.

When I got out of high school, I put my trombone away and never played it for years. Now I usually get it out at Christmas and try to play a Christmas song. But I soon realize that I can't play it anymore and the horn goes back in the case until the next Christmas.

I have to say that I am not very proud of my days in high school. I was not motivated. I needed to do some growing up. My brother Floyd ahead of me was a good student and one of Rockwood's best basketball players. Maybe he was a hard act for me to follow. For years after high school and after my days in the navy, when I would come home to visit with Elaine we would go visiting and Elaine would introduce me to someone as her brother. When she did, more often than not, they would say "Oh, you're the one that played basketball and went on to college and got a PhD in Chemical Engineering" and I would say "No, I'm the other one that nobody talks about—they let me out sometimes on weekends."

The old high school building is long gone and now they have a new high school with a big gymnasium and big parking lot. Of course they also have buses to bring kids from all over. Brother Wilbur made the observation one time that if they had the kids walk to school for exercise like in the good old days, they could eliminate the big expensive gymnasium, the parking lot and the school bus.

The Carnival Strongman:

Every year the carnivals would make the rounds to the small towns in the area. During any given summer, there would be at least a half dozen within fairly easy distance from home so that before the summer ended, we would have visited several usually on weekends. On one such occasion when we were high school seniors, Al Kusch and I were selected by a so called Carnival Strongman to help him perform his feats of strength. He said that he would pay us twice as much as he paid the last boys that helped him which was of course nothing (i.e., $2 \times 0 = 0$). We would, for example, be asked by the strongman to hold a piece of wood while he drove nails through the board with his hand. He also showed how strong he was by bending spikes with his hands. He would wrap the spike in a cloth, or kerchief, and then using both hands he would bend the spike until it was shaped like the letter U, more or less.

When I got home, I though about the spike bending act and decided that it probably was not that hard. It seemed like the spikes that he used were made from steel that was fairly ductile. I found some spikes in our shed that looked like the ones that he used so I wrapped one in my handkerchief and guess what; I could bend it. Imagine that, a 125-pound weakling could bend spikes like the Carnival Strongman.

I showed Al Kusch what I could do so he started calling me Spike. The name stuck and followed me through the navy and college.

Chapter 2

My Time in the Navy
(1948-1953)

Remembering Pearl Harbor:

SOMETIME SHORTLY AFTER December 7, 1941, Floyd and I walked into the kitchen of our country home and Mom informed us that the Japanese had bombed Pearl Harbor. I was only eleven years old at the time. In the days, months, and years to follow, the war became the news. They made movies about war stories with the likes of John Wayne and William Holden. National support for the war effort was 100 percent. Patriotism was everywhere and political party affiliation didn't matter. Support for President Roosevelt was overwhelming. They stopped building automobiles for several years during the early forties and converted the assembly lines to accommodate the building of tanks, jeeps, war planes, liberty ships, and other implements of war. Women joined the work force as riveters and such while most able bodied men went off to the battle front. Those left at home were encouraged to plant victory gardens and collect aluminum foil and other metals to be used for building airplanes. Even little kids helped. They instituted rationing of gasoline and other hard to get items. I wanted to go fight the bad Japanese but I was too small and I was too young. Saying that may sound strange but maybe it was because I was too young to enlist so it was safe for me to act brave. Shortly after that Day of Infamy, Merle went into the Medical Corps of the army and went to India. Paul was eventually drafted, as well, and remained stateside for a short while before the war was over. Wilbur didn't pass his medical and so he stayed at home and helped the war effort by farming. Floyd was also too young initially and the war was over by the time he came of age. In the meantime I was wishing that I were older so I could join up. By the time I was seventeen, the war was over so I could not get in to fight the Japanese or the Nazis.

Boot Camp:

Several days after I graduated from high school I joined the navy, but not so much to be a war hero but rather for the adventure. I was not yet motivated to go to college and Pop couldn't afford it anyway. As it turned out, my time in the navy helped me mature. By the time I got out, I was ready to go to college. I was motivated to study. Had I gone to college right out of high school, it would have been a mistake.

Al Kusch, Bob Ringer, and I all enlisted together. We were all from the same graduating class. Red Engle, from the same class, also joined but at a slightly different time. We would meet him later while stationed in New London, Connecticut. When I signed up Pop did not want me to go. The recruiting officer had to come down to the farm and talk him into letting me sign up. (See photo of the four of us later).

The last job that my nephew Bob and I did on the farm before going off to the navy was to cultivate corn. Each of us on separate tractors (I on my little Allis Chalmers and Bob on the Farmall). The next day we walked down the road together as we left for boot camp. Our mothers cried while they watched us from the kitchen window of the old farmhouse.

Shown on the following page is our high school graduation photo. Notice the jacket and bow tie. All four ridge runners wore this same jacket and tie for our graduation. I couldn't find the photos of Al Kusch and Glen Baer. You might think that we were poor and couldn't afford more than one jacket and tie for all four of us. Actually, I think that it was my idea for us all to dress alike for the photo. The jacket and tie were mine. This article was in the local paper when we went to boot camp

Shortly after getting to Great Lakes Naval Station, I found myself in this huge airplane hangar with an acre or so of naked men all getting a short arm inspection. How humiliating.

We went to the Great Lakes Training Center for our boot camp training. There we spent three months learning how to tie knots, march, obey orders, clean our barracks, wash our clothes, make a bed, row a boat, swim and other stuff. I couldn't swim a stroke when they told me to jump in the pool at the training camp. I soon learned how to swim a little bit but I am still not a good swimmer. I may have known how to tie knots when I came out of boot camp but I think I can only tie a granny knot and a square knot today. Jean still laughs at me every time we make the bed. She reminds me that I was in the navy and was supposed to know how to tuck the sheets in at the corners.

At Great Lakes

Robert Ringer

E. Jay Romesberg, son of Mr. and Mrs. E. J. Romesberg, and Robert Ringer, both of Wilson Creek, are undergoing "boot" training at the Great Lakes (ILL.) Naval Training Station. Both were graduated from

E. Jay Romesberg

Rockwood High School in the class of 1948 and plan to enter submarine training upon completion of their recruit duties. Romesberg is an uncle of Ringer. Their address in USNTC, Co. 240, Great Lakes, Ill.

Ringer and Romesberg Make local paper

One day while there at the training camp, I walked into the barracks and saw some of the men of our company (Company 240) holding down a sailor and they were painting him with black shoe polish and covering him with feathers from a pillow that they had torn apart. I asked my next door bunk buddy what was going on. He told me the guy was queer. I thought that was pretty harsh treatment for a guy who was a little funny. My bunk buddy had to explain to me what a queer was. I was shocked. So if you are paying attention to what you just read, there were two things very shocking here. One, I was seventeen years old and I didn't know about homosexuals. Two, the military in 1948 considered a simulated tar and feathering applicable punishment for a homosexual in their ranks. Apparently I had led a very sheltered life since I didn't realize that some folks like members of the same sex and not the other sex. But how can that be I thought. I had never heard of a queer, or in today's speak, a gay. When my bunk buddy explained it to me, I was shocked and stayed shocked for days. The whole concept didn't make any sense to me. Male and females were built different for a reason. How could two males, or two females match up? Why would they want to was the bigger question. It was like a dairy farmer who had all bulls and no cows and expected to raise cattle and produce milk. It was like trying to make an electrical connection with two male, or two female, connections. It didn't make any sense no matter how hard I tried to understand it. Imagine Noah loading the ark with two males or two females of various species. Picture this, if you will, God calls up Noah and says, "Hey Noah, you better get a move on. I don't know how long I can hold off on this flood thing." And Noah responds with "Give me a break, I'm doing the best I can but I keep having same sex couples of various species showing up to board the ark so what am I expected to do." So what's God going to say? Will he say "don't worry about it, if that's what they want let them board?" I don't think so. Talk about endangering the species. The animal rights people would have had a fit. Also, regarding the tar and feathering job on the queer guy, pretty much everybody agreed that it was the correct thing to do. After all, the guy was queer.

Sorry, but that's how it was back in 1948. Fortunately, it's not that way today and I am better educated now then I was then. I have no problem with homosexuals. Remember, I live on the left coast. It just took me some time to understand and accept the real world.

Al Kusch got out of the navy early though I don't remember why. He was a pretty smart guy and after he left the navy he went to school and ended up working in the San Francisco area in some state of the art field involving, I believe, the development of uses for laser light. Bob and I went to New London, Connecticut to submarine school.

New London, Connecticut:

Shortly after arriving at New London, Connecticut and while still in Submarine School, Bob and I decided to go to New York City. It was the winter of 1948. We were both eighteen years old at the time and we were as back-woodsy as you could get, still wet behind the ears, as they would say in those days. We took the train on Friday and we spent the first night, all night, pretty much moon gazing at the large buildings and playing the machines in the penny arcades. They really did have penny machines at that time. At one point we found one of those quarter machines where you could cut a record. So we decided to make a message for our mothers. We spent some minutes rehearsing what we were going to say and then got into the booth and deposited our quarter. As soon as the record started to turn, we started to laugh. I think the record was only a minute or so long and we laughed nearly all the way through it. We sent it to my sister Mary, Bob's mother, and she just loved it. She most likely had it until the day she died. I heard her talk about it many times during my visits to Rockwood and the home farm.

During our second night in the big city, we decided that we really needed a good place to sleep. But that presented a problem because we only had a few dollars between us. So I came up with the idea of sleeping on one of the benches at the railroad station. I had read, or heard somewhere, that bums do it all the time, so why not a couple of tired sailors. So we asked someone how to get to the Pennsylvania Railroad Station. So we followed their directions, we thought, and entered into this very swanky room with very high ceilings, fancy chandeliers, fancy carpets and lots of big soft arm chairs. We though this was a bit fancy for a railroad station but since we were not familiar with the big city ways, we decided that stations in New York were not like the station in Rockwood, and so we didn't ask questions. Instead, we each found a nice big armchair and snuggled down and went to sleep. Several times during the night and early morning hours, I noticed men in uniform going back and forth but I didn't give it much thought. Then at about 6:00 or so in the morning, one of the uniformed men came up to me and very politely said, "You gentlemen will have to leave now because the guests are starting to come down." Well, I guess at that point we finally realized that we were not at the Pennsylvania Railroad Station. We were in fact in the lobby of the swanky Pennsylvania Hotel.

Part of the submarine school training is to go through the pressure chamber and then come up from one hundred feet in the diving tank using the Mumson lung. The first time I tried the chamber, I had a head cold and my ears hurt too much so I had to abort. I tried it two more times with the same problem. They normally only give you three tries and you're out if you can't make it. They gave me a forth try and I made it but the pressure had ruptured my eardrums. They had me go to sick bay for several treatments where they shoved probes up my nose. At the ends of the probes was some radioactive substance which gave off alpha particles designed to cause scar tissue to form on the eardrums. I have always suspected that I was being used as a guinea pig but in any event it worked and my hearing was always okay. I learned from that experience that the holes from my nostrils go straight into my head and not at an upward angle.

Spike Romesberg USN mug shot

Just two weeks before graduation, I came down with the mumps so I didn't graduate with the rest of the class. I graduated two weeks later and they assigned me to the USS *Sarda* (SS-488) which operated out of New London with the mission of taking submarine school men to sea for training purposes. I had wanted to go to Pearl Harbor but because of coming out of school two weeks later, my orders were changed for reasons that I didn't understand.

USS *Sarda* (SS-488):

I went aboard the *Sarda* and the first night there I slept on a top bunk in the after torpedo room. During the night, I had a nightmare and I sat up suddenly and my head hit a chain fall which was hanging just above my head. I just about knocked myself out. At that point I wondered what the heck had I gotten myself into.

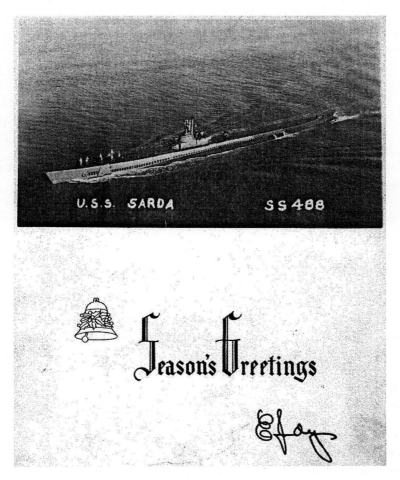

USS Sarda

My main job as a seaman when on watch aboard the *Sarda* was to stand lookout when we were on the surface or to man the bow or stern planes when we were submerged. There would be two of us standing lookout along side of the conning tower at a level just above the officer of the deck. We had binoculars and we were supposed to be looking out for other ships especially enemy ships (it was peacetime). When we heard the dive alarm which went like "ga-uga, ga-uga" and the officer of the deck would call out "Dive, Dive," we would scamper down through the hatch to the conning tower and then through the hatch to the control room. I never timed myself but I think it took less than thirty seconds from the dive order to the time we were in the control room. One time after coming out of the lookout station, I looked forward just before ducking down through the conning tower hatch, and I could see the bow sliding under the water. Also, on one such occasion, I hit my right elbow on the side of the hatch and chipped my elbow. It still bothers me a little bit and I can feel where a little chip was removed. The officer of the deck was the last man down. He would close the hatch as he came through and the sailor on duty in the conning tower would dog it down. When we, the two lookouts, got to the control room, we would go straight to the control station for the bow and stern planes which were used to help control the depth and level of the submarine. The Captain, or Officer in Charge, would provide directions such as: "Ten degree down bubble, level off at one hundred feet."

In the meantime, I was supposed to be "striking" for something such as torpedo man, machinists mate, sonar man, etc. I helped tear apart one of the engines one weekend and thought maybe I should be an engine man. I eventually decided I wanted to be a torpedo man. Of course being seasick most of the time I didn't do much studying. When I left the *Sarda* after being aboard a little over one year, I was still a seaman.

The *Sarda* was one of the fleet boats before the development of the nuclear navy. As such, it was powered by two diesel engines while on the surface and two large battery banks when submerged. The air supply to the engines, and the crew as well, entered through the main induction valve. When submerged, the main induction valve closed and the ships propulsion power as well as other power was provided by batteries. In the act of submerging, we were required to visually verify that the main induction valve did in fact close. The reason for this added assurance came about as a result of the experience of the USS *Squalis* back in 1939. The *Squalis* had just come out of an outage and was on a shake down cruise. When they dove beneath the waters off

Portsmouth, New Hampshire, the control room instrumentation indicated that all valves were shut. But the main induction valve was not. It had hung up because apparently some tool or other object had been left in the valve during the outage. As a result, twenty-nine men died and the navy got a chance to test their rescue equipment on the remaining thirty-one.

I spent about one year on the *Sarda* and I was seasick every time we went out to sea. While on the *Sarda*, nothing really noteworthy ever happened. I do remember one time being on the starboard lookout, probably seasick as usual, when I spotted something coming at us off the starboard bow. To me it looked like a torpedo but we weren't at war so it was hard to imagine a torpedo. I reported it to the officer on duty probably like this: "Something coming toward us off the starboard bow, Sir, looks like a torpedo" I was eighteen and the officer of the deck was probably no more than twenty-three. He asked me to repeat what I said. "Torpedo closing fast on the starboard bow, Sir, heading directly for us," I repeated, but this time in a more urgent tone. So he orders left full rudder, which was the wrong thing to do. As a result, we turned broadside to the torpedo, and it was a torpedo, and it hit us dead center. It hit on the upper part of the ballast tank and bounced up out of the water slightly just below my feet. I thought to myself, "hey, we just got hit by a torpedo and it wasn't a big deal." Of course, it wasn't armed. One of the other boats in the area had fired it as part of playing war games and it ran erratic. We picked it up and eventually returned it.

During war game exercises we were lying on the bottom maintaining silent running while a destroyer tried to pretend they sunk us. When the game playing was over, the captain gave the appropriate orders to obtain positive buoyancy by blowing some amount of water from the safety and /or negative tanks. We initially didn't move and some old salt of a sailor told me that we were stuck in the mud just to get my reaction, I guess. Actually, I didn't have any reaction and we weren't stuck in the mud. We just had to overcome the excess negative buoyancy by blowing more water out of the tanks.

While tied up at a pier in Groton we were next to the USS *Cochino* for several days. I was on mess cook duty at the time (that's KP duty for you Army types). The mess cook from the *Cochino* came aboard the Sarda and asked if he could borrow a can of beans. I said no problem and got a can for him. We're talking big cans you know. Half gallon size I think it was. Maybe more. He told me that he would return it and I said no problem. I forgot about it, since it really didn't matter if he returned it or not. However, some months later I was visiting my sister Helen in Washington

DC when I saw a startling headline in the newspaper. It read, "USS *Cochino* sinks in the Arctic Ocean." I was shocked and immediately thought of my mess cook buddy who had borrowed the can of beans. Needless to say, I never got repaid for the beans. Sometime later after I got back to the base I heard more of the story. It is a story of a peacetime tragedy with both good and bad results.

The details of the sinking of the Cochino during a severe Artic storm are beyond the scope of these writings here but suffice it to say that all of the crew of the Cochino were saved as the result of perhaps one of the most difficult and daring rescue efforts in Naval history. That's my opinion but I think that very few would ever disagree. However, one civilian aboard the Cochino at the time (I don't know why he was there) and six sailors from the USS Tusk which made the heroic rescue did unfortunately perish.

When the USS Tusk which was operating in the area got the distress call from their sister ship they came immediately at top speed to help. What they saw when they came along side was startling. The Cochino was dead in the water completely at the mercy of extremely rough seas. Most of the ships crew were topside lashed to the sail with the icy waters washing over them with every wave. Some were in their underwear, some were burned and injured, and only some were in life jackets. The crew had to abandon the subs compartments in a hurry due to hydrogen explosions and fires. Since the bridge only holds about 7 men, they were being supported on the sides of the sail by temporary lines and they were slowly freezing to death. In addition, the sub was taking on sea water and was slowly sinking. It was imperative that they be rescued quickly.

How the rescue was made with the north sea raging was nothing short of a miracle. Somehow, using lines, rafts, and a plank (I don't know where they got a plank) they were able to transfer all of the Cochino sailors one at a time onto the Tusk. The Captain was the last to be transferred and shortly after he came on board, the Cochino turned bow up and with a blast of spray she took her last dive.

A guy named Hafley was on the *Sarda* while I was there. He had an old Model A convertible that he had painted red and yellow. Hafley was a hell-raiser but I regarded him as a good friend, and vise versa. On several occasions, he took me along as his driver so that he could drink adult beverages and I could drive him home. He almost always had too much to drink. For a while he lost his license and he allowed me sometimes to use his car without him. The car was something that people noticed if you drove it down town. Remember, it was an old convertible and it was painted red and yellow. One time on the way home from Willimantic, Connecticut, he had had a few too many drinks. I was driving as I always did and was totally sober and suddenly without any explanation or reason, he put his fist through the windshield. I took him to sick bay on the base to get his hand stitched. The doctor asked him if it hurt. He looked at me and said, "Does it hurt?" and I said, "Yes just a little bit." So he turned to the doctor and said, "Yes, just a little bit." I told the doctor that he had a little too much to drink and that there was no other problem. The doctor came pretty close to putting him on report.

In spite of his being somewhat rowdy Hafley had class. He introduced me to the song "Malagenia." To this day, it is still my favorite song especially when done by Roy Clark on his guitar.

There was another sailor named Connover on the *Sarda* during this time period. His girl friend's name was Donna. He had her name tattooed on his arm. I asked him what he would do if they broke up. He informed me that a break up would not happen. It wasn't more than a couple of months until they did in fact break up. Sometime later the question of what to do with the name Donna on his arm came up. I told him he had better find another girl named Donna. I lost track of him so I don't know what ever happened.

One time one of the guys aboard ship was trying out a brand new rod and reel on the ships fantail while the ship was tied up to the dock. One of his buddies asked if he could try it out. So his buddy makes a vigorous cast and the rod slipped out of his hand in the process. The brand new rod and real sailed through the air and landed in the water about fifty feet from the boat. And that was the end of the brand new rod and reel.

The *Sarda* was a fleet type submarine which operated mostly on the surface and it always seemed to me that the motion was a lot like a cork floating on the water. So I was seasick almost all the time when we left the dock. They didn't have any seasick remedy at that time, at least nobody offered me any. I became known as the guy who was always calling for O'Rourke. An old Chief would hear me in the head heaving and he would comment on my calling O'Rourke. O'Rourke is the sound I made when I was throwing up. Also, aside from being seasick most of the time, I was also just a little bit claustrophobic. So let me recap. I was a sickly kid while I was growing up on the farm, I joined the navy and I couldn't swim and I didn't really like the water, I got seasick as soon as we would leave the dock, I got my ear drums busted while trying to pass the pressure test to get into submarines, and I was a bit claustrophobic. So what was I doing on a submarine? After about one year, the Captain or the Exec, I forget which, suggested that maybe I should settle for shore duty. So I transferred to the Engineer and Repair Dept (E&R Dept) at New London. So ended my seasick sea duty. For the remainder of my navy days, I was in the E&R Dept for over three years after which, I spent a winter in Ontario, Canada, on a snow compaction project.

Engineer & Repair (E&R) Department:

When I was transferred to the E&R Department they needed help in the office so I decided to become a Yeoman. As such, I worked in the office and reported directly to the Lieutenant who was second in charge of the Department. For those of you who don't know what a yeoman does, a yeoman is like a secretary. Old salty sailors would sometimes call a yeoman a "titless wave." But they didn't dare call me that because part of my job was making out the watch list and handing out liberty cards. I was in a position where I could get someone his liberty card a wee bit early on a Friday which might allow an early start on a long weekend trip. Or, I could put someone on an undesirable watch station for the graveyard shift. Not that I necessarily would of course. Also, since a yeoman works closely with the Officers in charge, sometimes the position can be used as a position of influence. I was a second class petty officer by the time I was discharged which is still two promotions below a Chief Petty Officer. But that's another story.

While working there my best friends were Robert Reese, Arnold Prather, and Bobby Hulse. I lost track of Prather and Hulse but still get together occasionally with Reese.

One time Bobby Hulse brought his car into the shop at the E&R Dept and I was helping him install a new fender. We got it all installed and put the wheel back but did not tighten the lugs because he was taking it to another shop just around the corner to do some more work on it which he told me required taking the wheel off again. I told him to be sure to tighten the lugs when he was done. But unknown to me, he changed his mind and didn't go to the other shop for the additional work. He forgot about the loose lugs nuts. That Friday he and Prather and Reese went to New York. They had asked me to go but I said no. It turns out that Hulse had never tightened the lugs and the wheel came off on the trip. In the process it tore the fender off that he had just put on. Fortunately, no one was hurt. I always felt a wee bit responsible for not insisting that the lugs were tightened.

We had a lot of spare time while being stationed at New London. Sometimes I would feel a bit guilty if we were not doing something constructive. I found out one time that we could check out fishing gear. So Prather, Hulse, and Reese and I tried going fishing a few times. We never really caught anything interesting but it was fun.

They had a gymnasium and plenty of sports equipment to work out. I met a black athlete who could put his feet up on a stool about the height of a chair and then with his hands on the floor would do two hundred pushups without stopping. I felt so inadequate that I decided to try to get into shape. I tried the pushups but could only do a dozen or so. But they had other things. I liked to climb a rope with just my arms. I was pretty good at that since I wasn't all that heavy. Also, I tried to get us into running occasionally. We did go out on the highway near the station and run a few miles on several occasions but it never really caught on. We would usually have a special sandwich, known locally as a grinder, and maybe a beer or two after running. What ever we gained by the running we lost in the grinder and beer. Some twenty-five years later, I would take up running again in a more serious way.

I had a 1950 Ford during the last two years or so while I was stationed ashore in New London. We had to stop at the gate when we left the base so that the marines could check us for contraband. I never had any. One time the marine, or Jar Head as we called them amongst ourselves, wanted to check my glove compartment more carefully but it was dark and he didn't have his flashlight. So he used mine that was lying on the front seat. It turned out that the flashlight was navy issue. I had been using it for years just like everybody else was doing. He sited me for taking Government property off base.

While working at the sound analysis laboratory one time, two of my buddies were horsing around and they put my navy jumper on me with my arms not in the arms of the jumper where they were supposed to be. The jumper when put on in that fashion is much like a straight jacket. My claustrophobia kicked in and I panicked. They thought it was funny. Eventually they realized that I was seriously claustrophobic with the straight jacket type situation they had put me in so they got me out of it.

Hitchhiking as the Primary Way to Travel When on Shore Leave:

I went home to Rockwood, Pennsylvania on long weekends (seventy-two-hour pass) on quite a few occasions while stationed at New London.

The total distance was about four hundred miles from the base to my home in Pennsylvania. The acceptable way of traveling at that time, before I got my 1950 Ford, was hitchhiking. Sounds risky, but not so much then as it would be now. One time I got a ride with a guy who was tired and he asked me to drive. We were on the Pennsylvania turnpike, it was night, and it was wintertime. He was asleep and I was at least half awake. We came out of one of the seven tunnels on the turnpike and it was icy. The car did at least two complete 360-degree turns and came to rest along side of the road. He woke up and I asked him if he wanted to drive and he said no and almost immediately went back to sleep. The man had nerves of steel.

Bob Ringer and I were hitchhiking home one time and we were momentarily stranded on Route 22 in a small town in Pennsylvania. It was so cold that I went into an entryway of an apartment house and waited for a car to stop for Bob. When it finally did, I high-tailed it out and got into the car with him.

On another occasion I had hitchhiked home for the weekend, and on Sunday afternoon Mom and Paul took me to Somerset and dropped me at the Bus Station. I had planned to take a bus to New York City or to Newark and then take a train to New London. But when I inquired inside, they told me that the buses weren't running on Sunday. I went back outside and told Mom and Paul to go on home that the bus would be coming later. I didn't want them to worry. So they left and I hurried to the outskirts of Somerset to a truck depot. I found a driver heading for Newark and he was okay with me going with him. I got into Newark in the middle of the night and was able to get on a train that would take me to New London. I was tired so I fell asleep on the train. Next thing I knew was the conductor waking me up to inquire if I was going to New London. I said yes and he responded by telling me to look back real quick because we had just passed New London. Next stop was Rhode Island where I started to hitchhike my way back to New London. Some nice young lady picked me up and dropped me at the gate to the Base with just a few minutes to spare. That was the closest I ever came to being AWOL.

Hitchhiking wasn't all that bad. We could usually get rides without long waits. However it was usually hard to get a ride home the last twelve miles from Somerset. I could get from Somerset to Rockwood and then it was almost impossible. Many times I would just walk the four miles from Rockwood. I would get home sometimes after daylight on Saturday and had to leave on the return trip by usually no later than noon on Sunday. So it didn't leave a lot of time at home.

On one trip home I was shocked to see the old summer house, which had been turned into a chicken brooder house, had burned down. Apparently the incubator set the place on fire one night and caused quite a commotion. Paul jumped out of bed exclaiming, "The brooder house is on fire." Then he jumped into his car and drove to Rockwood yelling "fire" all the way. Those who might have heard him, and there weren't many, didn't know what to do since no details on location where provided. Meanwhile, Mom went out with a bucket and poured water on the gate on the path between the house and the brooder house. She saved the gate, but the brooder house along with all the baby chicks was a total loss.

On one long weekend trip home I arrived, as I usually did, in the middle of the night and found all the doors locked. I didn't want to disturb anybody so I took the back screen door off by the hinges and laid it on the grass and went in the house and went to bed. In the morning I heard Pop ranting and raving about somebody must have broken in because the screen door was on the ground. I decided I'd better show my presence and clear things up.

World War 2 Veteran:

Toward the end of my tour of duty I remember sitting in the local tavern in Rockwood having a beer with a WWII veteran. I forgot his name but he told me that he had it pretty good because he was on disability and the navy was taking good care of him. He was proud of his service to his country and was glad that he had the opportunity to serve. He appeared to be happy and had no complaints. His disability was quite obvious when you looked at him straight on. While on the battlefield, he had taken a shell or piece of shrapnel right in the face, which had taken away both of his eyes and most of his nose.

Wine, Women & Song (and not much of either):

In the last paragraph, I described sitting in a tavern with a local hero. In that particular case, I only went there to buy a WWII hero a beer. We did, however, inhabit the local bars around New London, Connecticut, occasionally. However, I was never much of a drinker. Generally, about two beers were all I could handle. There was a favorite bar in New London the name of which has long been forgotten but I do remember the name of the barmaid who worked there. Her name was Ruthie. One of my buddies would often suggest, usually on a Friday night, that we should go there and pat Ruthie on the butt. I won't tell you which of my best friends made this suggestion, because his wife Joan might hit him upside his head if she found out about it. It was just a fantasy anyway. I am pretty sure that neither Reese, Prather, Hulse, nor I ever did that. But it was fun thinking about it.

What we did instead when we went to this bar was to see who could go the longest without going to the men's room. Who ever had to go first had to buy a round of beer.

Before I met Jean, two of my buddies (I think it was Al Prather and Bobby Hulse) and I dated several student nurses who were all Catholics. I don't mean to pick on the Catholics but it just seems like most of the girls we met happened to be Catholic, and of course that included Jean. The student nurses lived in a dormitory (I called it a convent) which was located within striking distance from the submarine base. Three of us and three of them went out one night in one car which of course had only a front and a back seat. I think they believed in the old adage that there is safety in numbers. When we took them home that night we were late and the doors to the dormitory had been locked. As a result, all six of us had to spend the night in the car until the dormitory doors were unlocked in the morning and they were able to sneak in to their rooms. Imagine, three sailors trying to sleep in the front seat with three student nurses in the back seat. What was wrong with this picture?

Going Steady:

One night Robert Reese came back from a date with Joan Portelance from Norwich, Connecticut and asked me if I wanted to go on a double date with him and Joan. Joan had a friend named Jean. It was late when he asked me and I told him no and let me sleep. He kept pestering me so I finally said yes. Actually, I think that he mainly wanted me to go because I had a car, a 1950 Ford. So soon thereafter, we went on our double date and my date turned out to be my future wife, Jean.

Jean and I starting dating regularly shortly after that first meeting. We often double dated with Joan and Robert. Eventually Robert completed his tour of duty and he and Joan were married. About the same time, Jean and I got engaged and planned to get married after I was discharged.

Beach Scene ~ 1952. From left to right in the photo are: Robert Reese, Joan, Joan's mother Louise, Joan's brother Tommy, Spike, Jean, and Jean's mother Loretta

Snow Compaction Project:

My tour of duty at Kapuskasing, Ontario, Canada was a bit unusual. As it turned out, they needed a yeoman on a Snow Compaction project. My job in Kapuskasing went quite a bit beyond the standard yeoman (the titless wave) function. I had a U.S. Navy Lieutenant as my boss but I actually worked for one Capt. Fowler of the Canadian army. The job that the group performed was to build snow roads and an airstrip for the purpose of learning how better to do such a job in wartime. I got involved in a lot of things in addition to the strict yeoman duties. For example, I volunteered to make the breakfast run using a big British made truck, which had the steering wheel on the wrong side. I would get up early and drive those who wanted to go into town to a place called Wally's. After breakfast, I would bring back a load of locals who worked for the project. Sometimes in the afternoon, I would drive workers home. One time one of the workers, who spoke only French which I didn't speak at all, had to go home out in the country. He gave me directions off the main road onto a road that was plowed but only about the width of the truck. I dropped him at his house and he started to go in but I tried to ask him how to turn around. It was about 30 below zero and I wasn't interested in getting stranded but I couldn't figure out how to turn around when the plowed part of the road was so narrow. He eventually realized what I was asking, he should have from the beginning, so he guided me to drive a little farther where turning around was just barely possible. But I always remember that trip back because I was alone and it was mighty cold and the roads were snow covered and slippery.

My tour of duty in Kapuskasing lasted about three months and the coldest that it got while I was there was 50°F below zero. When it got that cold, most of the equipment was left running all night. But the truck that I used always started right up when ether was injected into the carburetor by means of a small either capsule.

One day we drove out into the bush with two big tractors and a couple of sleds. I went along just for the ride. We went past a house or two where the folks who lived there didn't get out to the city until spring. Actually, later in the spring we saw a husband and wife from one of these places come into town on a tractor. The husband was driving and the woman was riding on the draw bar. But back to this trip into the bush. As we were approaching what appeared to be a snow covered clearing with a small shack near the edge, the lead tractor suddenly disappeared except for the back end and the intake pipe and the exhaust pipe which was directed up at the midpoint of the tractor. The clearing turned out to be a small lake and the tractor hit thin ice where a stream fed into the lake. We then spent the entire day getting the tractor out with the aid of the other tractor and by cutting down timber to build a ramp for the tractor to back out on. All of the time that it was nearly fully submerged, it continued to run because both the intake and the exhaust were still above the ice and water. When I got back to the barracks that night, I couldn't get my overshoes off; there was a layer of ice between the shoes and my woolen socks.

Return to Civilian Life:

I was discharged from the navy after serving five years. My youthful idea of joining the navy to be a hero never came true. My life as a sailor was interesting at times and also mundane at times. Some would say a waste of time. But I did mature quite a bit during my time in the navy and I believe that I became a better person for it. It was by no means, a waste of time for me.

In the meantime, my nephew and long time friend Bob Ringer made a career out of the navy. He went to a special school in Pittsburgh and in Arco, Idaho to learn how to be a crewman on a nuclear-powered submarine. He became one of the first crewmembers of the USS *Nautilus*, the world's first nuclear powered submarine. He served on the USS *Nautilus* until he retired after over twenty years of service. He now lives in Utah with his wife Joyce. When I graduated from college I went on to work at General Electric's Knolls Atomic Power Laboratory in Schenectady, New York, where we designed and developed reactors, especially reactor cores, for the nuclear submarines, including the *Nautilus*.

Right to left: Red Engle, Al Kusch, Bob Ringer, Spike Romesberg
(All four graduates of Rockwood High Class of 1948)

CHAPTER 3

Hunting
(1944-1976)

Hunting for Food and Sport:

WHEN I WAS a kid, hunting was a big part of our family life. It was a method for gathering food. But it was a lot more than that. It was an exciting adventure. As a little kid, I couldn't wait until I got old enough to go hunting with my dad and big brothers. Not my sisters, of course, hunting was a man's game at that time. As a kid, I can remember Pop coming home in the evening from squirrel hunting with a number of squirrels in his hunting coat. I would have the privilege of unloading the coat and counting the number of squirrels. Then sometimes I would help Mom skin them so that we could have squirrel meat for dinner, perhaps we would have squirrel pot pie.

Once when I came around the old farm house on the way home from school at Wilson Creek there were three deer hanging on a scaffold in the yard between the house and the shed. It was like an early Christmas because it represented a successful hunt and the guarantee that there would be food for the table. To this day, the memory of seeing those deer hanging there is still vivid.

When I was fourteen, I finally got my first hunting license. I remember the first day of small game season that year, Pop and several of my brothers went hunting on their own, leaving the new kid-me on his own. When they came home for lunch, I had already gotten three squirrels and one rabbit, all shot with a .22 rifle. They were impressed. I suppose that was the day that I became a man, so to speak. (Note: On a trip to Pennsylvania in 1990, I saw that same .22 rifle at my niece Joy's house. A flood of memories came back to me.)

The first day of deer season in Pennsylvania was typically considered a holiday so there was no school. One time during the deer season, I took the day off from high school to go hunting. The other three ridge runners, Bob Ringer, Al Kusch, and Glen Bear, seeing that I wasn't at the corner to go to school with them, decided to skip school also. But instead of going hunting, they went to Somerset to hang out at the bowling alley. Later in the morning, the principal called Mom to find out where the boys were. She, without any hesitation said, "They went hunting." Well, with that the principal was satisfied. Hunting was, of course, one of the few legitimate excuses for not going to school on a school day. Of course I was the only one who was legitimately hunting. Mom had actually covered for the other three.

Hunting Primarily for Sport:

During my navy and college days, hunting took a back seat to other activities. But I never got very far away from the subject because every time that I came home to the farm to visit, the subject of hunting always came up. No matter what time of year, one of the main topics of discussion during the visit would be hunting. Typically, on these visits, there would be at least one big meal served, usually Sunday noon, where most of the local brothers and sisters and their families came. The women would do all the food preparation as usual, while the men gathered to rest and talk. When the meal was ready, the men sat and ate while the women waited on them. Sometimes, the women would not eat until the men and the kids had finished. As soon as the men were finished, they would move off to some comfortable corner to talk and maybe fall asleep while the women washed the dishes, cleaned up and probably started to get ready for the next meal. The conversation among the men sooner or later, and usually sooner, would get around to hunting. The men would take turns telling hunting stories and over a period of years, many of the stories were told several times. Perhaps a little bit like some fish stories that we have all heard, these stories would have a tendency to get better with age. Somewhat like a good bottle of wine.

As the years went by, I found myself having less to say at these gatherings primarily because my number of hunting experiences was limited. Still I always found the stories interesting and I missed being part of the hunting experience. I was never interested in being a trophy hunter like I think my brothers were to some extent. I just liked the idea of being a hunter for the adventure and for the food gathering purpose, Hunting remained a part of me, but during this time it was just dormant.

One time while in the navy, Red Fraunfelder and I borrowed guns from my future father in law and we went squirrel hunting near Norwich, Connecticut. We all had squirrel for dinner that night. What a way to impress my city girl friend and her parents.

Hunting with the Bow:

In about 1959, I bought a longbow from Larry Bosworth's basement in downtown Schenectady for about $15. Hank Truran and I would practice shooting at a bale of straw at noontime in the field near work. Soon after that, I was back into deer hunting again but this time with the bow.

The first deer that I shot with a bow was a small doe. I shot it in the evening near my mother-in-law's cabin in Grafton, Vermont and then I couldn't find it because of the darkness. The next morning, I took Tricia, Tom and Gary with me to help find the blood trail. It was hard to find red blood on red leaves in Vermont. Tricia was the best at finding the trail. She was small and her eyes were closer to the ground.

In Vermont, the bow season came in October which is the peak of the fall colors. It was like hunting on a post card. There was no more beautiful place on earth than being in a Vermont woods in October.

Many times I would hunt alone. Maybe that wasn't too smart. I was always careful, but there were a lot of "what ifs" one could postulate.

When I hunted in Vermont, I would stay at my mother-in-law's cabin in Grafton. I'd always get up early in the morning when it was still dark so that I could get to one of my favorite tree stands before daylight. One time my alarm went off in the dark and I got up, but it seemed unusually dark and cold. Also, I felt very tired, like I hadn't really slept much. But after some coffee and several layers of clothes, I managed to get out the door. I kept thinking that it was really dark and cold and the frost on the car was really thick. After getting the car warmed up and a small hole cleared in the windshield so I could see a little bit, I drove about a mile or so and parked. It was still really dark when I got out, climbed the fence and started up the old logging road. It was the darkest that I had ever seen it at this point before so I decided to take another look at my watch. It was around 2:00 AM. Apparently, I had set my alarm at 1:00 AM instead of 5:00 AM.

Hunting in the Catskills and the Big One That Got Away:

For about five or six years in a row during the sixties, I went hunting in the Catskills south of Schenectady with Carmen Palmer and Walt Andrus. We hunted on farm land that was no longer farmed and was grown up in brush and weeds. It was perfect for deer especially with us hunting there because the chance of us shooting any of them was pretty slim. We were all rather relaxed hunters and were there mostly for the outing. If we got a deer, that would be a bonus. I think I only ever got one deer from those trips and neither of them got any. But we did enjoy the outings.

On these hunting trips, we would get there about daylight so that we could take a morning stand on one of the deer trails that we were familiar with. During the day we would walk about looking for a good stand for the evening. Or we would sometimes have a nap in a sunny spot using a log for a pillow.

On one of our trips to that area, I was hunting from a tree stand just off what appeared to me to be a well-used deer trail. I climbed into the tree at just about daylight while Carmen and Walt went on to another spot further down the hill. I stayed very alert anticipating that a large buck would be coming down the trail anytime. But nothing happened so finally at about 9:00 AM or so, I decided that the prime time for a deer to come by had passed so I decided to relax. I hung my bow on a tree limb, took out my pack and started to eat one of my sandwiches. In the meantime, unknown to me, Walt and Carmen had abandoned there stands and were walking back toward me along the deer trail that I was standing by. In so doing, they had apparently spooked up some deer that were moving toward me. So right in the middle of my sandwich, I looked up and saw a small yearling walking toward me on the trail and in back of the yearling was a large doe. At that point, I started to figure out how to put my sandwich away and get my bow into shooting position without being heard or seen with the yearling almost directly beneath my feet. Just about that time, I looked up again, and what I saw almost gave me a heart attack. My heart started pounding so hard, I could see my shirt jumping in and out. My hands were shaking so bad, I was afraid of dropping my sandwich on the yearlings head. What I saw, coming down the trail in back of the doe, which was in back of the yearling, was this huge buck. Have you ever seen the Hartford stag on the Insurance commercials? This deer was the Hartford stag's big brother. I have never seen a deer to match this one. The first thing I saw was the rack. How could I miss it? The base of the antlers was as big as my wrists. Both sides were perfectly symmetrical. The horns swept forward and up to about three feet wide and a good two feet or more above his head. There was a least five points on each side, maybe six. I was in shock. I was shaking like a leaf and I was sure that the sound of my heart beat would spook them away.

So what could I do? They had caught me with my pants down, so to speak. I couldn't move because the doe and the buck were facing me and were only about thirty to forty yards away. And the yearling was right under my feet. All I could do was freeze and watch.

As they approached, it was obvious that they were nervous. The yearling wandered on by and eventually, so did the doe. But the buck must have sensed something and he veered off to the left somewhat and instead of passing under me, he passed about thirty yards to the side. As he went by, and was not looking directly at me, I managed somehow to put the sandwich back in the pack without dropping it to the ground, and then to hang the pack on a limb and pick up my bow which was hanging on another limb. An arrow was knocked in the string so I had to be careful not to brush against the tree and drop the arrow or make any noise or fall out of the tree my self. It was a very tedious task especially with my hands still shaking and my heart nearly jumping out of my chest. I finally got around into a position where I could draw and release an arrow and by this time the buck had gotten to a position about thirty-five yards (I stepped it off later) and was angled slightly away from me. It was a perfect angle for a shot. He had stopped for a moment so I drew the arrow to the knock position and held for a second or two to make sure I was on the deer. I released the arrow and knew immediately that it was a good shot. The arrow arrived at the location of this giant of a buck and it appeared to hit it in or just back of the chest cavity. I heard a noise like an arrow makes when it hits something solid. The buck immediately leaped into high gear. I assumed it was a perfect hit so my eyes followed the deer as it entered a thicket. I made a mental note of where it entered the thicket so I could go find it later. After it entered the thicket, I looked again at the place where my arrow went, and there was an arrow stuck in a small sapling waving in the breeze. My heart sunk. I couldn't believe my eyes. The sapling couldn't have been more than two inches in diameter and I had hit it dead center. If I stood up there in that tree and tried to hit that sapling, I don't think I could have done it in a dozen tries.

The buck was gone. I had missed the chance at the biggest deer I had ever seen. Shortly after, Carmen and Walt came by. I was distraught. They tried their best to soothe me but it was no use. Weeks later, we went gun hunting in the same area and we heard locals talking about a large buck that was taken out of that area. I asked if it had antlers as thick as my wrists at the base. They said yes. That was the buck that was almost mine.

By the way, remember earlier I said that I was not a trophy hunter. I think I lied. I only said that because I never got a trophy.

The three of us drove to a different hunting spot one time when we were hunting in that area. We all three rode in the front seat of Carmen's big American car. It was one of those cold crisp autumn days but with a lot of sunshine so that inside the car, with the sun shining through the windshield, it was tranqualizingly warm. When we parked the car at our destination, we all three sat there for quite some time, sound asleep in the sunshine.

The Ralph Teamer Place:

One of my favorite hunting places was on the old Ralph Teamer place which was located on the Hudson River adjacent to the Saratoga Battlefield. Somebody—can't remember the name—lived there but it wasn't Ralph. It was a husband and wife from California. I always stopped to visit them when I hunted there. One time I was in the old barn talking to the man who lived there and I noticed that I was leaning on an old piano. I looked up and said, "Hey, you got a piano in your barn." After some bargaining, he said he would sell it to me for $25. I said that I would take it but didn't know how to get it home. So, included in the $25 he said he would also deliver it. And he did. It was about forty miles and he even brought a friend. What a bargain. Jean and the kids and I later put it in the basement. We got it down the stairs using ropes and a block and tackle. Later, I took it completely apart and restored it. It was a good piano. Later we sold if for $150 when we were in Pottstown, Pennsylvania. We sold it so that we wouldn't have to move it back to California.

But getting back to hunting on the old Ralph Teamer place. One day I was at work and it was during the bow hunting season in New York State. As the day wore on, I began to feel physically ill. So about 2:30 in the afternoon, I couldn't take it anymore, so I left work and headed home. It was one of those crisp autumn days when the leaves are starting to turn and with the feel and smell of autumn in the air. As I got closer to home, I began to feel the sickness leaving my body. When I got home, I rushed into the house and changed into my hunting clothes, grabbed my hunting equipment, and headed for the Teamer place. I parked my car by the farm house, waved to the tenants, and headed into the woods. The place where I hunted was right next to the Saratoga battlefield. There was also an old Cemetery there. I remember seeing head stones from the 1700s. I had a tree stand which I had made from a plank extended between two trees. It was at a height of about twelve feet off the ground and was very easy to get into. So on this particular day, I went straight to that stand. By the time I got there, it was about an hour or less before dark and there was a slight rain falling. I had been in the stand for about an hour and it was beginning to get dark when a young buck came down the trail. He never saw or sensed me and he walked directly under the plank. My feet could not have been more than six or seven feet from his head as he went under. I waited until he passed by and then shot an arrow down through his midsection. He ran about seventy-five yards and dropped. It was late by the time I field dressed and dragged the deer out to the car. The woman at the farm house was worried and the husband had fixed up an old lantern and was about to come looking for me.

Memorable Places:

There were many places in New York State and Vermont where I went hunting and I can still remember many of them. My memory fades on a lot of things but seemingly less on places where I have gone hunting. I remember the contour of the land, the look of an old snag or downed tree. I remember meadows and streams and big rocks just like I was there yesterday. I remember the old Frenchman's house near Berne in the Helderbergs south of Schenectady. I never got a single deer there but it was great country and I had a lot of good outings there. Gary and Tom and I went camping in that area one time and we went to dinner at a big restaurant and we were the only ones there. Both of the boys were wearing their red sweat shirts with hoods and snotty sleeves. They served us family style in a big old room with old wooden boards for flooring. It was home cooking like you would get at home and they served much more than we could eat. The boys were brought up not to waste food and they thought that they had to eat everything that was placed on the table. I had to explain to them that we couldn't possibly clean up everything because as soon as one dish was nearly gone, they brought more.

There were areas north of Schenectady near the town of Cambridge where Phil Gagnon and I hunted several times. We met a local resident there by the name of Stephen Stephanovich. He had a pet deer which he had raised from a fawn. He kept it in a stall next to a couple of cows. We surmised that the young buck would provide meat to help him through the winter.

There was also a woman in that same area who owned a bunch of horses and she also had a pet deer and each year during hunting season she would put a red coat on it. One year some thoughtless low down person shot it even though it was wearing the red coat. Land owners in that area weren't very friendly toward hunters after that.

Hunting was a way of meeting people. I always spoke to the land owners first before going on their land. Almost all land owners in the Northeast would welcome hunters providing the hunter showed respect for the owner's property. They didn't want to have their cows shot or their fences torn down.

Shooting a Six-Pack:

One time I came home from hunting and Jean asked me how I made out. I told her that I had shot a six-pack. She growled at me saying that I should not be boozing while hunting. I explained to her that I didn't have a drop to drink but that I had actually shot a six pack. Here's what happened. While hunting, I came upon a small stack of hay. I went up to it and checked to see that there was nothing underneath the hay besides the ground and then I found a piece of paper to be used as a target. I stood the paper up in front of the hay and then backed off about thirty yards or so and proceeded to shoot several arrows into the target just for practice. When I went to pull out the arrows, one of them was attached to a six-pack of beer. The arrow had gone through two of the beer cans. I had missed seeing the beer when I checked earlier.

Hunting in Vermont:

I took Ernie Karner and Bud Crockett hunting from the camp in Grafton, Vermont several times during the Vermont Yankee startup in 1970. Crockett had never been hunting with a bow before that. On our first trip, I suggested a spot for Crockett which was in a tree on a well-traveled trail. He was in the stand for only a few minutes and he saw several deer. That led him to believe that this was going to be easy. As it turned out, those were the only deer that he saw while bow hunting.

The three of us went gun hunting later along with my two sons Gary and Tom. We went into the woods near Grafton and we all took up positions along side the mountain except for Tom. He walked around the backside of the mountain below the top thinking that he might chase out a deer that would come over our way. He was right. I was the first person to see it and it was a good sized buck. I saw it sneaking through the brush and I took one shot at it with my 30-06 but missed. When it left me, it was headed right for the general area where Karner and Crocket were and within a minute or so, I heard about six shots. I thought for sure that they had gotten it so I walked over to where they were expecting to help them with the field dressing. As it turned out, they had missed. Crockett told us later that as he watched the deer coming toward him, he could see the venison frying in the pan and he was already calculating how we would divide it up among all of us participating hunters. That's a good example of counting your venison before it is shot.

Moose Hunting in Newfoundland:

After hunting in Vermont with both bow and gun and not succeeding, Karner and I decided to try moose hunting in Newfoundland. I got all the details from my old friend Harry Schrader in Schenectady on where to go. So in late November, we left on a Friday evening and drove one thousand miles to North Sydney, Nova Scotia. We arrived there Saturday afternoon. We took the car and our selves and boarded a ferry boat which departed for Port Aux Basque, Newfoundland at about 11:00 that night. We had our own little room with bunk beds where we spent the night, at least part of the night. We had not slept the night before as we had been driving all night. The crossing was rough as I recall and we happened to be roomed next door to a bunch of rowdy merchant marines who were drinking beer and making a lot of noise. I finally got annoyed because we were really in need of a good night sleep so I got up and knocked on their door and calmly requested that they tone it down a bit. They responded with a few choice cuss words which I can't repeat here. I went back to bed hoping that the noise would abate. Surprisingly, it did get quieter eventually which probably had nothing to do with my request. In the morning Karner told me that I had more nerve than brains for what I did.

We arrived at Port Aux Basque at 7:00 in the morning and had breakfast of ham and eggs, which by the way was pronounced as "am and heggs" by the waitress. We then drove another 325 miles to Millertown. At Millertown, we stopped to ask a couple of school girls how to get to the outfitters office. One of the girls gave me an answer, and Karner said to me, "What did she say?" And I said "I have no idea." "What language were they speaking?" he asked. "I think it was English with some really weird accent," I said.

· Millertown is a town of several hundred. We found the outfitter, bought our licenses, picked up the cook and headed out into the Bush. We drove forty-five miles into the wilderness with no signs of life except an old logging camp and the camp where we were to stay. There we met our two guides and had supper and went to bed.

Next morning we got up at about 4:30 and drove another ten miles down an old logging road to a lake they called Victoria. Here we boarded two small boats, Ernie and a guide in one, and I and a guide in another.

We went to the other end of the lake, about thirty-two miles. It was calm in the morning but got rough later in the day. On the way across the first time we scanned the banks for moose along the way. About halfway down the lake, my guide cut the engine and whispered "moose." About a hundred yards away stood a big cow. I hesitated because it was the first day out and I was hoping to get a bull. I didn't shoot and later I realized that the guide was slightly irritated. Still later I realized that the guides and the cook had not filled their tags and they were interested in some moose meat for themselves. They are not allowed to carry guns while they are guides so they did not get very many opportunities to shoot one themselves. So we continued to the far end of the lake, tied up the boat and started down a logging road. On the way, we saw moose droppings and some old tracks. Eventually we came upon some fresh tracks and just about the same time we saw two moose at about a hundred yards walking through a timbered out area. They were both cows and so again I didn't want to shoot. I had the scope on the first one and the guide kept saying "shoot, shoot." So I did. When the smoke cleared, there were about six or more empty shells at my feet and two dead moose in the bushes. When we field dressed them, each had been hit three times. One had been hit in the heart, liver, and the neck. The other was hit just in back of the heart, just below the heart, and once near the liver. I was using a 30-06 and was surprised at how much it took to bring them down.

We brought the boat up a creek and got to within less than a quarter of a mile of the moose. Karner and the other guide had arrived by this time and the two guides quartered them and we all carried them to the boat. Actually, Ernie and I didn't do much because the quarters were too heavy and the terrain was too rough. By the time we got all eight quarters loaded, had lunch and finished the thirty-two-mile boat ride, it was nearly dark.

In order to keep hunting for the two bull moose that we wanted, it was assumed that the cook and the one guide would tag the two moose that we had gotten. We hung the eight quarters in a shed in back of the camp.

Tuesday morning we repeated the trip to the lake only this time we all got in the same boat. Ernie, myself and the two guides. We had gone about twenty-five or so miles along the lake when we saw another moose. As soon as we saw it, we all immediately looked for a rack, but there was none. When it saw us, it started to run up the bank away from the lake. The guides were yelling at us to shoot. I told Ernie to shoot but he couldn't find it in his scope. So he told me to shoot. I felt that I shouldn't since I already shot two. In the meantime, I had it in my scope and was following it up the bank and the brush was getting thicker. It was now or never so I fired. To my complete amazement, the moose drooped in its tracks. We pulled into the bank, struggled up through the brush and found the moose, a spike horned bull, shot through the head. It was an amazing shot at about a hundred yards while running away in the brush, and me in a rocking and turning boat.

We quartered this one and deposited it by the bank to be picked up later, marked the spot with a red life jacket and went on down along the lake. We had not gone more than a few miles when Ernie spotted a bull in the heavy timber. He shot and then I saw it running. We each took a few more shots and it disappeared in the woods. We found blood and followed the trail about two hundred yards. Then we saw him, fired a few more shots each and he dropped. He had a nice rack with fourteen points. I don't know what it weighed but the guides said that it was about nine years old and weighed about 750 to 1,000 lbs. I think that it was no more than 750 lbs. As we stood there looking at the fallen moose, one of he guides pointed out that the bull we just shot was not the same one we wounded earlier. So while the guides quartered the one we just shot, Ernie and I got back on the blood trail. We followed it about a hundred yards or so before we saw it. We both shot a few more shots before it dropped. It was about the same size as the first but had only twelve points.

The boat was pretty low in the water going home that evening and the shack in back of the camp looked like a slaughter house. The moose that we had shot earlier but left by the bank was left for them to pick up the next day and give to the other guide who still had an unfilled tag.

Ernie and I each ended up with a lot of moose meat in the freezers. And the cook and both of the guides I presume got about the same. The meat was very good and did not have any wild taste to it at all. During that winter, I would occasionally catch Jean buying some beef for which she would get a scolding from me. "But," she said, "I get tired of moose meat." So we occasionally had other meat and we gave a fair portion of the moose to friends.

The Motel Maid, Judy's Mother and the Deer Heart:

In 1971 I had to go back to Vermont periodically for testing at Vermont Yankee. Usually, I would stay for a few weeks at a time. One of those trips was in October. So I took my hunting gear along. Jean wanted to know how I would find time to go hunting, and if I did go hunting, did I really expect to get anything, and if I did get a deer, how would I get it out by myself, how would I get it field dressed, how would I get it frozen, where would I keep it, and how would I get it home to California. I told her not to worry, I would cross all those bridges as I came to them.

Before making this trip, Denny Turner called me and requested that I bring his German Lugar, which was stored at a friend's house. Meanwhile, John Salisbury requested that I bring along his shot gun. At the same time, I wanted to bring my own rifle, my bow and a bunch of arrows. To make it interesting, airplane hijacking was at its peak about this time and airports were starting to get strict on the transporting of firearms. So picture me arriving at the San Jose airport carrying one German Lugar, one shot gun, one 30-06 rifle, one hunting bow, and a dozen hunting arrows. All I needed was a Fidel Castro outfit and beard. Some guy in line in back of me said "Oh No" and changed lines. Maybe he changed airlines too, I'm not sure.

I did go bow hunting on that trip and I did get a deer. I shot it late Sunday evening near the spot where Karner and Crockett and I missed the buck the year before. I followed the blood trail and then couldn't see well enough to follow it any further. When I finally looked up, I was deep in the forest in an area I hadn't been before. And it was dark. I knew if I walked down hill I would eventually come out to the road. So as I walked out, trying to walk as straight as I could without falling over rocks or stumps or running into trees and brush, I used my knife to blaze a trail to be seen coming back the other way. I did that until I came out to the road near a farmer's house.

I returned to the hotel and called John Salisbury, Ken Burke and Russ Serenka. We agreed on a plan. Since the next day was Monday, Russ and Ken agreed to go to work and John and I would go find the deer. The job was such that all four of us weren't needed that day. Early the next morning, John and I followed the blaze trail to where I had left the blood trail the night before. We then got back on the blood trail and after following the trail for a short distance we found the deer. We field dressed it and dragged it out. On the way, I gave the liver to the farmer.

I left the deer on top of the car until the end of the day and then took it to our Secretary's parent's house and hung it in their smoke house. Meanwhile, I had left the heart in my motel room sink during the day. Later when the motel maid was cleaning the rooms, she was seen and heard running out of my room screaming about finding a bloody heart in the bath room sink. Fortunately, the clerk remembering that I had just shot a deer the day before, was able to clarify the situation. That evening, I took the heart to Judy's mother's house (Judy was our secretary who later married Ken Burke who was one of our startup test crew members). Nobody was at home at her mother's house so I went inside and put the heart in the refrigerator. I left a note on the kitchen table which read as follows: "To Judy's mother. I hope you will forgive me for what I am doing. I gave my heart to your lovely daughter Judy. I put it in the refrigerator on the upper shelf beside the jar of mayonnaise." I then signed the note. I never did find out what Judy's mother said when she found that note and the deer heart in her refrigerator.

The venture all worked out perfectly. Within a few days, I had a butcher cut up the deer and quick freeze the meat. This was the same butcher that butchered the moose for Karner and me one year earlier. The tricky part after that was to find a freezer to store the meat in. Dick Wentzel volunteered his freezer, but I didn't trust him, he liked venison too much. Bob Tetrault had room in his freezer and neither he nor his wife liked venison. So that was where I stored it until my next trip back to San Jose. The airlines provided boxes and even helped me pack it in dry ice for the trip back. It all worked out well.

Hunting in California:

When we first came to California, Gary, Tom and I were all interested in hunting. It seems, as I look back, that I played a dirty trick on them. During our last days in the Northeast, I got them interested in hunting, and then we moved to California where it was much more difficult to hunt because we had to travel far from home to do it. Also, the attitude of many Californians' was very negative toward those who shoot animals, even legally. Consequently, we didn't go hunting very much. At first we made a few trips but these trips became outings more so than a hunting trip; such as our several trips to LaPorte.

LaPorte is an old gold mining town at about seven thousand feet elevation. At that time there were only fifty or so permanent residents. Now, I understand, there are a lot more. On our first trip to LaPorte, we visited a ghost town called Gibsonville just above LaPorte. While we were there we decided to drive to Quincy for lunch. According to the map, we figured it was about a one hour drive. But we were about to get introduced to California mountain roads. It took us about three hours and it was a bit scary. These were real honest to goodness mountain roads; dirt, narrow, curvy, steep, bumpy, hanging on the side of the mountain, and with no guard rails.

Bob Lutman, Tom and I went to Sonora Pass one weekend to hunt with guns. On the way up, some deer crossed in front of us and one of them came so close it brushed the rear of the camper trailer. Lutman got all excited thinking that we would see lots of deer. I told him to relax because it could very well be as close as we would get to a deer. It turned out to be true. We never saw a single deer after the encounter on the road. We were hunting at about six thousand feet of elevation or higher and we saw a lot of deer signs. They had probably already migrated down by the time we were there. At one point during that hunt, I was on the side of the mountain and I saw a little red dot near the peak. I sat there and watched it for about a half hour as it came closer and got larger. It turned out to be Tom coming down off the mountain top.

One year they had a late season for doe in the coastal region south of Monterey. The Jardeen Ranch allowed bow hunting for $10 per day. It was a ten-thousand-acre ranch, more or less. I went there just before Thanksgiving. I arrived at the ranch house just before the evening meal and they invited me in for coffee. The man in charge, the Chief, was sitting at the head of a huge table and about twenty-five young boys lined the sides. There were several women preparing and serving the meal. It reminded me of my youth back on the farm. The ranch was a foster home for boys without parents or homes. It looked like an ideal setting. I used their phone while I was there to call Jean. I told her that if I wasn't home by Thanksgiving with a deer, to go ahead and buy a turkey.

While I was there, I did get a deer. It was the only deer I ever shot in California. I shot it on the side of a hill and when it was hit, it ran down the hill for about fifty yards or more and fell over dead right by my truck. All I had to do was field dress it and then pull it easily down a few more yards and put it in the back of the truck. It was a very accommodating deer to run toward the truck like it did. On the way out to the ranch gate in the dark, several boys stopped me and asked me if they could follow me out. They had a tractor pulling a wagon with a water tank and they had no lights on the tractor. So I drove slow enough for them to follow me. The old man in charge of the ranch took one look at my deer and told me that I should skin it before I left for home. So he yanked it out of the truck, hung it up on a scaffold, and skinned it right before my eyes. He had to be the fastest deer skinner in the west.

Probably the most outrageous hunting trip that I ever went on was with Bob Lutman. It seems like a lot of outrageous things that happened over the years was with Bob Lutman, now that I think about it. Bob and I worked in the same office along with Russ Serenka. Bob claimed that he knew of a hunting spot where there were so many deer we would probably have to beat them off with a stick. It was somewhere in the foothills near Placerville, I believe. So we set up a trip that was originally planned for Bob, Russ Serenka, and me. Then Russ decided to bring his son Russell. Jenny Lockhart who also worked in the same area, heard us talking about the trip and she asked if she could go along. We were a little uneasy about bringing a woman with us but she assured us that she would stay out of the way and that she just wanted to camp out and do some hiking while we were hunting. So we took her with us.

The five of us left on a Friday in my station wagon and my little tent trailer. The weather was fine when we left but clouds started to roll in as we approached the hunting area and light rain started to fall. As we got close to the hunting place that Lutman had bragged about, we had trouble finding it and we got lost, or at least confused. We ended up on this long dirt road in the dark and we were no longer sure if we were at the right place. By this time it was raining harder, it was dark, we were deep in the mountains on this dirt road, it was late, we were tired, we were hungry, we were grouchy so we decided to park and camp wherever we were.

We found a flat spot where we could get off the dirt road and we stopped and set up our camper trailer. We had a small tarp that served as a porch and to cover the cooking area and we set that up too. By now it was raining pretty hard and it was cold. So there wasn't much to do except go to bed. Of course the sleeping space was rather limited. This camper had two fold out shelves with mattresses for sleeping. It was ideally suited for two people, or at most four if the four were either small or friendly, or both. Lutman and I took one of the shelves and Russ and Russel took the other. Jennie slept on the floor between us.

The sleeping worked out fine as it turned out. But when we got up early in the morning, a cold rain was still coming down. And a rather large puddle had formed outside and in front of the camper.

Well the first day, Russ, Bob and I went hunting. We each went our separate ways. I'm not sure what Jennie and Russell did. They went for hikes and hung around the camper. But it was cold, wet and depressing.

The second day was the same or worse than the first. The puddle in front of the camper had grown to lake size and almost everything we had was wet. I had a gas heater which helped some but not enough.

It rained all weekend. It never let up. I kept thinking that it would stop, but it never did. I wore a poncho or raincoat the whole time I was there, except while I was sleeping. The poncho looked like a tent. Only my head stuck out of it. The rest of my body, even my arms and my rifle, were under the poncho. I think Jenny loaned it to me. Once while I was walking up a muddy bank (everything was muddy), I accidentally stepped on the bottom edge of the poncho. As I took another step, my other foot also stepped on the poncho but further up on the inside of the poncho front. This action pulled me forward and forced me to run up the inside of my poncho pulling my head down toward my feet. I ended up in a little tight ball in the mud on the side of the bank.

We had a lot of laughs that weekend. Especially when we would try to cook the evening meal under the tarp in the rain beside the puddle that had grown to lake size. We never saw a single animal that whole weekend. I don't think we even saw any birds, squirrels, or anything. They were all holed up due to the rain.

One year we tried hunting in Northern California in the Trinity Alps. We did equally well in this region at not seeing any legal deer. We camped at night in my tent trailer and we had trouble sleeping due to the sound of the deer running around outside. Where they went during the day, I couldn't say.

That was a brief look at my hunting in California, and my hunting career in general. I essentially gave up hunting. Running and hiking has taken the place of hunting. Long distance trail running has worked well for me in place of hunting. I still have that small moose rack over the fireplace in the family room and one day I heard Tricia explaining to one of my granddaughters that Pappy (that's me now) and Nana (that's Jean now) ate the meat that Pappy got from hunting because we needed it for food. Hunting here in California at this time is really not the" in" thing.

Several years ago I gave my hunting rifles to Gary and now he is the hunter in the family. He has done better than I did. He recently shot two deer in the Trinity Alps. He has a unique way of handling his deer after he shoots it. He guts it, brings it home, then takes all the shelves out of his refrigerator and stands the deer inside until he butchers it. He and his sons have shot wild boars on a ranch near where they live and they have now become avid duck and quail hunters.

PART 2

Family Portrait ~1999
Family Portrait 11/26/99. Back row: Gary, Carla,
Tom, Laura, Tricia, Bryan
Front row: Emily, Callan, Jason, Jean, Graham, Old Ephraim,
Olivia, Austin, Young Ephraim.

Introduction

RUN IT MIGHT Be Somebody has been written in two parts primarily because the two parts cover two distinctly different time periods in my life. The break from part 1 to part 2 represents the change from adolescence to adulthood. I consider that my marriage to Jean as the time at which I became an adult. Right after marriage, I started to college and perhaps for the first time in my life, I had a clearly defined goal. Up until that time, I didn't seem to have any direction.

Part 1 of *Run, It Might Be Somebody* contained a collection of memories and anecdotes recalled from my early childhood through a tour of duty in the navy. This period of time essentially represented my adolescent years. At that time, I had no clear direction and didn't know what I wanted to do with the rest of my life. Those were my growing up years especially my time in the navy.

Part 2 begins with my marriage to Jean and the realization that I needed to find a direction in my life.

CHAPTER 4

Married Man with Children Goes to College

1953-957

Marriage:

WHEN I WAS discharged from the navy in July of 1953 after five years of service, I drove away from the Submarine Base at Groton Connecticut in my 1950 Ford with all of my worldly possessions in my car. My home address was still Garrett, Pennsylvania although I had not lived there for five years. I no longer had a room there nor did any of my belongings or memorabilia remain after my five-year absence. At that moment I felt a certain freedom that I had never felt before nor since. I had no job to go to, no home that I could call my own, no lawn to mow, no cows to milk, no mortgage to pay, no captain to serve, no duties to perform, and no one to tell me what to do. At that moment, I was a free man—free to go anywhere or do anything I chose.

Having said that now, I of course realized then that there was in fact a plan in place for me to start a new life and I would not have wanted to do otherwise. Learning a profession, getting married and starting a family of my own was my top priority.

After a quick trip back to Pennsylvania to say hello to my mom and pop, I went to work in Norwich as a painter for a small outfit called "Ryan and Tenant." I got paid $1.00 per hour. I helped paint the Greek Orthodox church in Norwich. After two weeks, I told a fellow painter named Pete Schafer that I couldn't save money for college on the $1.00 per hour salary so he and I found a job doing construction work that paid $2.10 per hour. The new job involved tearing out old entry ways and building new ones in a navy housing project near the submarine base. It was hard work but after a week or so the boss gave me the job of driving the company truck which was used to make regular runs to get sacks of cement and cement blocks.

I stayed on the construction job for about two months until Jean and I got married. During this time period I lived in temporary quarters in a downstairs bedroom at Jean's parent's house. I should point out that Jean's bedroom was upstairs and her parent's bedroom was downstairs right next to mine. So, clearly there was no messing around before marriage. In those days, couples did not live together before they got married, especially Catholics.

So on September 12, 1953, just two and a half months after serving five years in the navy, Jean and I were married at the Sacred Heart church in Norwichtown, Connecticut. Most of Jean's relatives were there since they all lived in Norwich or the surrounding area. From my side, my mother and father, my brother and best man Floyd, and several of my navy buddies were there and that was it. While Floyd and I were waiting for my future father in law, N. Ervin Whitehill, to bring his daughter down the isle, we were off to the side in our designated area and Floyd was telling me hunting stories about some of the deer he shot with his bow in Michigan and Ohio. Floyd's hunting stories some times get pretty involved and as a result, we almost missed our cue to come out to the alter for the marriage ceremony to begin. When we did come out, a few seconds late, I felt nervous seeing all of Jean's Connecticut Yankee good catholic relatives sitting there on both sides of the isle (both sides because there were only a few of my friends on the groom's side). I was just a small town farm boy from Pennsylvania, not one of them. I wasn't a Catholic and I didn't even have a real job, nor did I have anything in the pipeline. I had a feeling that I would have to prove myself before they would consider me worthy of marrying one of theirs. Jean has told me, more than once, that they really approved of me and that I shouldn't have felt that way. Perhaps it was a lack of confidence on my part.

After Jean and I were married, we left for a two-week honeymoon in Vermont. Just before we left, I overheard two of Jean's aunts wondering what I had given my new bride. It was a requirement, or at least common practice for the husband to give the new bride something before leaving on the honeymoon. I think that I was aware of that and I had bought some cheap jewelry which I had forgotten to give her. I gave it to her later but I don't recall ever seeing her wearing it. So it seemed that the non catholic country boy, with no job, dug the hole that he was in even deeper.

We didn't tell anyone where we were honeymooning because we didn't know. We just took off and stayed at a different motel each night. I guess convention would have dictated that we should have stayed in the bridal suite of a fancy hotel but we did it our way. Or maybe it was my way. After one week, we made a side trip back to Storrs, Connecticut so that I could register in the agriculture school at the University of Connecticut. Since I was still a farm boy at heart, even after my time in the navy, I decided that I would like to do something associated with farming but not actually farming. The University of Connecticut was known as an excellent agricultural college. When I got to the registrar's office, it was suggested that I might want to consider trying the engineering school first and if I didn't like it, I could switch after the first or second semester. The man gave me a multi page test which he suggested that I could take right away to determine if I had the appropriate aptitude for the engineering school. I sat down in an empty office and took the test which took about an hour or so. The test was graded immediately and I was told that I did quite well. So I said, okay, I'll try Engineering. I think that he was pushing the engineering school, which was rather new at the University of Connecticut, while at the same time the Agriculture School, had an excellent reputation and had no problems getting students. So that's how I choose to study Mechanical Engineering. This decision, which of course had a major impact on my life as well as Jean's, and ultimately many others, was made on the spot without any detailed thought or consideration.

Back to School:

After completing the registration, we continued on the rest of our Honeymoon. When we returned to Norwich, we moved into the second floor of Jean's parent's house which they had converted into an apartment. I commuted to school at the University in Storrs which was about a thirty to forty-five minute drive from Norwich. I went to classes every day and came home in the evening. Jean continued to work at the Norwich Bulletin while I received $150 per month on the GI Bill. It was like a job except that I had a lot of homework.

I was motivated to learn when I began college but I was scared. I had been out of high school for five years and I lacked the confidence that I would be able to compete with the students fresh out of high school. The first semester, I took three math courses; trigonometry, geometry, and analytic geometry along with all the other necessary courses. After one year, I went to summer school to take some extra courses where I felt I was not very strong. One course was English. This was a course in simple

English that anyone who was born in America should have already had. The teacher looked like Ichabod Crane and one day, during the early part of the course, he gave us a test. The entire class flunked it. The only way anyone could have passed it would have been if he graded it on a curve. What made this even worse was that it was a test that he had given to his seventh grade class and most of the seventh graders had passed it. The fact that my class mates had done poorly made me feel better. At that moment I knew that I would make it through college. I realized that the other students weren't so smart either.

Birth of Sons While Working and Going to School:

Our first child was born on Christmas Eve in 1954. We had been married over twelve months, which was greater than nine months so all was well with the relatives. When I had taken Jean to the hospital, the doctor told me to leave because she wasn't quite ready. At that time, men were not part of the birthing process. It was pretty common for the husband to go home and wait for a call. In my case, it was also important for me to take advantage of any opportunity to make a few extra dollars especially with a new baby in the house and Jean not working. When the call did come in, it was Christmas Eve and I had just returned from delivering mail in Norwich which was standard practice for me during my college days. The call came in to my father in law and he handed me the phone. I was told that it was a boy and all was well with Jean and the baby. When I hung up Grampy (we could start calling him Grampy now) anxiously asked "Is it a boy? Is it a boy?" I smiled at him and made him wait. I asked him if a girl would be okay and he said "Yes," but I could tell he really wanted a grandson. He could hardly contain himself when I told him that it was a boy.

So our first born was a boy and we named him Gary Wayne. Jean and I celebrated Christmas morning in her room at the hospital and Gary was brought in by the nurse with a little candy cane in his hand.

With Gary's arrival and Jean not working anymore, I worked during summers, weekends and during time off from school. I worked for a gardener on weekends, delivered mail on holidays, especially Christmas, and worked during the summers on a surveying crew for several years. We were living on about $150 per month, which was the amount allowed by the GI Bill. We also used up some savings that we had accumulated. During my second year in college we moved to Willimantic, which was near the University. We first moved to a third story flat in town and then, after a few months, we moved again to a housing development which cost us $28 per month, including utilities. Jean's parents would come to visit us every Saturday night and they would bring dinner.

Up until my third year in college, we didn't have a washing machine. Jean took our clothes to a Laundromat or she washed things at home by hand including Gary's cloth diapers. During my third year, I was awarded $500 from Westinghouse Electric Company as a physics achievement award. We used the money to finally buy a washing machine.

During the summers of 1954 and 1955, I worked as part of a surveying group whose job was to survey areas where road work was planned. There were four of us in the group. The lead guy used the transit, which is basically a telescope sitting atop a tripod. Another person used a long cloth tape measure and a third person held a numbered pole. The idea was to determine the elevation profile of a given area as the first step in building a new road or road widened, etc. A fourth person would serve as a traffic director. We worked an eight hour day however part of the eight hours included driving to and from work which used up at least one hour and another probably thirty minutes for a coffee and donut stop so we only worked about 6 to 6.5 hours each day. If it rained, or even looked like rain, we would sit in the truck and play cards. One time near Old Saybrook, Connecticut, it was raining so we couldn't work. Instead, we went crabbing in the rain. We couldn't work in the rain but we could go crabbing in the rain. I recall one other time sitting in the truck playing cards when we were having a hum dinger of a storm. We were inside the truck and didn't realize how bad the storm really was until we saw an old woman going to fetch her cows and a tree blew down in back of her and appeared to be chasing her across the field. It was then that we decided to go home. As it turned out, many of the roads were closed and trees, power lines, and debris cluttered the roadway. We were in the middle of Hurricane Carol which was one of the worst hurricanes to hit Connecticut in many years.

While working near a housing project, some of us were looking through the transit one day when we spotted a young lady in a backyard sunbathing in the nude. That kept us occupied until she discovered that we were watching her and she felt compelled to go inside.

Tom was born on July 12, 1956, which was after I had completed my third year in college. About a week before his birth, Floyd and his wife were visiting us and we had eaten a lot of watermelon. Jean suddenly thought that she was ready to deliver so I took her to the hospital in Norwich. The doctor said that she wasn't ready and the false alarm was probably from the watermelon. Probably no connection, but Tom always liked watermelon. When he was small, and even now, when he is nearly fifty, he still requests a watermelon with candles instead of a cake for his birthday.

That same summer I worked at Pratt and Whitney Aircraft which was a step up from the surveying joy of the previous two summers. So during my fourth year in college, we had two little boys. Jean's brother Jack brought us an old television with a very small screen. We had it sitting in our $28 per month flat on my desk where I did all my homework. On more than one occasion, I remember having both boys sitting on my lap watching TV while I was doing homework.

College Life:

They gave us plenty of homework during my four years at UConn. I always felt that I had to do more than the other students because of the five years I'd been out of high school. If a professor told us to do all the odd number problems at the end of the chapter, I did all the odd number ones but then did some or all of the even numbered ones. It usually paid off.

I did not spend a lot of time on campus. I went to classes, took exams, and then went home to do homework and be with Jean and the boys. Occasionally Jean and I would go to a sports event. College for me was more like a job. I did stop by the student union sometimes for coffee and some deep discussions on things like space, time and other dimensions. I remember a lengthy discussion with a guy named Heinz Kappel about the practicality of space flights. We decided that it would never be practical because of the high fuel load to pay load ratio. Shortly after we graduated the Russians launched their first sputnik which started the space program race and showed us how wrong we were.

Heinz and I also got into deep discussions on things like infinity. Heinz would argue that the Cosmos was infinite in size and therefore there were infinite other worlds like ours. That being the case, he argued that there were two people sitting at a table in another world discussing infinity like we were. I disagreed because even if there were an infinite number of other worlds, the probability of two worlds being alike was infinitely small so you had a case of infinity divided by infinity which was indeterminate.

The concept of infinity always fascinated, and in some ways frightened, me. I thought there had to be infinity in all directions. That is, the cosmos was infinitely big and infinitely small, and if I thought about it very long I would get dizzy. It also seemed to me that the Big Bang was just one in a cycle of Big Bangs. In other words, there have always been Big Bangs. There was no beginning. This Big Banging has been going for an infinite amount of time and to infinity in space. So it would answer the question of when did this all start. The answer is, it never started. It was always here.

I once dreamed that I saw a man holding a book. On the cover of the book was a picture of a man holding a book. On that book was a picture of a man holding a book. On that book was a picture of a man holding a book. It was like I was riding on a light beam heading into the book and it continued without stopping. That was my dream, or vision, and it caused me to get dizzy and break out in a cold sweat.

I eventually came to realize that I was a deep thinker with a shallow mind. That's a bad combination. Someone suggested to me that all such deep thinking was unhealthy and that one should be content to gaze up at the night sky secure in the knowledge that you won't fall off the earth and that none of the stars above will land on your head, then how much more do you really need to know or need to worry about. So I decided to not think about infinity and relax with the comfortable belief that God made the heavens and earth and when I die I will show up somewhere else, perhaps in another dimension.

Our thermodynamics professor gave us a surprise quiz one day which had something to do with a rocket flight at speeds greater than Mach 1. The entire class flunked it. So he spent another class period explaining it and then gave us the same quiz again. All, but a very few, flunked it the second time. I didn't fully understand the concepts then and I probably still don't understand then now. That surprise quiz helped me realize that I wasn't, or didn't want to be, a rocket scientist.

During my senior year, I was somehow elected to be president of the engineering class. I really didn't want to do it but it turned out to be interesting experience. A class mate named Joe Peralta and I decided that the school should have an engineering magazine so we started one. It was a lot of work but it was also fun and provided us with some good experience.

I graduated in 1957 from the school of engineering with a degree in mechanical engineering. When I graduated, it was the best of times for engineering graduates. Companies came on campus to interview graduates. There were many job opportunities. My interview with General Electric was especially interesting. I was invited to a group dinner at a nearby restaurant but I had to decline because I had another interview at the same time. I agreed to come when I could hopefully in time for dessert. So I came just as the main dinner was over and I was invited to sit down at a place saved for me. Just after I sat down, I was being introduced to someone behind me so I started to get up to shake his hand. In the process of getting up, I put my right hand down on the table to push myself off and just as I was dong that the waiter put down a big fat gooey dessert in front of me. Well, my hand landed right on top of the gooey dessert and in the same motion I started to extend my hand for the introduction. I pulled it back in time to avoid contact. That was the first impression that I gave to the interviewer of the company where I would eventually choose to spend my engineering career.

Decision Making Time:

After many interviews, my choice boiled down to three possibilities: I had an offer to work in the MIT Instrumentation Laboratory in Cambridge, Massachusetts, while taking classes to obtain an advanced degree. The job involved the development of guidance systems for rockets. The other two offers were both involved in the design and development of Nuclear Power for the navy. One was at the General Electric Knolls Atomic Laboratory in Schenectady and the other was at the Westinghouse Bettis Atomic Laboratory in Pittsburgh, Pennsylvania. I eliminated the MIT job because I thought there was no future in rockets. Besides, remember that surprise quiz that I twice flunked in thermodynamics class that had to do with rocket flight. That probably had something to do also with my decision as well. Well, regardless, I thought the nuclear direction offered a better future. The Bettis job was better in the sense that I was offered a PhD program. The KAPL program included a Masters program and I thought the location looked like a better place to bring up kids. I was having a major problem deciding which to choose. Jean said that it was up to me and she would go wherever I decided. Finally one day I discovered the tie breaker. I read an obscure article in the Willimantic Paper and I threw the paper up in the air and told Jean to pack her woollies, we're going to Schenectady. What I had seen in the paper was a little obscure article that said the following: "Construction halted at the Knolls Atomic Power Laboratory prototype facility to allow the hatching of a nest of birds." I figured if they would do that for birds just imagine what they would do for people, including me.

And so it was. I finished college, accepted a job with General Electric, and we moved to Schenectady, New York. Another big decision that had a major effect on me and my family was made because a bird decided to make its home in the middle of a construction site.

CHAPTER 5

Living in Schenectady
1957-1969

The Move:

WHEN I ACCEPTED the job offer from General Electric's Knolls Atomic Power Laboratory (KAPL), I didn't realize that they would pay for my move to Schenectady. They didn't tell me that or if they did I didn't hear it. So with the help of a friend, I rented a truck and we moved all our household belongings from our $28 per month flat to a house that I had rented in Schenectady. I didn't tell Jean at the time but during the move we dropped the washing machine (the one that we bought with the Physics achievement award money) off the back of the truck in the unloading process. Fortunately, it didn't seem to affect the machines performance.

Working At KAPL:

During my first two years at KAPL I was enrolled in a program called the KAPL/RPI program. Essentially, I worked half time while completing a Masters program at RPI in Mechanical Engineering with a minor in Nuclear Engineering. My annual starting salary at GE was $6,000 but while I attended RPI I received just half of that amount. Even so, we felt rich after living on $150 per month.

My early jobs at KAPL were involved with the design and development of nuclear power plants for Admiral Rickover's Nuclear Navy. During my time there, 1957 to 1969, we did not have desk top computers. My first job involved the design of radiation shielding for the USS *Triton* and the

Triton prototype. The *Triton* was built at the shipyard at Groton, Connecticut and the prototype was located at West Milton, near Schenectady. The prototype was used as a training facility. I used a desk top mechanical calculator and a slide rule to determine gamma ray and neutron shielding requirements, and later, for designing other fluid and mechanical systems associated with the plant. It wasn't until sometime in the late seventies that I started using personal computers. I always complained that I was born too soon for the electronic age.

I spent much of my working time at the West Milton prototype facility with an occasional trip to Groton, Connecticut to the *Triton*. The *Triton* was the first dual reactor submarine and was the first to circumnavigate the earth submerged. I just threw that in because that's the only thing that I can think of that the *Triton* did that was noteworthy. One time I went there when the ship was in dry dock to make some radiation measurements inside of the ballast tanks just opposite the reactors. I was using a gamma ray detector like a Geiger counter and I wasn't getting any response. I thought maybe the detector wasn't working so I tested it by monitoring the dial of my watch which was an old watch with numbers painted on with a radiation emitting substance and the detector needle jumped telling me that it was, in fact, working. I was a little surprised to see that the shutdown radiation level just outside the reactor was lower than the level just outside of the dial of my watch. I decided to deep six my watch soon after that and I got a new one without the radiation in the dial. As a point of lasting interest, after one of my trips to Groton, I submitted an expense report that included $7.50 for the hotel and $3.50 for dinner.

KAPL had just one customer and that was Admiral Rickover. He was the father of the nuclear navy. During my twelve years of working there, I never met the man but I heard many stories about him. On one occasion, he did a short tour of the West Milton site and found some lights that were still on and it was in the middle of the day. He asked that they be turned off but the location of the switch could not be readily found. When he left the site the lights were still on and he requested that he be called and informed when the lights were turned off. This incident reminded me of my dad who often told us to "outen the lights when we leave a room."

There was another time when he told our water chemistry expert, Sherman Williams, that he had gotten too fat and that he should lose some weight. He even called Sherman's wife and got her involved in a weight loss effort. He expected that the next time they met, there would be less of Sherman to see. We thought it might be fun if we selected some really skinny guy, like me, to go in his place to their next meeting and pretend to be Sherman. Of course, we didn't actually carry out that interesting idea. I think that the final outcome of Sherman's weight loss effort was some minor weight loss but probably not as much as Rickover had in mind.

I've been told that Rickover had chairs in his office that had the legs cut short, especially the front legs so that his subordinates during meetings and candidates during job interviews would feel small and uncomfortable.

Since all of the work that we did at KAPL was under contract with the U.S. Navy, we were required to have a "Q" clearance to work there. It also meant that we had to pass through a security gate to and from work and we had to keep all of our work locked up when we were out of the office. Our working routine required that the first thing after arriving in our office, we had to open the combination safe and take out our work for the day. At the end of the day, the work went back in the safe. The purpose was to prevent the work that we did from falling into the hands of our competitors, or the enemy. In this regard, I often thought that the stuff I had in my safe would only confuse them and would set them back instead of forward.

While working at KAPL and living in Schenectady I heard a lot about Charles Protius Steinmitz. Although he was only four feet tall, he was a genius. He worked for GE in the late 1800s. After he retired in 1902 he was called back to work on a problem that no one else was able to solve. He was soon able to locate the problem as a failed part which he marked with a piece of chalk. He later submitted a bill to GE for $10,000 and I guess they thought it was pretty high so they asked him for an itemized account. He responded with: (1) making chalk mark—$1.00, and (2) Knowing where to place it—$9,999.

One other story that I heard involved two young engineers who thought that they had found a problem that he wouldn't be able to solve, at least not in a hurry. They approached him in his office with the question of finding the exact amount of material that would be removed from a one-inch diameter rod by drilling a perpendicular hole in the rod with a one-inch diameter drill. The young engineers knew that in order to solve this problem exactly would require the use of triple integration with hard to define integration limits. They presented Steinmitz with the question and they immediately started to leave thinking that this would take awhile. They were asked to wait while it did some fast scribbling on the back of an envelope and within a few minutes he handed the young engineers the answer.

An interesting fallout from this story came when I went home and at the dinner table I was telling this story to Jean. Gary was about eight or nine years old at the time and he was listening. After a few minutes of silence, he suggested that they should have just weighed the material to find out how much had been removed. I think this was a good example of the old proverb that says: "There's more than one way to skin a cat."

After nearly twelve years at KAPL, I was passed over for a promotion to a unit manager position that I thought should have been given to me. I interpreted that to mean that I should look elsewhere if I wanted to progress. A number of my peers had already transferred from KAPL to the commercial nuclear power generating business in San Jose, California, which at that time was booming. So I decided maybe I should follow. The move to California is covered in a later chapter.

Birth of Daughters:

When we first moved to Schenectady we rented the first floor of a house on Patrick Court in a nice section of Schenectady. For us, this was a big step up from the $28/month place in Willimantic. It was about seven miles from KAPL which was a nice drive through the country. After one year at Patrick Court, we bought a house at 147 Willow Lane in Scotia, which was actually a part of Schenectady. It was a little Cape Cod-style house with two bedrooms and one bath downstairs and two bedrooms upstairs. It also had a full basement with a very high ceiling and an attached one car garage. It had a big lot with lots of trees and nothing but woods behind it. It was a great place for the kids.

During the buying process, Jean and I worried because of what seemed to us to be a high price for the house. We worried about being able to make the payments. The price we had to pay was $10,200. That was the total price. As I write this, it sounds more like the cost of getting a new drive way. We were somehow able to come up with around $2,000 for a down payment which left us with a mortgage of about $8,000 with monthly payments somewhere in the range of $75 per month. I know it sounds like we shouldn't have had to agonize but remember my full time salary was $6,000 per year and since I was still on the KAPL/RPI program I was only getting paid just a little over half that amount.

As a new home owner, I always found things around the place that needed improvement or repair. Gary will always remember and remind me often that on one of those repair jobs while I was up on a ladder, I dropped a pipe wrench on his head. I've actually forgotten the exact circumstances but occasionally he reminds me of it. Also, while during some preliminary work on converting a portion of the basement into a play area, Tom, who was only two at the time, fell down the basement stairs. I was near the bottom of the stairs when I saw him coming. I made a frantic dive to catch him but missed. I think that I did get him on the first bounce. This incident came at the time when Jean was about nine months pregnant with Tricia. I took Tom to see Dr. Mauet, our family physician, and after checking him out he thought that he was most likely fine, but we should watch him for a few days. We never did see any adverse effects.

The following day, October 5, 1958, Jean went to the hospital and gave birth to Patricia Lynn. We should have named her Tricia because that's the name she uses.

When she was still only a month or so old, she wore casts on both of her feet because her feet turned in an excessive amount.

When Tricia was just a few months old, we hired a lady during the daytime hours to help out with taking care of Tricia and the boys and for helping with the house work. It was also a test, of sorts, to see if she could handle the three kids while Jean was in the hospital for planned surgery to remove cysts from her ovaries. It turns out, she wasn't very "child friendly" so we let her go. We decided instead to have Jean's mother, Loretta Whitehill or "Nana" to come in her place.

A few days after Nana got there, Jean went into the hospital for her scheduled surgery. During her second day in the hospital, I went to visit her and while there I started to feel sick. I came home and the sickness got worse. It's a good thing Nana was there because my condition deteriorated to the point where I decided to go to the hospital. I should have called an ambulance but I called a taxicab instead to take me to the Emergency Room. When the cab arrived I told the driver that it was an emergency, but he insisted on picking up another fare. I kept telling him to hurry because I was in severe pain but he pretty much ignored me. When we finally arrived at the hospital, the fare was only a few dollars but all I had on me was a $20 bill. I handed it to him and he tried to take advantage of my condition by suddenly having a big problem finding any change. I insisted on change in spite of the fact that I was in a whole lot of pain. He finally managed to get close but I insisted that he give me all that was due. I was prepared to strangle him if he didn't come through with the correct change. He finally did and you can be sure that I gave him absolutely nothing for a tip.

I went into the emergency room and literally crawled up onto a gurney. Attendants thought I had appendicitis. They rushed me off to surgery while I signed papers along the way. It turns out that my appendix was okay. I had something that I'd never heard of, Meckel's diverticulum. This is a congenital condition where a sac protrudes from the final section of the small intestine. The condition sometimes causes twisting of the intestine and apparently cuts off the intestine and causes blockage along with severe pain. The operation, that they performed, included removal of the sac and patching the intestine wall. They, of course, removed the appendix while they were in the vicinity.

When Nana found out that they were keeping me at the hospital along with Jean, she was suddenly stuck with taking care of three kids. So she decided to call for reinforcements. She called her husband "Grampy." Sometimes parents, or in-laws, come in handy.

When I was out of the hospital and fully recovered, I was telling an older man who lived in the woods behind our house about my surgery. He seemed familiar with my problem. He told me that I would probably have related problems later in life. I really didn't want to hear that but it turns out that he was right. I would be reminded of his statement on at least six occasions starting about twenty-five years later.

It looked for some time like our family of two boys and one girl would be the final count. But in 1963 while bowling with Forrest and Shirley Rathbun and Don and Kathy LeGrand, the subject of more babies came up. Somebody asked us if we planned to have any more and I said "Yes, we plan to have another daughter." They asked when and I responded most assuredly that it would be "nine months from tonight." As it turned out, almost exactly nine months later on October 27, 1963, Laura Jean was born. Our family was complete with two boys and two girls.

Schenectady Summers:

There were many jokes told about Schenectady summers. Like for example, "we had a very good summer last year, both days were nice." Though a bit of an exaggeration, the summers were a bit short and the winters were long. I personally liked both the summer and the winter. For me, summer time meant camping, fishing, hunting, hiking and an occasional trip to Nana and Grampy's house in Connecticut or to Grandma and Pappy's house in Pennsylvania. Winter meant sledding, skiing, building a big snowman, fires in the fireplace, snow covered trees, the kids playing in the snow, and of course shoveling the driveway.

The most memorable summer time activity for all of us was camping. We had been in Schenectady about a year when I went to Goldstock's Sporting Goods store in downtown Schenectady and bought a complete camping outfit including a very large rectangular shaped tent, a Coleman stove, Coleman lanterns, cots, sleeping bags, a hatchet, shovel and other things that we might need. I had them in my car and then worried about what Jean would say when I got home. I hadn't told her of my planned purchase. At that time, we had two little boys and I don't think that Jean had any imminent plans to go camping. She was not exactly excited at the idea of going camping with two boys still in diapers but she warmed up to it after we tried it a few times.

For the twelve summers that we lived in Schenectady, we went camping during summer weekends and sometimes on our vacation. Our favorite places were in the Adirondack Mountains north of Schenectady. We formed a family bond with Forrest and Shirley Rathbun and Don and Kathy LeGrand. The majority of our camping trips were made with this group of six adults plus kids. Toward the end of the twelve-year period, the number of kids increased from about six to about ten or more.

During those camping trips we encountered a lot of rain. There were times when we considered ourselves to be rainmakers. I recall one trip where it was just the Rathbun's with their kids and Jean and I with our kids when it rained all the time that we were there. The locals told us that it had not rained for forty days and forty nights until we arrived. They took our phone number so they could call us the next time they had a drought. It rained so hard the first day we stayed most of the time in our big tent. I remember all twelve of us eating pizza in the tent and under the canopy.

On another occasion, just Forrest and I and our four boys went to the same place and once again it rained pretty much all weekend. We spent a lot of time by the fire and then went for a hike in the rain. We had to cross a river at one point and in order to do it we found a spot where the river was narrow but the flow was pretty fast. With Forest on one side and I on the other and with both of us standing in the water at the edge of the stream, we passed each of the four boys across one at a time. As we did so, their feet would drag in the stream so that the force of the water would turn them almost horizontal. We all got rather soaked in the process. We later stopped in a roadside tavern which served both food and liquor. It was a honky-tonk type place with a fat lady piano player. They had Forrest and I and the four boys seated near a wood burning stove so that we could dry off but also away from the other regular patrons. We had some lunch and hot chocolate. Later after we dried off a bit, we all went to a movie. We noticed all the people near us moved away. I guess we smelled funny from camping out and from all the rain and the camp fire smoke that our clothes had absorbed.

Once while we were in one car and Forrest and family in another, Forrest made a sudden stop. He got out of the car and walked back to tell us that he had just heard on the radio that Marilyn Monroe had died.

After tenting for about eight or ten years, we graduated to a tent trailer. This was a step up from the tent. We expanded our range and went as far as Prince Edward Island one year and to Florida another. Laura was only three years old when we went to Florida and on that trip she learned to swim. In 1967, we spent the entire summer camping in the tent trailer. It was Jean and I and the four kids and Nana. This was just one of the many adventures that we had over the years and the details of this are discussed later.

When we had a chance during the summer months, we would go fishing. Usually we would rent a boat and I would use my little 5 HP outboard motor so we wouldn't have to row. We would go out on one of the many lakes in the area and find a quiet cove where the water was calm and where we could fish near the Lilly pads. We would catch blue gills or similar fish and then take them home and have them for dinner. It was a lot of fun for me and for the kids and eating the fish was always a special treat for all of us especially the tail fins, which were crisp like French fried potatoes.

Gary and I went on a Boy Scout outing one time which involved a canoe trip and sleeping on the ground in under designed sleeping bags. It was early spring and we got one of those late spring weather conditions where you have to wonder whose idea was it to go on a canoe trip. We started out with many canoes with two or three people in each canoe but we had to cut it short when several of the canoes nearly capsized due to high winds and rough waters. Not only that, the boys, and some of the dads were freezing. None of us had come prepared for cold weather. That night we camped in the woods near the water and we slept right on the ground. I remember laying down a piece of plastic, then our two sleeping bags on top of the thin piece of plastic without any air mattress. I rigged a piece of tarp over us to keep out the rain or snow if it should happen. All through the night I was worried about Gary getting too cold so I rigged our sleeping bags so that part of mine would cover him as well. He slept like a log. I was shivering all night and got very little sleep. When we awoke in the morning, the landscape was white. It had snowed during the night. At this point, I swore if they had another camping trip, the boys were on their own.

After living on Willow Lane for some time, we decided that we needed a second car. I found a used Desoto two door with a very big trunk. It had an automatic transmission but it was designed with push buttons for changing gears instead of a standard gear shift handle. I stored much of my sporting equipment in the big trunk so that I was always ready for any occasion. I had a five hp outboard motor along with fishing equipment, camping equipment, hunting equipment except for the hunting weapons themselves, artifact digging equipment, rain clothes, tarps, tents, sleeping bags, etc. I always liked to be ready for the outdoors. I only had the Desoto for about two years and then I traded it in on a nice new red Volkswagen bug. The bug was a much more reliable car but I missed the Desoto, especially the big trunk.

Every fall, I went hunting for deer with my bow, and occasionally with a gun. I found a place, some distance north of Schenectady, where I had been a time or two. There was a small lake about two miles up hill from where I parked the car. According to the map, the lake was referred to as Mud Lake. I took Gary and Tom there one time and we hiked in to the lake with our back packs and sufficient gear to stay one night. At the lake was an old boat which had much of the seat chewed away by some animal which we assumed was a beaver but I was never quite sure what did the chewing. There was a small open sided structure by the lake which would serve as a place for us to sleep. We tried fishing but I don't think we did very well so it's a good thing that we had brought something along to eat. After dinner, we settled down under the open sided shelter in front of a nice fire in our sleeping bags and talked until we fell asleep. We hadn't been asleep very long when one of the boys nudged me awake saying, "there's something out there." "What did you hear?" I asked. "There's animals running around," was the reply. The three of us lay there straining our ears and eyes to figure out what it was. We, of course, thought bears, or worse. I fished around in my bag being as quiet as I could until I found my flashlight. I turned it on and scanned it across the ground between us and the lake and much to our surprise what we were hearing were rabbits. Large rabbits. After seeing the rabbits, we could relax and go back to sleep since we felt pretty sure that the rabbits wouldn't eat us.

Once again the under designed sleeping bags failed to protect me from the cold Adirondack nights. Along about four in the morning, I was so cold I couldn't sleep. So I got up in the dark and started to rebuild the fire. Both boys, who weren't all that warm either, got up and helped. So there we were in the cold darkness foraging for wood. We got the fire going again and managed to get a few more hours of sleep before we awoke to see a young buck come down to the edge of the lake for a drink of water. We watched from our sleeping bags until the sun rose over the trees surrounding the lake before getting up for a meager breakfast. We spent several more hours at the lake and then hiked back out to our Desoto and headed home.

Where we lived in Schenectady was only a few miles from the Mohawk River which was part of the old Erie Canal. We found a place along the river where archeologists had spent considerable time digging an ancient Native American site which was inhabited about three thousand years earlier. I believe the inhabitants were referred to as "The Normanskill." The site had been worked for some years and was then opened up to the public. We discovered this place, and Tom, Gary, and I went there many times and dug for artifacts. Sometimes Jean and the girls went along and dug or just watched.

But usually, it was just Tom and I. It was a very relaxing activity. Actually, it was much more than just something to do to relax. While we chipped away on the sides of the trench, we would feel a certain anticipation about finding something man made that dated so many years before. When we would find anything that had been buried there by the river for thousands of years we would wonder about who it was that made and used it. What were they like? What did they eat and how did they keep warm in the winter? We would sit in a trench and pick away at the sides with small tools looking for items that would be recognized as tools that the ancient people used. In the course of probably a few dozen or more trips we found many cutting edges that would have served as knives or arrow and spearheads, gouges, celts, and net sinkers. Tom showed the most interest in these projects and he still has many of the artifacts that we found.

Surviving the Schenectady Winters:

Jean and I still remember the sound of the snow plow clearing the street past our house in the middle of the night. To us, it was a pleasant sound because it meant that we would awake to see a fresh layer of white covering the landscape. It was especially nice if it occurred on a Friday night because that meant we, and the kids, could play in the snow on Saturday morning. Even if it came in the middle of the week, the drive to work for me, and the walk to school for the kids, was rarely a problem. Tricia also remembers falling asleep during those frequent snow storms thinking that the morning might bring a "snow day" when school would be cancelled.

There was another sound in the night that was not so pleasant: The sound of limbs breaking due to the weight of ice during one of those nasty ice storms. It seems like there would be at least one bad ice storm every winter. When these occurred, our birch trees would become so laden with ice that they would bend over until the tops of the trees would touch the ground. The morning sun would sparkle off the snow and ice and the icicles lining the edge of the roof. When this happened, the place looked like a Winter Wonderland. Our house looked like something you might see on a post card.

The birch trees could bend without breaking until the tops touched the snow covered ground, whereas the limbs of the pine trees and sometimes the power lines would break. During several of these storms, the power was lost due to the loss of the power lines. I recall one time in particular when we were without power for three days. We slept in sleeping bags in the living room by the fireplace. We burned up all our available firewood and finally burned the wood box. I was beginning to look at the furniture when the power came back on. We were lucky because some people in outlying areas were without power much longer. Tricia once told me that this is a favorite memory of hers that she has retold countless times.

During one of those ice storms I had to go to Albany and pick up a new car. We had bought a brand new 1964 Chevrolet station wagon and I had to drive it home during the ice storm. Jean was at home awaiting my arrival and she was a wreck just thinking about me and the new car on the icy roads. As it turned out, the main roads had been salted and sanded to remove the ice, but the roads close to our house were totally covered with "black ice." There was a little upgrade as I entered Willow Brook Park and I had to drive in the ditch to get enough traction to get up the hill. On the level part of the street there was no way to control my direction. When I tried to turn on to Willow Lane, the car wanted to continue straight. Fortunately, I was the only car in sight. As I got close to our house one of our neighbors came down the street on ice skates. Honest, it's true; I saw it with my own eyes. He helped me make the turn. When I got to our house, it would have been impossible to turn into our driveway. So I let the car sit in the middle of the street while I ran into the backyard and dug up ashes from an ash pile which I kept for such emergencies. I spread several buckets of ashes in front of the wheels on the street and in the driveway. The ashes, along with the weight of my available kids in the back seat, did the trick and I managed to get the new car home safely. And Jean breathed a sigh of relief.

During our very first winter in Schenectady, before Tricia and Laura were born, we had a major snow storm. It started snowing on a weekend and before it was time to go to work Monday morning I received a call from my boss Henry Stone that work was cancelled. School was also cancelled so Jean, the two boys and I had a fun day playing in the deep snow. We built this big snow man in our front yard at Patrick Court. Things in the city were back to normal the next day but some places in the country were snowed in for weeks.

By early January of our first winter in Schenectady I knew that we had to find a wintertime activity. So we took up skiing. There were a few places to go near Schenectady and one of the places even had lights. Jean and I went there occasionally because we had a season pass. But places that we really learned to like were farther north in New York state and in Vermont. It was always cold and sometime the slopes would be icy. It was not the greatest skiing in the world but we still liked it.

Gary, Tom, Tricia and I (Laura was only two at the time) went to Pico Peak in northern Vermont one time and it was cold, very cold. Tom and I got on the chair lift to the top where we were completely exposed to the cold winds. I was scared that if the chair stalled we would freeze to death. I think the wind chill factor made it equivalent to about 60 or more below zero. When we got off the lift we decided to ski to the lodge and quit. But the run down the mountain was so good that we looked at each other and immediately decided to do it again. We made many more runs because the run down was worth the cold ride up. In the meantime, Gary and Tricia and one of Tricia's friends were doing the same thing.

On one of our trips to Vermont we passed by Big Bromley, which is one of the best places to ski in the northeast. We never stopped there because I considered it too expensive to buy lift tickets for four people. On this occasion, I saw a sign that read "$8.00 adult, kids under 14 free." This was a special price for one day only. So for this one day the four of us could ski all day at one of the best places in the Northeast for just $8.00.

When we got to Bromley, Tricia and I went straight to the top of the mountain. They had an intermediate run that was about two miles long to the bottom. This was one of the best skiing days we had up to that time. On one of my runs, while standing in the lift line, I got my skis crossed up with the man in back of me. It turned out to be Lowell Thomas. Of course you all remember him don't you? I listened to him on the radio for years when he brought us the news.

Laura started to ski when she was just three years old. I first took her on the rope tow and held her between my legs. Then I would ski down the bunny slope with her between my legs for the first few times and then she could do it on her own. It was pretty apparent from the very beginning that she was destined to be the skier in the family. A few years later after we had moved to California and when she was still only six or seven, she and I along with Jim Klucar and Danny Mangin went skiing at Boreal Ridge. I turned her loose on the Bunny Slope and gave her some small change for hot chocolate and then proceeded to ski with the other two leaving her alone on the slope. Jim Klucar was shocked. He would check on her occasionally, as would I of course. She was very independent and had become quite expert at using the lifts and at getting back down the slopes.

Aside from skiing, we tried ice fishing in some of the nearby lakes, but we didn't do so well. We would clear the snow and then dig a hole in the ice before we could get started. It was hard work. We didn't have a shelter so we would get pretty cold especially if it got windy. One time Gary, Tom and I were out on the ice and it did in fact get very windy. The snow on top of the ice was dry so the wind blew the snow around so much we could hardly see. We packed up our stuff and high-tailed it back to the car in what seemed like a blizzard. Once inside the car where it was warm and protected, we all had a big laugh about the situation.

After living on Willow Lane for several years, I bought a little red Volkswagen. They were notorious for not having a good heater or defroster. Since we had a one car garage, the little red Volkswagen had to sit outside during those numerous days when the temperature hovered well below 0°F. So when I got in it to go to work on those very cold days, it was hard to see out of the windshield. So picture me in my McGregor coat with the hood up over my head and just my nose and eyes sticking out, with my hands covered with big mittens, and my car windshield covered with ice and frost. I would scratch away a small hole to look out of so I had to lean forward with my face near the hole to see the road. I looked like Nanook of the North going to work.

For a short while, we had a little dog named Augie which I had picked up at the animal shelter. We hooked him up to a sled and he could pull the kids down the street. If I had put a deer rack on Augie's head, he would have looked like the dog who pulled the sled in the *Grinch That Stole Christmas*.

Another thing we did in the wintertime, we tried to build an ice rink in the backyard. We didn't have very much success at Willow Lane but later when we lived on Cedar Lane we were able to actually have a small rink. We even had lights so the kids could skate at night.

After we moved to California, we missed those Schenectady winters. But we learned to live without them.

Trips to Pennsylvania and Connecticut:

We usually made at least one trip each year to my home in Pennsylvania and probably two trips per year to Jean's home in Connecticut. Those were always fun trips especially when you take into account that most of our kids would at least on some occasions get carsick. One time when we went to Pennsylvania, by the time we arrived Jean was wearing only a raincoat. Kids, I don't remember which ones, threw up on her repeatedly until her skirt, blouse, and to some extent her under things, were all reeking of vomit. So she stripped down to nothing more than her raincoat by the time we reached our destination. She was a bit annoyed at the time but to tell you the truth, I found the situation a little provocative.

Being able to visit the farm was something special for the kids. I still remember the boys helping one of their cousins fetch the cows down the old country road to bring them to the barn for milking much like I, and my dog Rex, did twenty odd years earlier. Except for a new barn and more modern machines, including milking machines, the old farm was much like it was when I was a kid. My kids, along with their cousins, got a chance to slop the hogs, feed the chickens, gather the eggs, feed the dogs and cats, feed the cows hay and grain, and ride on the tractor. They also were able to run barefoot through the cow pasture and feel the warmth of fresh cow paddy ooze up between their toes as did my sister Luella nearly forty years earlier.

My father died in 1964, and my mother joined him one year later in 1965. Laura was too young to remember either of them. After they died, our trips to Pennsylvania became less frequent and when we did go there, I always felt their absence.

In the meantime, we made trips to Connecticut more frequently because it only took about five hours instead of ten hours that it took us on our trips to Pennsylvania. As it was in Pennsylvania, there were a lot of cousins in Connecticut. Jean's brother Jack had four kids and her brother Bob had five. They were always excited to see their cousins but in some cases, getting together would bring out the worst in some of them. It seems like every time that our two boys got together with Uncle Bob's boys, all hell would break loose. We attended a wedding of one of Jean's cousins one time when all of our kids and their cousins, both boys and girls, were dressed up in their very best. The boys all wore white shirts with ties and jackets while the girls all wore nice dresses as you would expect at a wedding. They made it okay through the wedding but at the reception, the boys, as you might expect, got a bit rowdy. By the time we were ready to leave, the jackets and ties were dirty and in some cases torn, the pants were dirty and grass stained, and they looked pretty much like the kids in the Little Rascals movies of long ago. I guess you could say that when they got together, they acted like boys. Even to this day, when Gary and his cousin David get together they get a little out of hand.

On our trips to Connecticut, we always tried to travel thrifty. There was a place somewhere between Schenectady and Connecticut where we would stop to pick up something to eat. We could get seven hamburgers to go for $1.00. We brought our own drinks. So we would have our food for the trip for $1.00.

Neighbors Move to California:

A young couple with one small daughter moved from our neighborhood to the San Francisco Bay area of California sometime in the early 1960s. We really didn't know the people but we were aware of their move. A few years after they moved, I am not sure of the year, but I believe it was around 1963 more or less, the priest in our local church made a sad announcement during the morning mass. He reported that this same young couple along with their two young children, a baby boy and one girl, had died in a plane crash in California. They were in a small plane heading from the San Francisco area to Tahoe when they crashed during bad weather while trying to get over the Sierras. We all heard the news with much sadness but since life goes on, we put the event out of mind and went on with our lives. This memory would come back to me in a very sad and shocking way about twelve years later.

The Rathbuns:

I first met Forrest Rathbun while taking a class at RPI in Troy, New York, across the river from Schenectady. I was taking a class as part of the KAPL/RPI program and he was taking the same class as part of another GE Advanced degree program. We became instant friends. We often did homework assignments together, sometimes with other people involved. We once worked on a difficult math problem in the basement of our rented house on Patrick Court. It was one of those types of problems where the exercise is to reduce a complex equation down to its simplest form. I remember when we finally got it after page after page of calculations by about four of us, it reduced down to something like x = pie/2

Forrest was a major in the Army National Guard. As such, he went off to duty for several weeks every year. He was quite military in his demeanor. I on the other hand was much more disorganized and disconnected but we, I think, were a good pair. Besides the few classes we took together, our biggest activity together was camping. For a time period, I considered Forrest my best friend. He and Shirley had two boys and then two girls. It was the same with Jean and me. So we had a lot in common.

When we first knew the Rathbun's they lived in downtown Schenectady in a big old house. Shortly after we moved to Willow Lane, they moved to a house just around the corner from us. The LeGrands lived just down the street in the other direction. We three families were the best of friends and we were also neighbors. In the wintertime, which seemed like all the time, we went bowling together. Forrest was left handed and rolled a wicked ball. When the ball hit the head pin, the pins exploded. His score usually was no higher than Shirleys, she was the best of the bunch, but Forrest was the most dramatic.

About five years after we first met, on a cold rainy day in the northeast, a commercial airplane crashed while making the final approach to the runway at the Cleveland airport. We soon learned that Forrest was on that plane. He was heading for Cleveland on a business trip. They gave him a military funeral with a twenty-one-gun salute in his hometown of Providence, Rhode Island. In a formal ceremony, they presented Shirley with a United States flag. She received a financial settlement for her loss but she was left without a husband, her four kids lost their dad, and I lost my best friend.

On the afternoon of the day that Forrest died, Jean went to their house which was just down the street from ours to provide some solace for Shirley. While she was there, she parked the car in Shirley's driveway. She was still there when it got dark which was longer than she expected to be there. In the meantime, Tricia had gone there with her and was outside with Shirley's and Forest's daughter Linda. They were best friends at that time. Jean had told Tricia not to bother Shirley during this time of grievance. When it got dark, Tricia felt that she couldn't go inside because of her instructions not to bother Shirley, and there was a standing instruction not to go out on the street after dark, so Tricia didn't know what to do. So she got in our car in Shirley's driveway and waited for her mother to take her home. In the meantime, I am at home with the other kids wondering when Jean and Tricia would be home. So I called Jean at Shirley's and found out that Tricia wasn't there. I immediately started to comb the neighborhood looking for Tricia. She wasn't at Shirley's and she wasn't at home. I checked other neighbors and nobody had seen her. Almost immediately word got around that Tricia was missing. I had neighbors showing up with flashlights ready to form a search party. This all happened within minutes. It was around supper time and several men were beginning to gather by our house when Jean drove home from Shirley's with Tricia. She had been waiting in our car at Shirley's house because she had no other choice. Her instructions from her mother were to not bother Shirley at her time of sorrow and she had a standing order not to go out on the streets after dark. She was a very obedient child.

Ed Hanna:

Ed Hanna and I both worked at KAPL so for several years we interacted during work for some time before we became friends socially. He was single and was still living the single life style during those twelve years so we didn't socialize very much. I would invite him to our house for dinner sometimes if he didn't have a better offer. One time when I invited him, I think it might have been the first time, I called Jean to tell her that I had invited Ed, she said, "Hell's Bells, there's nothing in the house to eat," So I said that I would bring home pizza. I told Ed that we were having pizza so he said, "sounds good, I'll buy the beer." But when I went to get the pizza I realized that I didn't have enough money so I had to borrow the money from Ed. As it turned out, I invited him for dinner and he had to pay for both the dinner and the beer. For years after this, Ed would advise people that if they were ever invited to dinner at my house, they better decline. Of course he didn't really mean that. Or did he?

Ed was a lot of fun. One time Gary, Tom and I were fishing on Saratoga Lake and we came upon a large dead carp. We pulled it into the boat and then delivered it to the front porch of Ed Hanna's house. He wasn't home at the time. He came home later with his lady friend and somehow he knew who put it there. Have you ever smelled a carp that had been dead for several days? I guess leaving it on Ed's deck was a pretty dirty trick.

Within a year after I accepted a job transfer to GE Nuclear in San Jose, Ed did the same. I was a little surprised when he made the move because Ed had lived all his life in the Schenectady area. I don't think that his move was influenced by my actions. The business in San Jose was booming and he probably made the move pretty much for the same reason that I did.

One other story that involved Ed that neither he will forget, nor will I, involved our dog and it occurred after Ed had been in California nearly one year. I had just finished my assignment in Spain which involved the startup of the nuclear power plant called Nuclenor which was located in northern Spain near Vitoria. When we finished the job, Jean and I and Tricia and Laura wanted to spend several weeks in Europe before we came home. Gary and Tom were still in school in Sevilla in southern Spain and they would be coming home later. The problem that I had was what to do with Cali. Cali was our little beagle who was very much a part of the family but we really didn't want her while traveling around Europe. So I made arrangements with Ed to have him pick up Cali at the airport in San Francisco a few days before we left Spain. Being a good friend, he agreed that he would keep her until we returned to San Jose. So we put Cali on an airplane and advised Ed of the shipment details. On the anticipated day of arrival, Ed and Liz (Ed lost his single status sometime after we moved from Schenectady) went to San Francisco airport to pick her up but there was no Cali. Turns out, Ed was a day early so he had to make a second trip. He was probably already regretting his agreement. Actually, he was probably starting to regret that he ever met me.

Fortunately, on his second trip to the airport, they found Cali. However, when she arrived, it turns out she was in heat. This was a surprise to us and to Ed. To make matters worse, Ed and Liz had a male dog at the time. I was unaware of that also. So that presented a major problem. For a week or so, Ed and Liz had to keep the two dogs separate which presented a bit of a problem since they lived in a small house in the middle of San Jose.

That wasn't the only problem. Cali was not a well-mannered dog. Ed noticed after Cali had been there a few days that for some reason the full glass of orange juice that Liz was setting out for him while he was getting ready for work had been reduced to just a half glass. At first Ed assumed that they were low on juice so Liz was simply rationing it out. But after this happened several times, Ed became suspicious. By keeping an eye on the filled glass, Ed observed that after Liz would fill the orange juice glass and leave the room, Cali would get up on the chair and lap out of the glass until the level was too low to reach it with her tongue.

There was another incident that tops the orange juice story that Ed would be heard telling many times. It occurred one evening when he and Liz had invited another couple for dinner. The main course was a healthy sized eye of the round roast. This was a somewhat fancy affair that they were having which involved the best set of dishes, the best tablecloth, cloth napkins, and of course wine. It was a special occasion for Ed and Liz and was intended to be a memorial event. And that it was. Following the meal, everyone had moved to the living room leaving a large portion of the roast on the table. At this point, Cali made her move. She grabbed the rest of the roast, which was probably going to serve for Ed's lunches for the rest of the week, and was feasting on it when she got caught. To this day, I am not sure exactly what happened after that but I am pretty sure that Cali became airborne out the back door before landing in the backyard pool. On the positive side, the evening definitely was memorable.

After several years in San Jose, Ed accepted a new job at KAPL and he and Liz moved back to Schenectady. At this writing, Ed is retired and they live in a beautiful house on a hill in Rexford, New York which is just outside of Schenectady. Their house overlooks the Mohawk River. Although we rarely see them, they are still good friends. I hope.

I recently told Ed by e-mail that I was writing a book. Ed said that was a good idea because it would keep me off the streets.

Uncle Bill's New House:

Jean's aunt Marie, who was married to Bill Hill, lived on an old farm in Norfolk, Connecticut. They lived in a big old house which had many rooms, old interesting pieces of furniture, and a big attic. It was very hard to heat in the wintertime. We went there many times, mostly in the summer, and the kids loved it and so did I. It had been a farm house but when we went there the land around the house was no longer farmed but there was plenty of space to roam.

Uncle Bill was one of my favorite people on Jean's side of the family. He was a veteran of World War 2. He had been in the Army Corps of Engineers, I believe.

During football season, he could often be found watching at least two TV sets the same time in order to watch two football games. They didn't have Picture in Picture at that time. In the winter months he was also an avid curling player and he was good at it. He would attend curling matches in the area. He had a hat and a jacket with a whole bunch of participating ribbons on each. Not too many people knew this but he completed the Boston marathon wearing street shoes when he was in high school.

Some time in the mid-1960s, I helped him tear down an old house which was in the path of a proposed dam. He wanted the building material to be used to build a new house for himself and Marie. The house represented free, or essentially free, lumber. So we needed to use reasonable care in removed boards, studs, rafters, etc., so they could be used again. It was a pretty hard job. I think that I helped him over one or two weekends. The lumber was put aside for a year or two until they decided to build a new house. The new house was a ranch style home and much smaller and easier to heat than the old one.

A small amount of the lumber from the old house went in my station wagon to 147 Willow Lane in Schenectady where it was used by me to build a small playhouse in the backyard for the kids. The playhouse had a window on each side and one window and a door in front. We put a little flower box under the front window. The kids painted the house white to match our white cape cod. As of a few years ago, the playhouse was still there. The present owner uses it as a garden tool shed.

Getting back to Uncle Bill's new house, he got me to help him do the electrical wiring. At that time, I had some experience with house wiring but the wiring scheme that he was using was a bit different then the normal. His was the only home that I have ever seen that used the system that he used. I think at the time, he though that it was going to be the system of the future, but it didn't turn out to be the case.

As everyone knows, our homes use 110-volt wiring for the lighting and 220 volts for things like dryers and ranges. So did his. However, the lighting scheme that he had utilized a second system that ran on 12 volts. The 12-volt system was used to control the switching. In other words, instead of having the 110-volt lines go through the switches which we use to turn lights on and off, his scheme used relays located near the light. In his case, the switches that were used to turn lights on and off were located in the usual places but they were connected to the relays by the 12-volt system. You got that?

He told me that it was a General Electrical System so he expected me to know all about it since I worked for GE. Boy was he wrong. I had never heard of it. Anyway he got me to handle the switches, the 12 volt wiring, and the relays. I would go there on weekends and crawl around underneath the house and run the 12 volt wires from switches to relays. The wiring was color coded using about six different color schemes to keep from making the wrong connections. Everything was going okay until we ran out of wiring so he went out and picked up some more wire. However, when he did, the new wiring used a different color code. When I used the new wiring after having half the house done with the old wiring, I had to make a color matching table which looked something like this: Black is red, white is tan, blue is red and white, gold is pink, yellow is orange and yellow, etc. Somehow when we finished, everything worked as it should. To this day, I have never seen another system like this.

Uncle Bill and Marie eventually sold the farm and moved away. Jean and I and the kids were sad when they moved.

Transfer To Nowhere:

In 1967 I was scheduled to be transferred to Vallejo, California as part of a KAPL team with the job of refueling the USS *Bainbridge*, a nuclear powered frigate. At that time, we lived at 147 Willow Lane in Scotia, New York. Since we needed a bigger house, we decided to sell our house and then upon our return in a year or so, we would buy a new one.

So we planned our move for the summer after the kids got out of school. We had a buyer for our house and we were all excited about moving to California for a year or two. Jean's mother, who was living with us at the time, would go with us.

Shortly before the scheduled move, my Boss, Herb Pagano, decided that it was the wrong move for me. He felt that I should go instead to Groton, Connecticut, to handle a job associated with the USS *Triton*. It was said to be a job with more responsibility and so surely it would be better for my career. He insisted that I go there. So we started to change horses in the middle of the stream by planning to move to Connecticut instead. But believe it or not, before our new plans got very far, Mr. Pagano changed his mind once more and decided that I should take over a supervisory job at the KAPL prototype facility at West Milton which would require no move at all.

Believing that we were going to move away, the neighbors had scheduled a party for us which came in the midst of this turmoil. We went to the party and when asked where we were going, we said we didn't know. At that time, we really didn't know if we were going to California, to Connecticut, or to nowhere. The moving van came to pick up our furniture and we didn't know where to tell them to take it. We decided to have them take it to storage. It turns out that we were the first family that KAPL had ever transferred to nowhere.

The decision to stay and take the supervisory job became final just about the time we moved out of the house. So we decided to go camping. At the time, we had a large tent trailer that had room for six or eight people to sleep. We packed our station wagon and the tent trailer with lots of camping gear and we headed north. Included in the group were Jean and I, our four kids and my mother-in-law.

We first tried a campsite on the Sacandaga Reservoir. We camped on the lake and I commuted to work from there, which was a reasonable commute. After a week or so, we decided to move to Lake Lonely near Saratoga Lake. We camped there for several weeks but now my commute was slightly farther and the accommodations were somewhat more primitive. But it appeared to be more interesting for the rest of the family. During one of the weekends while there, I rented a boat and with my little outboard motor to provide the power, my two boys and I went for a ride down a shallow river which brought us out into Saratoga Lake. Along the river, it was like a jungle. We felt like we were in the middle of Africa during the trip. We had to navigate around logs, rocks and very shallow places. We got hung up several times on the rocky bottom which required my getting out and pushing.

After about two weeks at Lake Lonely, we relocated to a camp site on Saratoga Lake. We stayed there for the rest of the summer vacation period.

During those months, they referred to me at work as the migrant worker. I was the only one in the group that was homeless. But there was one big advantage: they couldn't call me after hours very easily because being homeless, I didn't have a phone (cell phones hadn't been invented yet).

The kids had a lot of fun during this extended camping trip. Actually, we all did. Life is full of experiences and that summer camping trip certainly was an experience. With our little outboard motor, we would rent a boat on weekends and go for boat rides and fishing on Saratoga and Lonely. Once on Saratoga Lake, we found a large 30 pound carp which we picked up and put on Ed Hanna's front porch as a joke. It turned out to be embarrassing when he brought his lady friend home and found this large dead stinky fish on his porch.

We were camped next to families of musicians who were performing at the Saratoga Performing Arts Center. The three husbands were all

Musicians and all had to wear a tuxedo during performances. It seemed strange to see them come out of their tents in the middle of the woods dressed in a tuxedo. But it also seemed strange to some that a GE Engineer was spending the whole summer camped in a tent trailer as his primary residence.

The kids had plenty of friends during our stay at the campsite. The musician families had lots of kids. One time we went on an outing with our four kids and a bunch of the musician's kids. On the way home, the kids started singing Ninety-nine Bottles of Beer on the Wall. They were still going strong as we pulled into the campsite.

Near the campsite was an amusement park and it had a carousel. Near the amusement park, was a little store. I used to send Tricia to the store with a hand written note to get me some cigars. Tricia has fond memories of the campsite, the amusement park, and her trips to the store. Several years ago, she and her husband Bryan went back east and they visited the campsite. It was still there but the Amusement Park was gone to make room for condos. A tattered and worn carousel building was still there but probably not for long. The carousel itself was long gone.

In the meantime, we found a beautiful house at 8 Cedar Lane which was just a stone's throw from the Willow Lane house. We bought it but we couldn't move into it until November. So after about three months of camping out, we rented a cabin on Saratoga Lake. We lived there until the house was ready. Now instead of just me commuting to work, the kids had to commute to school. They commuted with me when I went to work.

In November we got our furniture moved out of storage and into our new house and our life finally returned to normal. But for sure, it was a summer to remember.

8 Cedar Lane:

If you were to ask me what was the prettiest house we ever lived in I think that I would have to say that it was 8 Cedar Lane. It was a cape cod like our 147 Willow Lane house but it was much bigger with lots more storage space and had, in my opinion, a better setting. There was a creek in back which we could get to by going down a rather steep hill. In back of the creek was a trail that went through the woods to a shopping center with restaurants, gas stations, etc. When we first moved in, I proclaimed that we would never move again. Two years later we would pack up and go, this time for sure, to California.

Chapter 6

The Move to California
1969

Leaving Schenectady:

THE DAY WE left Schenectady, I will never forget the last moments at 8 Cedar Lane. We had packed up the Chevy Station wagon and the tent trailer, Jean and I were in the front seat, the four kids in the back two rows of seats, and Mattie, the renegade beagle, was somewhere in the back. We paused momentarily in front of the house before starting our long journey. There wasn't a dry eye in the car. The only words that I remember being spoken was Jean saying between sobs, "let's go."

The Trip:

I did a lot of thinking as we drove on down the highway on our three-thousand-mile trip to California. There was a lot of second guessing going on in my brain. Why did we leave such a pretty house with a beautiful setting in an excellent school system? Why did we uproot the four kids, especially the older ones, when they were beginning to form social ties? Even worse, this was just the first move of many that would come later. The job that I had accepted with GE Nuclear in San Jose was in Startup Testing which would require transfer to the site of the commercial nuclear power plant where ever it happened to be, stay there for about one year, and then move on to another. I am not sure that I had really thought this through carefully before accepting the new job. Since that time, I have second guessed the wisdom of my decision many times. It was fun for me but was it good for the four kids? I guess I will never know for sure but in any event, it is an academic question. It's water over the bridge, or under the dam. There was no turning back.

We spent over a week traveling across the country on our way to San Jose. Jean and I made an earlier trip and had bought a big house on Mojave Drive which is located in Almaden Valley of San Jose. When we bought it, Laura asked if it had a pool and we had to tell her no. However, we assured her that there was a neighborhood pool right nearby that was much better than a backyard pool because she could meet lots of neighborhood kids.

We stopped in Pennsylvania for a short visit with my sister Elaine and to drop off our renegade Beagle named Mattie. They agreed to take him and make a rabbit hunting dog out of him. "Good luck," I said. When we were leaving her house on the country road, we encountered a small and totally unexpected problem. When I tried to make a quick stop due to another car coming the other way on the narrow road, the brakes on the camper trailer locked causing the wheels to slide. As I was to learn later, the camper was not really designed for brakes even though it was sold with brakes. When the wheels locked, the frame was not strong enough to keep the axel from being pulled toward the rear of the camper. This resulted in both wheels pulling back to the rear of the wheel wells. In other words, the wheels and the axle were literally pulled almost free of the trailer. I lay there under the trailer, wondering how I am going to deal with this. It turns out that Gary, Tom, and I were able to fix it temporarily. First, I disconnected the brakes so that there would be no significant force on the axle directed toward the rear if we were to somehow continue. Then we used the jacks to hold the trailer up and totally disconnected the axle from the springs which were attached to the trailer. We then slid the twisted axle forward along the spring bundle until the wheels were centered in the wheel well and clamped them back on the springs in an off centered position. This allowed us to go on until we could get a more permanent fix, which we did when we reached my brother Floyd's house in Michigan. While there, we had it fixed properly and had additional iron welded into place to strengthen the frame. I later wrote a letter to the trailer manufacturer and told them that they had a poorly designed trailer. They never wrote back.

One thing the little problem in Pennsylvania did for us, it forced us to address the present problem which helped us get our minds off of the past.

At one of our overnight stops somewhere in the middle of the country, we rushed inside the motel in time to see Neil Armstrong make his famous "one small step for man, one giant step for mankind" statement as he stepped down on the surface of the moon.

We stopped for several days in Yellowstone National Park and while there we went fishing off of the Fishing Bridge. We caught some nice trout. Laura had probably the biggest one of all but due to getting entangled with other lines, she lost it before she could walk it off the bridge. She was so disappointed that she almost cried.

One other thing we did while at Yellowstone was to sign papers on the sale of our Cedar Lane house. Although we had made the sale before we left, there were some legal papers to sign that were not ready when we left. We made arrangements to have them sent to Yellowstone and they were there waiting for us when we arrived. That's probably not the best way to do business, but that's the way we did it.

The Job:

When we transferred to San Jose in 1969, the nuclear business was booming. GE Nuclear had a backlog of orders a yard long. Our part of the business was to provide the nuclear steam supply system which included the reactor core and pressure vessel, the recirculation system, the nuclear safety systems and the turbine generator. The U.S. suppliers of the nuclear steam supply systems were GE, Westinghouse, Babcock and Wilcox, and Combustion Engineering. GE and Westinghouse were the two major suppliers. The GE Steam Supply System utilized a Boiling Water Reactor (BWR) design whereas the Westinghouse system utilized a Pressurized Water Reactor (PWR).

The group that hired me was responsible for field testing of the nuclear steam supply system after the building of the plant was completed and before it was turned over to the utility customer. The group was actually two groups. One group performed the preoperational testing and the second group did the startup testing. I was hired as part of the second group which was responsible for the startup testing.

As part of the startup testing group, several months of test preparation in the home office in San Jose was required and then when the preoperational testing was essentially complete, the job would require relocating to the plant site for six months to a year or so. Usually it was a year or more.

During the next 8 years more or less, I would be involved to some extent with numerous plants. I would spend time without the family at Dresden in Illinois, Quad Cities in Iowa, Duane Arnold in Iowa, Millstone in Connecticut, Browns Ferry in Alabama, and others. I would also move the entire family to Nuclenor in Spain and Vermont Yankee in Vermont. I would also move the family, without the boys, to Limerick in Pennsylvania and I would also relocate alone to Caorso in Italy.

When I first arrived in San Jose, my boss, Bob Brugge, put me in a large cubicle with Bill Brown, Steve Jones, and Howard Smith. He told me that he needed a Romesberg to break up the bland created by having a Smith, Jones and Brown in the same cubicle. At that time it tentatively looked like my first field assignment would be at the Millstone Plant in Waterford, Connecticut. However, after I had been there for a month or two, he asked me if I would like to go to Spain. I thought about it for about 5 seconds and then said, "yes, I would be happy to." And so it was, my first extended field assignment was to be the Lead Test Engineer at the Nuclenor Plant in Santa Maria de Garona near Vitoria in the Basque country of northern Spain.

Chapter 7

Spain
1970

The Move:

WHEN THE PROJECT manager was notified that I was to be the Lead Test Engineer he initially objected because transferring me to Spain represented a transfer of a lot of baggage. I had a wife, four kids and a dog. The company policy was to cover the moving expenses of the wife and the kids so they always preferred to send people with minimum dependents. They didn't care about the dog because that would be at my expense. The convincing argument that my boss used was that when considering the total test group of five people, there were two single men, three married men, and just four kids. The fact that I was responsible for one wife and all four kids should not be taken personal.

Once again, we moved in the spring when the kids were out of school. We turned our big Mojave Drive house over to Bob Stover, the Realtor, and he had already found a renter for us before we left. We had sold our little red Volkswagen and had put our station wagon and furniture in storage once again. We also had put together a shipment of items that we wanted or needed during the anticipated one year of living in Spain. The shipment had already left our house. The night before our flight we drove to a hotel in San Francisco with our luggage plus the dog Cali. Our bags were packed with the assumption that we would not see our shipment for several weeks so we had a lot of luggage.

By the time we finally left the house and had made sure that we locked the doors, we were all dog tired and grouchy. Here we go again was probably on everyone's mind. The kids were being uprooted one more time. They had just started to get settled in the California environment, including school, and we were moving again. When we got to the hotel in San Francisco, slightly over fifty miles from Mojave Drive, we realized that all of our clothing that we planned to wear on the trip were left behind in the entryway hall closet at Mojave Drive. After contacting the Realtor so that he could unlock the door so that we could get in, Tricia and I drove all the way back over fifty miles, picked up the clothing, and then returned to the hotel. The start of our trip was not so good.

The next day we flew into Madrid, stayed overnight and then took the train to Vitoria. Based on information given to us previously, we went to the train prepared to have Cali shipped in the baggage compartment so we had given her a tranquilizer earlier. But as it turned out, she rode with us in the passenger space. Tricia and Laura took turns holding her. But shortly after starting, Cali got sick from the tranquilizer and threw up in Tricia's lap. I've never been quite sure what she did with the dog vomit. I thought it best not to ask. During the trip, when the Conductor came around collecting tickets, he appeared to be more than a little surprised and perhaps a bit annoyed when he saw the little beagle dog on Tricia's lap. He spoke to us in Spanish but we were never quite sure what he was saying. We did however recognize some of his hand waving and we were able to understand 2,000 pesetas. After giving him the money he seemed to be satisfied. I never did know whether that was a fare, a fine, or a bribe. But it was academic since it worked whatever it was.

When we arrived in Vitoria, Vern Grayhek, the operations manager, and his wife Betty met us at the train station in his little Fiat. There were six of us, one dog, twelve suitcases, and one dog shipping crate. We decided to load the suitcases and the dog in the car and we let the two women drive back to the hotel. The rest of us walked.

Living in a Hotel:

We stayed for about two months in the Conciller Ayala Hotel in downtown Vitoria. We occupied three rooms, which represented a substantial portion of the second floor, until we could get into an apartment. During those first weeks in the hotel, I thought that I would die from lack of sleep. In order to get a decent breakfast at the hotel and still catch a ride to work, I had to get up by 5:00 in the morning. But in Spain, as is typical of Europe, you can't get dinner in the evening until about nine or ten o'clock. And then when you do get served, it is very slow. Eating was more like a ritual; it was not something you do in a hurry. Even getting the bill was difficult. As a result, it would be near midnight by the time I got to bed and then it was with a stomach full of rich and spicy food so I would be too uncomfortable to sleep. To make matters worse, we had arrived just at the beginning of some fiesta, Fiesta de la Virgin Blanca, I believe, which involved a lot of noise making which sometimes lasted all night. And since we did not have air conditioning, we had to sleep with the windows open in a room facing the main street where all the action was. Well, I was convinced that I would not survive this ordeal until one day Jean told me not to worry about it. Sounds simple enough, so I took her advice. I stopped worrying and by grabbing a few z's here and there, I survived.

One way that I managed to get a few more z's was to sleep during the morning meeting. Although I was required to go each morning to the "morning meeting," I soon discovered that those morning meetings had little or nothing to do with the work that I was doing at this time in the startup program. Regardless, I was required to be there. Out of necessity, I very cleverly developed a technique for nodding off without having my head falling down and banging on the table making a big noise which would disrupt the meeting to say nothing of the embarrassment that it would cause me. I would place my notes and papers in front of me and with my head bent forward so that it looked like I was looking at my papers, I would lock my both thumbs under my chin with my elbows on the edge of the table and I would fall asleep. This technique usually worked but I did get caught a few times. Of course I couldn't do this later in the program when startup testing, which was why I was there, became part of the morning discussion.

While still living in the hotel, Steve Jones came from San Jose to help out with testing on the recirculation system. I told Jean to contact him when he arrives and help him out with anything that he might need. So she went to the desk shortly after Steve was scheduled to arrive and asked for Steve Jones. They said nobody by that name had arrived. She was certain that Steve had arrived so she asked the man at the desk again but with the same result. Then she realized that maybe they were having problems with translating her English. So she went back again and asked for Stebay Honas since the *J*'s are pronounced like *H*'s. Sure enough, they said, "yes, we have such a person."

When I told the plant manager that Steve Jones would be on site for a week or so he suggested that I put a bell on him. It seems that Steve had a habit of wandering about the plant sometimes doing his testing without telling anyone. This is a big no-no at plants since some of his actions could cause an unwanted plant shutdown.

My working hours during the approximately one year in Vitoria were ten hours each day Monday through Friday and a half day on Saturday.

We did get time off when there were delays in the schedule or problems which didn't involve the startup test program. While still in the Hotel I would sometimes go with Jean and kids and of course our dog Cali on little trips on Saturday afternoons and/or Sundays. On one of our little trips in our Volvo, which we had bought for personal use while there, we drove into farm country and then took a walk where there were cows, and of course cow manure. Some dogs, especially those who were bred to be hunting dogs, will oft times roll in cow manure to eliminate their own doggy scent. Well, Cali, being a beagle, was one of those dogs and she did roll in cow manure until the only scent you could get, within a hundred feet or so, was fresh cow manure. When we returned to the hotel, where they really were violating there own good judgment in allowing Cali in our room, the girls sneaked her up to our room hoping no one would see, or smell, them. We threw her in the bathtub and scrubbed her really good hoping that the smell would not linger. I think that the hotel people were glad to see us go when we finally were able to get into our apartment.

The Drive to Work:

The ride from Vitoria to the plant site was very scenic but tough to make every day. The last half was over mountain roads, through small Pueblos, over narrow bridges, through tunnels and around many sharp curves. The curvy part went along side of a dam and before I started my job assignment, one of the company cars failed to make a turn and ran into the dam. The driver walked to work dripping wet. When they hooked on to his car to bring it up, it turned out to be the wrong car. Inside were two bodies, two Frenchmen. As it turned out, they had been missing for two years. Later, just before the job ended, two of the GE pre-operational engineers also failed to make the same curve and they drove into the dam. They were lucky to get out alive. Jim Miller, the driver, managed to kick the windshield out of the car so the both of them got out but it was a pretty close call. I came into the plant just after it happened and saw wet clothing, wet wallets, wet important papers, wet money, etc., all spread out in the control room along with Jim Miller himself asleep on several chairs pushed together.

The Log Entry:

It was standard policy during the Startup Program to us a log book to provide instructions especially for the swing and graveyard shift crews. Upon reviewing the log book entries one morning I found a comment from both shift engineers that they could not read one of the instructions that I had made before leaving the previous afternoon. I had a little trouble myself deciphering the instruction which read; "Please write legibly in the log book."

Our Apartment:

After about two months of living in the hotel, we got our shipment and we moved into an apartment in Vitoria. It was nicely furnished and it was on the third floor. There was plenty of room for Jean and I and for Tricia and Laura. Gary and Tom would be living most of the time in southern Spain in Seville where they would attend a British run high school. There was room for them too when they came to visit.

Shortly after we got there we found a place for Cali because we found out that the landlady didn't really appreciate having an American Beagle living on her beautiful carpets and sleeping on her stuffed chairs. So we needed to find a place for Cali. Well, it turned out that this old couple had a shed out in back of the hotel where they kept a pig and some rabbits and some of their garden tools as well. They agreed to keep Cali in the shed. For payment, they wanted something like 250 pesetas per month. I can't remember the exact amount but in dollars it was only about $4.00 per month. On top of that, shortly after they agreed to do it, we discovered that they had done a lot of work just to make her more comfortable. They had built her a little house to sleep in and it was lined with straw. She was kept on a leash out of reach of the pig and rabbits. We, mostly Tricia and Laura, would visit her often and feed her and take her for walks and bring her up to the apartment for visits. One time Tricia had her in the small grocery store nearby, and a member of the Guardia Civil was there and he decided that he wanted Cali for himself. But Tricia pretended that she didn't understand him and she high tailed it out of there not looking back until she got inside the protective gate of the apartment. In Tricia's mind, there was no way that anyone, even a member of the Guardia Civil, was taking Cali.

After we had been in the apartment for several months, we noticed one day that Cali didn't seem to be her usual self. She seemed lethargic. I checked her out and found a small hole in her side about a quarter of an inch diameter. I couldn't tell how deep it was. We decided to call a veterinarian. He came to our house and checked her out and then gave us his diagnosis. The only thing that I understood from his diagnosis was the word "superficial." So with that we stopped worrying. However, we were never sure what caused the hole. We were pretty sure that it was done with a BB gun.

Our apartment was always a little cold. They wouldn't turn the heat on until November and then they were not very generous with the amount of heat. One time the furnace broke down in the middle of winter and it was down for several weeks. I refused to pay the rent. The landlady complained and I told her that I would pay when she turned on the heat. She told me in response that all the other tenants paid their rent. I told her I would wait until we got heat. Shortly after that we got heat.

At Christmas time, we had a small tree and a small number of presents. Laura and Tricia remember it as their small Christmas. Near the apartment there was a full-size Nativity Scene which was lit up at night which we all enjoyed very much. Although it was our small Christmas, I think we all felt like it was one of our best.

During our stay in the apartment, we did not have a useable TV and all the radio that we got was in Spanish. Our record player that we had brought with us became one of our main sources of entertainment. Since our recorder was designed for an alternating current at sixty cycles per second and in Spain they use 50 CPS, I had to make a small modification to our recorder to make it play at the correct speed. I was able to do that by simply putting a layer of GE silicon resin on the recorder spindle to make the records turn at the correct speed. We had only taken a few records with us on our trip so some of them got played over and over. Our record stock included a set of children's records called *Grimms's Fairy Tales*. We played them so often that Laura, Tricia, and I could often be heard repeating words and phrases from the records. We still occasionally play act some of the parts even today.

There was a little park across the street from our apartment where we could take Cali for a walk and stop for ice-cream. On these walks, Cali would always get a lot of attention. I think that beagles were uncommon in Spain at that time, especially cute ones like Cali. People, especially women would make a big fuss over how cute she was.

On our way back to the apartment one night after eating out, Laura momentarily dropped behind us while we continued on for about a block. We noticed her back on the sidewalk talking, or so it appeared, to someone in a building. We walked back to check it out and we found her talking to a pig. It was not at all uncommon for people to have animals in their first floor, or basement, where they lived. It was convenient and the animals provided heat in the winter for the family living above. But talking to a pig was a bit unusual. It seems that Laura, then about seven years old, had developed a way of making guttural sounds similar to a pig so when she came past this particular basement window and heard a pig grunting on the other side, she decided to talk to it. She was definitely a source of entertainment for all of us during our stay in this foreign land.

School:

Tricia and Laura went to a British-run school that had been set up for English-speaking pre-high school kids. There were three teachers, plus a headmaster, all from England. When we were there, there were only twelve students. They used an old house in town for the school. They rode to school in a regular large bus. At the very end of the job, I think that Tricia and Laura were the only students who rode on this full-size bus.

Gary and Tom were in high school and we had to send them to another British run-school in Seville in southern Spain. It was hard for us to send them off on their own in a strange land however the plant manager's daughters were also going so I think they felt a little better about it. When they first went there, they lived with an elderly widow who had, as they described it, a toothless maid. The house was old and typical Spanish style with small rooms and very high ceilings and was located in the center of an old part of town. Tom's room looked like a closet. It was very small and dark and had an extremely high ceiling. Gary's wasn't much better. The old widow and her maid treated the boys well while they were there. They would make them big sandwiches for their lunch before they went off to school. After a month or so, they moved to an apartment-type place with the other school students which helped them be less lonely. However, at the new surroundings, I think that they had more of a social life but the classroom studies were pretty minimal. We figured that during this one year of their education they probably learned more about life than they did about the standard school stuff.

Laura and the Elevator:

We lived on the third floor of a twelve story apartment building. The Barretts lived on the twelfth floor. They had two kids who were about Laura's age so Laura would go to play with them almost daily. She would take the elevator. She had been doing this for a number of months when one day I noticed her getting on the elevator with a spatula in her hand. I figured that Mrs. Barrett must have wanted to borrow a spatula so I forgot about it almost immediately since I probably had important work-related stuff to think about. But that was typical for me since I worked a lot of hours, and even when I was home, my mind was often on some work-related item. So many of the daily family activities, and the cute things that kids do, went by me without much notice. And so the spatula thing was forgotten until about a month later, I saw Laura again getting on the elevator with the same old spatula in her hand. So this time my curiosity was finally aroused. So I asked Jean, "What's with the spatula?" Well, here's the story. From the very beginning, when she went to play with the Barrett kids, Laura would ride the elevator to the tenth floor and she would then walk the remaining two floors. At first, neither Jean nor I knew this. We naturally assumed that she was taking the elevator all the way. But as it turned out, she was too short to reach the button for the twelfth floor. The best that she could do on her tiptoes was to reach the tenth floor button. So she had to walk the last two floors. Of course, there was no problem reaching the third floor button so coming back was not a problem. Jean discovered this problem long before I did and her solution was to provide the spatula. By using the spatula as an arm extender, she could reach the twelfth floor button and ride all the way.

Sometimes Laura and the Barrett kids would play on the roof. Occasionally the Portera would find a big rubber ball on the grounds and he would smile and then give it to Laura or the Barrett kids when they came into the apartment. He also kept track of both Laura and Tricia. He would know and would comment to me if they were late coming home from school.

Franco and the Guardia Civil:

During this time period, Spain was essentially a police state under the control of Franco. He, with his Guardia Civil, ruled the country with an iron fist. Our apartment was right next door to a Guardia Civil barracks. Unlike our police force in the good old USA, the Guardia Civil members were not bound by so many rules of conduct. They didn't worry that their action might be politically incorrect, racially sensitive, or might result in bad public opinion or lawsuits. It was said that very few crimes were committed and if one was, they would show up armed with submachine guns and they would not hesitate to use them. Just the presence of them would calm a crowd and make criminals think twice before committing a crime. We heard of a situation where several Guardia members had their throats cut by gypsies. It was reported that about forty of them showed up with machine guns and completely wiped out the gypsy camp. No questions asked.

In order to get to their posts, the Guardia Civil members would travel by motorcycle, sometimes by car, sometimes even on horseback, but the most common way they would travel was on foot or by hitchhiking. On one occasion, on the way home from the site, our car pool was stopped by a Guardia member. When he saw that our car was full, he smiled and waved us on. He caught a ride in the car behind us.

One thing for sure, because of the strong unforgiving enforcement policy, the crime rate was low. All the American mothers felt completely secure about letting their young ones out, even after dark. We did as well. Tricia would go down town wearing her long blue coat with Laura hanging on to her coat tales. They would often go into a bar and have *tapas* (little portions of food such as sausage, hard boiled eggs, ham, or I can't remember what but lots of very tasty stuff). We never seemed to be concerned that they would be harmed.

During our stay, we were advised that if we were stopped for alleged speeding or some other minor violation we should not argue and just pay the fine no matter what it was. I got stopped one time and paid a couple hundred pesetas even though I had no idea what I did wrong. On another occasion, Jean drove right straight through a stop sign and got away with it. When confronted, she pretended that she didn't understand any of the language. He pointed out the stop signs and explained that a stop sign meant that you have to stop. The two daughters in the back seat had to refrain from laughing until we escaped without a fine.

Eating Out:

During our one year stay in Spain, we ate out a lot. The food was excellent and the price was so reasonable that there was little incentive to eat at home. Even when at work, we would often eat out if time would permit, which it usually did. One of my favorite places was in the little town of Frias which was close to the job site. Frias was first built on top of a large hill as a fortress by the Romans. A large part of the fortress and the palace still remained when we were there and no doubt still does today. It was said by the local people that it was one of the few fortresses that was never captured by the Moors. Just below the palace ruins, on a very narrow cobblestone street was a place to eat. There was always a chance that when we went there, they wouldn't have any food left because they did not have sufficient, or any, refrigeration to allow much storage. But if we were lucky, as we usually were, we knew we were in for a real treat. First, there was no language problem. There was no ordering because they have only one selection, *el menu de la casa*. First, they would serve a large bottle of the house wine and if that wasn't enough, they would bring more. Then comes bread, salad, and/or soup. Usually, we would have to cover the soup bowl or they would keep filling it. After the soup, they would bring a dish of either macaroni with sauce, a rice, an omelet or maybe fish cakes. With each dish, they ask if you want more. By this point, we would think that we can't eat any more, they would then bring the main course which would be either lamb or pork chops with some sausage on the side and fried potatoes, or roast beef. If you can possibly eat all that they bring, they will ask you if you want more. Then they bring dessert which might be a half of a melon, or maybe two pears or peaches, or sometimes ice cream. The cost of all this was 85 pesetas, which in American money was about $1.21. Even in 1970, this was amazing.

    Some of the restaurants in town were a little more expensive but were still amazingly inexpensive. One such place was referred to by the Americans as the Chuleta House. It was by far our favorite place. It was on a hill within a healthy walking distance from our apartment. There was a bar in the front part of the restaurant where locals would come to drink wine and talk. In the back, they cooked lamp chops in an open fireplace where they burned grape vines for the fire. The tables were all like our picnic tables and when you went there you would not get your own private table. You had to sit where ever there was space. To order, you only had to say one word, and that was the amount of meat that you wanted. For us, the one word usually was "Uno." This represented the weight of the chops in kilograms that you wanted. Sometimes you would have to modify your order if they felt that they didn't have enough to take care of all the customers. It was always full or nearly full. We would sit at one of the large picnic style tables, no table clothes, and the waiters would put out several bottles of wine, or course, several large loves of this wonderful Spanish bread, and large bowls of mixed salad. Then they would bring us the cooked lamb chops in the amount that we had ordered. There was nothing else served. But those who have eaten their will all tell you, the chops were the very best. Nowhere could you get a better meal.

    When we would leave there, we adults at least, pretty much always had a bit too much wine. I know Jean and I sometimes did, although Jean won't admit it. Under these conditions, it could sometimes be a bit difficult getting home since we had to walk down a long flight of outdoor cement stairs to get back down the hill and then on to our apartment. Walking down those stairs could be hazardous if you had too much to drink. But even much worse if you tried to drive your car down the stairs. Such was the case with our Control Systems specialist Bill DeLorme when he left one night after a bit too much wine. He took a wrong turn with his station wagon and soon found himself heading down the stairs. His wife and mother-in-law, who was visiting from the States, were with him at the time. As the car started down the stairs it would bounce up and down, and with each bounce, the back bumper would hit and drag across the cement steps, causing sparks to fly while making a very loud noise. After about the first bounce, Bill's mother-in-law says to Bill "Hey, Bill, you're driving down the stairs." Bill's reply was "I know that now, why didn't you tell me before we started?" Once started, there was no turning back. They bounced and scraped all the way to the bottom. I am sure the locals talked many times about the day the crazy American drove down the long flight of stairs.

One other memorable thing about the Chuleta house was the rest room. It always seemed to be that the Spanish were really good at cement and tile work but not so handy when it came to plumbing. I say this to help explain the Chuleta house rest rooms. They were, as I recall, a masterpiece of fine tile workmanship. But there were no toilets. They had just a hole in the middle of the floor which was covered with beautiful tile that had been placed there by skilled workmen. In the ladies room, according to my daughters, there was just a hole in the middle of the tile work with footholds, like foot prints, in the cement on each side of the hole. The idea was to squat over the hole with a foot in the footholds on each side of the hole. During our first or second trip to the Chuleta house, Laura, who was just seven at the time, had to go to the rest room. We had taught our kids to be independent so we told her to go. After she had been gone for quite a long time, we sent Tricia to check on her to see if there was a problem. When she got there, Laura had taken off her shoes and most of her clothes because she couldn't figure out how it was intended for her to use the hole and the foot holders. She though that she should not put her shoes in the foot holders.

The Road to Rhonda:

On one of our trips to see the boys in Seville we decided to go to the town of Rhonda by way of back roads instead of the main highways. I had a detailed map which showed lots of secondary roads which would take us through small Pueblos and many other out of the way places.

The trip started out fine, but at some point, where it appeared per the map that we were getting close to Rhonda, the roads started to look more like cow paths than actual roads. We kept checking the map to convince ourselves that we were on the right path, and path is a good word in this case. We considered turning around several times but we opted to continue. We were traveling in the country with no one to give us directions or advice. It had been miles since we had seen another car. The situation had become somewhat alarming.

We were driving in what appeared to be a large field on a road that consisted of two tracks worn by previous vehicle traffic and between the tracks and on the outside of the tracks was grass. It is the kind of road I recalled seeing as a young boy on the farm that was used with tractors or horses and wagons. The dirt road was fairly smooth and the terrain was more or less flat so if we did decide to go back we could turn around.

Just when we thought it couldn't get any worse, we found ourselves suddenly going down a steep hill which was too steep to come back up if we decided to do so. After a short distance down the hill, we came into a small Pueblo. We started to feel a little better until someone in the car pointed out that there were no cars in sight in the entire town. We though it was a ghost town at first until a bunch of curious kids came out to view our red Peugeot and the strangers within. They looked like they had not seen a car before.

As we pulled into the town, we realized that not only were there no cars, there were literally no streets. It seems that a large project to replace the sewage system was in progress. That meant that all the streets had been torn up and there were ditches dug along the side and across the open space were the streets should be. It appeared that we were dead ended in this little town.

I could see a short distance away on the other side of the town that there was a road, a real one, which would lead us back to a highway and then on to our destination of Rhonda. So all we had to do was get out of this little town. As it turned out, we actually had to do some bridge building to cross the open ditches which barred our way. The curious kids who had come to see us helped with the bridges and soon we were back on the road to Rhonda. As we thought about it afterward, we were glad that we had taken that route because of the interesting experience we encountered with the lack of modern roads.

Leaving Spain:

When the job was winding down, Bill Brown decided to have all of us involved in the plant startup over to his house before we departed. He called it "The get rid of his booze party." And so we did, but when the party was over, he had more booze than when he started. It was like the biblical story of the loaves and fishes. I guess everyone that came to his party brought their own drinks. So Jean and I decided to have another party after his with the same intent but it turned out to have the same result. When it was over, we still had a lot of booze left over so in order to get rid of it, we gave it away.

Before we left, we made one last trip to our favorite restaurant, the Chuleta House. As we were leaving, I stopped by the bar and tried to bid farewell with best wishes to the bartender in my best Spanish. Jean and my two daughters stood by and laughed at my poor Spanish. I never did learn much while there because the job was in English and I never really had many opportunities to practice. And it didn't help very much when my own family would laugh at me.

Jean and I with the two daughters left in our Peugeot and went on a trip through Europe before returning to San Jose. Gary and Tom were still in school in Seville and would return later. We visited my sister and her husband in Switzerland, then spent a few days in London, and flew back from there. We shipped our car back from France. Cali had been shipped earlier.

I remember stopping some place on our way to France and we all had hot dogs. It was a real treat for all of us. It was something that we didn't have all the time we were in Spain.

We flew back to San Jose with the knowledge that we would be leaving shortly for Vermont to join the startup group at another power plant called Vermont Yankee. We would only be in San Jose for a short stay. When we arrived, we took a taxi from the airport to a hotel. Laura soon realized that she had left her little stuffed animal which she called "Stuffy" in the cab. So my first assignment after I got in the office at GE was to find the little stuffed animal and return it to Laura. As I write this, about 35 years have gone by since we returned from Spain and Laura still has her little Stuffy sitting on a chair in her bedroom.

CHAPTER 8

Vermont
1971

Getting There:

WE DECIDED, OR Gary decided, I can't remember which, that Gary would fly back ahead of us to spend the summer working on Merle and Dorothy's farm in Pennsylvania. At that time, Gary had a large mop of hair as was the style at that time. Gary had curly hair so his long hair took on the Afro look. We informed my brother Merle of Gary's arrival schedule at the airport in Pittsburgh so he could arrange to pick him up. Merle decided to bring Wilbur, another of my brothers, along with him for company. They both waited somewhat anxiously because they had not seen Gary for several years and they weren't sure that they would recognize him. I had warned Merle ahead of time that they should be looking for a kid with a big mop of hair. When Gary arrived, he walked right past them and neither of them recognized him. After looking about for a few minutes, Gary spotted two worried looking farmers so he introduced himself and so the pickup was made successfully. Gary stayed on Merle's farm for the summer and I think that he would agree that it was good experience for him.

As in all of the previous major moves, we departed after the school year had ended. Our house in San Jose was rented, as it was when we were in Spain. We had shipped all of our furniture and belongings except our large collection of photo slides, which we took with us thinking that they would be safer with us. We no longer had our camper trailer, but in the meantime we had bough a Ford Econoline Van camper. We decided that Jean and I and Tom, Tricia, Laura and Cali would all go in the camper across country to Vermont by way of the northern route. We left San Jose and our first stop was at a campsite near Crater Lake, Oregon. We had our dinner at the campsite and then we decided to go see Crater Lake before turning in for the night. We loaded our outdoor items and made the camper ready for travel, we thought, and proceeded to go up the windy road, called the Rim Corkscrew, and then to drive around the lake on what would correspond to the rim of an ancient volcano. The lake was formed when the volcano named Mt. Mazama blew its top some 6,600 years earlier. The lake is about six mile across and about four thousand feet deep.

When we left the campsite, I asked Jean to drive so that I could view the scenery better. Then while driving up the Rim Corkscrew we saw several deer and I, for reasons I can't explain, shouted out "hey, look at the deer." So all three of the kids got out of their seat belts and ran to a window. Just about the same time, the refrigerator door flew open on one of the many turns because when we made the camper travel ready when we left the campsite, I had forgotten to put the pin in the door. When it opened, a bunch of cans and other food items flew out and some it hit Laura. When this happened, Laura screamed. Jean, being a mother, instinctively turned to look back. She was in the middle of a curve which was turning left when she turned to look back and her hands held the steering wheel in the same position. The curve in the road ended and the van, with the wheels turned to the left, ran off of the road on the left side. I was also looking back to attend to Laura when I heard a crash as the front bumper of the van hit a dead tree. The force knocked the tree down as the van wheels proceeded to straddle the tree and stop in an upright position for a few seconds before it rolled on its left side and stopped. My first thought was to get all of us out because there was still a flame going in the water heater so I was concerned about a fire. I told Jean to turn off the ignition key while I tried to open the door. My first reaction was to reach to my side for the door but it was above me since the van was turned on its side. When I released the seat belt, I fell on top of Jean. It seemed to take forever for me to get the door open. In the meantime, Tom in a very calm voice assured me that they were all okay. Also, by the time I got the door open, a man had stopped and came to our aid. I individually handed each person to the man and he helped them out the door and then down to the ground. Some of us, I can't remember which ones, brushed against the hot exhaust pipe on the way down to the ground. Tricia would not leave the back of the van without Cali who looked scared and confused with the situation.

When we were all safely out, I took a closer look at the situation and was quite startled with what I saw. There was a tree about 8 inches in diameter pressed against the roof that was preventing the van from rolling further down a long grade. If the tree hadn't been there, or if the tree hadn't been strong enough to hold us, we would have rolled over and over several times before the van would have come to rest.

All of us came through without any noticeable injury except Laura. She had a broken tooth and cut lip. As a result of that we thought it best that she get it checked out. She and I rode with the local sheriff to the hospital in Klamath Falls. We had to wait for some time to get her taken care of and while we were there, a young woman came in with an injured arm and a story that while in her sleeping bag she was bitten by a bear. I always wondered if that was really true.

Laura got her cut attended to, however the broken tooth would be a problem for her for many years. She eventually had a tooth transplant but even that turned out to be a mini nightmare for her.

A tow truck took our camper to Klamath Falls and within about 3 days they had it fixed so that we could drive it. They had to do wheel and front axle work to allow us to go on. In the meantime we stayed at a little motel in the country near our crash site. The people who owned the place were great and we kept in touch with them for some years after.

When we finally got on the road again, we traveled without any further problems to Merle's farm where we picked up Gary. We went on to Brattleboro, Vermont and moved into a little old house that I had rented on a previous trip. We moved our furniture in and tried to make it fit and we all looked at each other wondering, "whose idea was this anyway?" It was September 12, 1971. In all the turmoil with moving, I had forgotten that it was the eighteenth anniversary of Jean's and my wedding.

The Job:

The job was just like the job at Nuclenor in Spain. I was there in Brattleboro for the purpose of assisting in the startup and to perform startup testing on a General Electric supplied Boiling Water Reactor to be used for commercial power generation. The name of the plant was Vermont Yankee. The job was expected to last about a year. But as time passes, it is not the job that is remembered but rather it is family activities unrelated to the job that are best remembered. If you were to ask me for specific details about the job, I would probably not be able to answer them, at least not in any detail.

Winter in Brattleboro:

During our stay in Brattleboro, Gary was a junior in high school. During the winter months, he had a part time job working in a restaurant. He still had a girl friend but unfortunately she was still in Spain. He was saving his money so that he could go back to see her the following summer. Her permanent home was in Texas. I think that he was not very happy during our stay in Vermont and his school work showed it. I felt responsible for his situation.

Tom was a sophomore and he had a girlfriend who lived up the street from us. His biggest interest at that time was art, including wood carving and sculpture. Unlike Gary, he did not show much interest in skiing while we were there. When we left Vermont, he was clearly very sad when he had to say goodbye to his girlfriend. After we returned to California, he hitchhiked back to Vermont for a short trip. While there, he worked enough to buy airfare back to California. Hitch hiking across the country one time was enough, he preferred not to do it again.

Tricia was in eighth grade and at that time she liked boys and roller skating more than anything else. It always seemed to me that Tricia was pretty much okay where ever we were. I think that she adapted well to changing environments and new friends.

Laura was in third grade and she liked the outdoors. She became very good at skiing while we were there. She walked to and from the school bus stop down the street from where we lived and on her way home from school she would pick up trash along the road. She was way ahead of her time in that regard. She enjoyed Vermont probably more than any of the kids.

Jean and I both had friends that we knew from Spain. Some of the same people were transferred to Vermont just as we were.

We bought an old jeep station wagon as a second car while we were there. I used it to go to work and we used it for outdoor activities. I had a ski rack on top and we just left our skis on it all the time. We never had really expensive skis so we didn't worry about anyone stealing them. There were places to ski within a half hour drive so that if we decided at the breakfast table on Saturday morning to go skiing, we could be there in less than an hour. Of course, we also had a little ski place across the street from where we lived and we had a season pass to use it. Laura and I used it quite often. One time I watched Laura skiing there by herself and only her eyes were visible. The rest of her was covered with clothing. It does get cold in Vermont but if you dress properly it can be not only bearable, but actually it can be fun.

We lived pretty much on moose meat during the winter that we were there. Ernie Karner and I had gone to Newfoundland and brought back a lot of moose meat. I talked about that in my chapter on hunting. I growled Jean if I caught her buying beef.

Nana still had the cabin in Vermont when we were there and nobody was using it. I went there whenever I could for hunting purposes and just for the outdoors. She sold it while we were still there and I wished many times after that I had bought it from her.

We moved back to San Jose in the summer of 1971 after the kids finished school. Our total stay in Vermont was less than one year. When we were ready to leave, someone had to go find Tom who was saying a long and sad goodbye to his girl friend. The job wasn't finished when we left but I would take a number of trips back from California by myself until our commitment to the customer was completed

CHAPTER 9

A Summer to Remember
1975

Back to the Big House on Mojave Drive:

I HAVE A pretty good memory for family events but usually I have trouble putting them into the correct time period. There were a number of events that occurred during the summer of 1975 that were exceptions.

We were living on Mojave Drive at the time. In 1973 or '74, I am not sure which, I had moved out of the Startup Test Group and took a new job as the manager of a small group called Core Management Engineering. This job change was a good sign that I was through moving the family to different parts of the country and the world.

In the fall of 1974, we did a lot of concrete work and built a new deck out back and then when that was all done, we put in a new lawn. In preparing the soil for the new lawn, I used a friend's trailer and hauled several loads of rotted manure from a local dairy. With the generous amount of manure, we expected a lush green lawn. Then during the spring of 1975, we got an unusual amount of rain, unlike the previous 5 years of draught, and as a result of the rich soil and the rain, the lawn came in real good as expected. But then, due also to the rain and the manure, fungus took over and killed most of the new grass. In its place, came crab grass. So I spent most of the spare time during the spring and early summer fighting crab grass. Eventually it looked acceptable but never real good. I only mention that here because fighting crab grass had always been one of my major activities no matter where we lived. I finally realized that crab grass was green and hearty, so why not just go with it. So after all my work, we ended up with a crab grass lawn. I decided that it looked fine.

The Softball Game:

If you ask me to tell you what event had the most impact on my life, the softball game that I am about to tell you about would rank high on the list. It is right up there near the top along with the surgery that I had on my small intestine when I was twenty-seven. Both of these events would have an impact on what amount of physical risk taking I was willing to live with for the rest of my life.

Sometime during the early spring, I decided to play softball with a work league. I hadn't played for several years so I wasn't very good. But it was a low key league so being good wasn't necessary. Our first game was in May and I played second base. During the first game I remember getting on base several times but I also remember making about four errors in the field.

On May 14, we had our second game. I don't remember anything about it nor do I remember anything from about noon of that day until about four or five days later. Apparently, based on what others told me, I left work, changed clothes in the parking lot and drove to the park where the game was scheduled. As it turned out, our regular catcher didn't show up so I must have volunteered, or got elected, to catch. Maybe because I had made so many errors at second base the previous game, they decided I would do less harm as catcher. For whatever reason, I was the catcher during this second game. During the first inning with the other team at bat, a bigger than average guy hits a long drive to center which bounced under a fence. At this point it would have been ruled a ground rule double but the umpire didn't call it. The batter tried to stretch it into a home run. The throw came to me and I turned to put the tag on him. I was told later that he was out by a mile and he knew it. So clearly, his intent was to hit me hard so that I would drop the ball. He came in with his shoulder down like they do in the majors. His shoulder caught me square in the eye and I went over backward and hit the back of my head on the hard ground. I still had the ball in my hand when I hit the ground but as I lay there out cold for a moment, my hand relaxed and the ball fell out and the rampaging runner was called safe. I was only out for a short time and I apparently got up and said that I was okay. After some time, however, one of the ladies watching the game realized that I wasn't okay so she took me to the hospital. She told me later that the conversation between the two of us all the way to the hospital, which was about fifteen minutes, went something like this: "where are you taking me?" "To the hospital," she would respond. "What happened?" "You got hit on the head playing softball," she answered. Then about fifteen seconds later I would ask again, "where are you taking me?" and she would say again, "To the hospital," and I would again ask, "What happened?" to which she would again reply, "You got hit on the head playing softball." According to her, this went on all the way to the hospital.

I spent eight days in the hospital and most of it was in the intensive care unit. In addition to a torn ligament which controls the lower eye lid, and a damaged tear duct, both of which were fairly minor, I had a concussion, which was slightly more than minor. During the first couple of days, I only remembered, or was vaguely aware of, just one thing. I remember hearing something about a code 99 (Or code something) and people rushing around. Also, it seemed to me that I was watching them load someone up onto a gurney and rushing off for x-rays and/or MRIs. It was like I was off to the side and was watching an emergency and thinking that some poor guy is having a big problem. I was hoping that he was okay. Apparently, the someone was me. Jean was there at the time and she says that I had a major seizure (grand mal) or whatever they call those big seizures when you feel like your brain is exploding and you can't stop it. Gary was in the army and was in Germany and he was contacted to be prepared to come home. But fortunately, everything worked out okay except I had to go through a lot of testing and inconveniences afterward to avoid having more seizures. I was required to take Dilantin for several years but even with the Dilantin, I had several seizures later. The mere threat of having a seizure had a major impact on my life for many years.

The big guy who took me out with his shoulder has never identified himself to me. He never came to the hospital, he never came to my desk at work, he never called me to ask about my well-being, nor did he ever apologize in any way. Someone once started to tell me who it was and I stopped him. At that point in my life I didn't want to know. I was afraid of what my attitude would be toward him especially if it was someone that I would interact with at work which it most likely was. But you can be sure that at times I had some very strong feelings about him and probably still do.

The Roadrunners:

Laura was the real softball player in the family. She also played softball during the summer of '75. Her main playing position was catcher. She caught every game that year except two. This was her second or third year in softball. She played for the Almaden Roadrunners. The league that she played in was part of the Police Athletic League (PAL). They called themselves the "PAL Gals." She was in the minor division where the age range was up to twelve.

In 1974, the Roadrunners took first place in San Jose but then were beaten in the third game of the Northern California tournament. They were beaten by Vallejo, but at that time Vallejo, for some reason, had a different age cut off for their girls. Their minors were almost a full year older than our girls on the average.

In '75, the Roadrunners again took first place in San Jose with a record of twelve wins and one loss. But unlike the previous year, they went on to take the tournament by winning three straight games. They were given their trophies in a rather formal manner at the stadium by the President of the Police Athletic League with all the parents and others present. After the presentations, they then announced the most valuable player. It came as a very pleasant surprise to us when they announced that it was Laura. I was taking pictures at the time and I was so excited that I forgot to take pictures of her getting the trophy.

The Fishing Trip with Gary:

Gary was home from Germany for one month during the last part of June and most of July. While he was home, he and I went ocean fishing. It was his first fishing trip on a commercial fishing boat. We left the house about 4:00 AM and drove south to Monterey. He didn't get much sleep the night before so he wasn't much company for me while I drove. His head kept dropping as he would fall asleep every minute or so.

We had a big breakfast on the dock and then got aboard a chartered boat called *Miss Monterey*. We left the dock at about 7:30 and it was cold, damp, foggy, and just a little bit rough. We went south along the coast for several hours until we were just about off Big Sur. The boat used sonar to locate schools of rock cod. When we stopped, we fished deep at about 150 or more feet. We used a heavy sinker and a rig with about four hooks. We didn't use any bait except pieces of colored cloth and some foil. Once in a while a few people would put on pieces of squid. At times, we caught fish as fast as we could get the hooks down to where the fish were. However, getting the hooks out of the water wasn't always easy. If you didn't catch a fish, you often caught three or four of your fishing partners. Also, when you caught a fish and it swam sideways while you were pulling it in, then you also caught a few partners. Or they caught you.

So as a result, most of the time was spent untangling lines and hooks. Some people were seasick and were unable to work on tangled lines. So that made it even harder. Three fishermen beside us up near the bow were on leave from the navy and they were all sick to the point that they couldn't fish at all. Seasick sailors, I though that was strange. But then I remembered that I got seasick every time we went out to sea when I was in the navy.

Usually when we caught a fish, we would catch several at a time. It was hard work reeling them in from 150 feet down. By the time we were ready to head back to shore, Gary and I had caught over 100 lbs. of fish. Since we had more than our limit, we gave the extras away to those who were too sick to fish. We had our catch cleaned on the way in and then brought the fillets home to our freezer.

Mt Whitney:

When Laura was finished with softball, she, Jean and I went on vacation. Tom and Tricia stayed home to take care of the house and the garden. Both had part time jobs at that time. While they were home, the tomatoes, squash, and corn all started to ripen at once. Tom made Tricia eat three ears of corn every day so they wouldn't be wasted. They peddled tomatoes and squash to the neighborhood and they ate a lot of salad while we were gone.

On our vacation, we took our station wagon and our little camper trailer and headed south to Los Angeles. We parked the camper in a campsite in Anaheim and spent several days visiting Disneyland. We played tourist for several more days visiting Lion Country and Universal Studios.

From L.A. area, we headed north but this time on the east side of the Sierra Nevada. While going through the Mojave Desert, we picked up two teenaged hitchhiking girls. Some time later, one of our trailer tires overheated on the hot desert highway and threw the treads off which left only the tire cords. We couldn't use the spare because the stem was busted so we had to drive slowly with the treadles tire. While driving so slow, we had to use the flashers to warn other cars of our slow speed. After doing this for about fifty miles, the flashers burned up and so we were left without flashers or turn signals. So we had to speed up and hope the tire would hold together. It did and in the first big town that we came to, we bought a new tire and new turn signal switching equipment.

That night we camped in a desert campsite near Lone Pine, California which is near the base of Mt Whitney. The campsite was at about four thousand feet elevation. On our second day there, Jean drove Laura and I up toward Whitney as far as we could drive to an elevation of about eight thousand feet. She dropped us off at about noon (it was Sunday) and we started hiking up a very well-marked and well-kept trail toward Whitney. We both carried a pack, but of course mine was heavier. We brought warm sleeping bags, a small amount of food, water, and warm clothes. We did not bring a tent. We hiked slowly until about 6:00 in the evening. It was a very beautiful day and there were quite a few other hikers. When we stopped for the night, we were at a place called Trail Camp at twelve thousand feet elevation. We both felt the effects of the altitude from about the time we reached eleven thousand feet. At twelve thousand feet we were well above the tree line and the place where we camped was very desolate. Looking around at other campers reminded us of being in the presence of zombies.

At a spot which was level and fairly smooth, we pushed aside the rocks and spread our sleeping bags at about 6:30. We had our supper which consisted of one pop tart each, some hard salami, some peanut butter, candy and for dessert, we had apple sauce. We used the primitive outhouse provided and then since it was so cold and windy, and since there was little else to do, we crawled into the sleeping bags at about 7:00. When the sun went down, it didn't get very dark since the moon was nearly full and the stars were so bright. We stayed awake for quite awhile and watched the stars and talked. We didn't sleep very good because the ground was too hard.

We got up at about 6:00 and each of us had another pop tart, packed our stuff and then started hiking with just a small pack, leaving most of our equipment at the Campsite. We only took a camera, water, warm clothes, and a small amount of food. During the night some small animal had chewed through one of our packs and ate some of our cookies so we decided to donate the rest of them to whatever critter it was. We decided later that it was most likely a marmot.

When we left in the morning there was a lot of ice on the trail. The trail was steep when we left camp and within a few hours we were up to the crest of the mountain at over 13,000 feet. It was very windy and for the next mile or so, the trail was fairly level. Then toward the end, it got steep again. Our progress was very slow and we were in continuous oxygen debt. We didn't say very much to each other. We just walked in silence. Both of us were somewhat sick with headaches and slight dizziness. Every one hundred yards or so we would stop and rest and sit in the sun trying to avoid the wind.

At about 10:45 we got to the top. We were pretty tired but happy that we had made it. There is a log book provided at top for people to record their name. Laura was too cold so I signed for her. The elevation was 14,495 and we thought that was pretty high for a couple of flatlanders.

For us, and for Laura especially, who was only 11 years old at the time, we thought it was an accomplishment. Not so much, I think, that we had done it because hundreds of others do it every year. But rather, we had done it together. A father and his eleven-year-old daughter together had gone up Whitney. That's what was memorable.

We stayed at the top for only about forty-five minutes and about half of that was spent huddled together out of the wind. The view was great. From the highest point in the United States (not counting Alaska) we could see Death Valley which is the lowest point in the United States. But we were anxious to get back to the lowlands and our natural habitat so we started back at about 11:30 following the trail we took to get there. On the way down, we picked up our pack that we had left from the night before. As we moved down the mountain, dark clouds moved in behind us. Our timing was just right. Without a tent, we could have been in big trouble.

While we were gone, Jean had to stay alone at the base camp. When she had come to pick us up, high winds tore our camper apart. It had ripped off the canopy, knocked down the tent part of the camper and tore the canvas. We managed to tie it back together good enough for the rest of the trip. Had the bad weather come a day or two earlier, Laura and I would have been caught on the mountain without adequate protection. I realized that it had been a mistake on my part to be on the mountain without a tent. This time, luck was with us but I would never take such a chance again.

When we left the Mt Whitney area, we came back across Tioga Pass and on into Yosemite. We only stayed there one night and then came on back to San Jose. While we were there in Yosemite, we didn't see any bears. This was unusual because bear visits were common at this campsite. Two bears did however visit some campers nearby.

Fishing and Hiking Trip with Tom:

We stayed home for a few days after our Whitney trip and then Tom and I took off in our little Ford Courier on a camping trip of our own. While we were gone, Tricia went with some friends to Disneyland. Jean stayed home and canned some tomatoes and did other chores around the house.

Tom and I went back to the Sierras just south of Lake Tahoe. We drove off the main road into a place called Hope Valley. This is a very big valley with a stream going down the middle of it. We drove through the valley and on up further into the mountains to about eight thousand feet elevation to a place called Indian Valley. We drove on dirt roads and in some places we had to cross through small steams. At one spot the water was over the axle. There were no people other than the two of us. Each night for about five nights we would camp at a different spot, mostly along side of a small mountain lake. The first day Tom did some fishing in the lakes but didn't catch anything. I tried bow hunting but didn't see very many deer signs so I gave up on that. Instead, we concentrated on fishing in the small stream and just hiking on the mountains. We caught a lot of small rainbow trout which we ate for breakfast, lunch, and dinner. We used flour and oil and fried them tail fins and all. They were delicious.

Since it was just the two of us, we slept during those five or so nights in the back of our Ford Courier. We had a small shell on it and I had built a platform in it which went across the bed about halfway up along the sides. This didn't leave much room for sleeping. Tom said it was like sleeping in a coffin. I thought it was rather cozy.

While camped in Indian Valley one day, Tom decided to climb a nearby mountain which peaked at about ten thousand feet. I stayed back at camp and washed the dishes and cleaned and straightened out the truck. Then I even took a bath in the stream and then sat down and did some reading. It was a gorgeous day with temperatures just perfect, lots of sunshine and a beautiful view.

At about 1:30 or so Tom came back from his hike with a story about seeing an old plane crash site. It was across a gorge from where he was and it had crashed into the side of the mountain. He couldn't get very close to it because of the gorge. When he told me about it, we decided to go back up and take a closer look if we could get to it. We studied the topographic map and decided on a different route than the one he had taken. We left at about 2:00 in the afternoon. The first part of the climb was easy but then it started to get very rocky and steep. There was no trail to follow so we had to guess on which was the best way. There were large rocks shaped like pillars and we had to weave in and out of those and occasionally we would get boxed in and had to back track and then find another route.

We managed to get to the crash and it looked to us that it had been there for at least ten years more or less. It was a small single engine plane and it appeared to have crashed into the top of the mountain against a vertical wall or rock a mere one hundred feet or so from the top. The main body of the plane was still in one piece except the entire front end was completely crushed and one wing was separated and lay further down the mountain. There was a big X painted on the side which signified that the plane had previously been found. In looking around the wreckage, we determined that there had been a man, woman, small girl, and a baby boy aboard. We could tell this from the clothes that still remained scattered about the site. There was a little toy truck, baby bottle, rubber pants, small girls shoes, a woman's leather shoe with the toe turned up and all dried out, and other items that a family would take for a short trip. All of these personal items, bleached by the summer sun and worn away by the winter winds and snow were still there much as they must have been right after the crash. From the look of the clothing, especially shoes, it looked like the crash had occurred at least ten years earlier.

As I looked at the wreckage, a chill suddenly came over me as I remembered the words of the priest in Schenectady twelve years earlier, when he reported the tragic plane crash and death of the young family that had moved to the San Francisco area. I realized that this was the place where they died.

Tom and I came back down the mountain in silence. The mountain seemed different to us after what we had seen. When we got back to the truck, which was parked in the shadow of the mountain, we decided not to camp there anymore and we moved on to another place.

Chapter 10

Limerick Station
1976

The Urge to Move Again:

ONCE AGAIN, THE wander lust within me reared its ugly head. I had heard about a job opportunity in Pottstown, Pennsylvania and it aroused my interest in moving back to the East. Jean and I were both from the east and we often talked about going back before the kids got married and rooted in California which would then mean that we would never go back. We saw this as our last chance to go if we really wanted to go. If we took the job, our long range plan was that when the job ended I would stay at the site in some other capacity so that we as a family would stay in the east. We talked about it to the kids and they seemed to be okay with the idea probably either way. The job opportunity was to be the GE Site Manager at the Limerick Station during the construction and startup of the plant. The Limerick Station consisted of two 1,100 megawatt electric BWR units. When the construction and startup were complete, I would then switch jobs and stay with the Utility. Our relocation back to Pennsylvania would then be long term. The job would be a promotion and it sounded like something that I felt was more to my liking.

The Move:

Since the move was to be permanent, instead of renting our big Mojave Drive house as we did for the previous moves, this time we sold it and Jean, Tricia, Laura, and of course Cali took off once again for the east this time taking the southern route. Gary and Tom who were already out of the house and were living pretty much on their own. They both had plans for additional schooling either in San Jose or in Pennsylvania. Initially, at least, they would stay in San Jose. They were working and going to school at the same time. After we got settled in Pennsylvania, they would follow, or stay, that was a decision that would come later.

At Mojave Drive, we had this barrel cactus which we decided to take with us. Since we were taking the southern route we had to get a permit to take the cactus through Arizona. I don't know why we wanted to take the cactus in the first place. It was huge and very heavy. I still have visions of the cactus in the back of our station wagon covered with a box to avoid the spiny needles. It took up half the space in the back of the station wagon. Cali was in the same space and she avoided the cactus like it was the plague. At that time we had a station wagon instead of a camper.

While going through Mojave Desert in southern, California, Cali got sick and we had to make a stop at Barstow to see a Vet. We got some medicine and went on our way and Cali was soon feeling better. As we were approaching the Arizona border where we would go through the small town of Needles, I commented to Jean that I thought the air conditioning in the car was no longer working. It was on full blast but the inside of the car was still hot. When we arrived in Needles at about 2:00 in the afternoon we noticed that there were no people anywhere. We though that maybe Needles was a ghost town. When we arrived at our hotel, I parked and opened the door. When I stepped out, I thought I was entering an oven. The temperature was in the low 120s.

We went on to our destination of Pottstown, Pennsylvania without further incident.

Another Seizure:

Over a year had passed since I had any seizures resulting from the head injury during the softball game in May, 1975. I had taken Dilantin for some period but at the time of this trip, with the doctor's permission, I had taken myself off of the drug. I had become somewhat complacent about any reoccurrence of seizures. I assumed that there was no lasting effect of the concussion. So it came as quite a shock to suddenly have another one of major intensity. We were staying in a hotel while looking for a house to buy when this one came on completely to my, and Jean's, total surprise. When it occurred, I thought that my brains were exploding. If there ever was such a thing as a grand mal seizure, this was surely it. Jean and the kids were really worried. I ended up in the hospital in

Pottstown and was soon under the care and advice of a neurosurgeon. He immediately put me back on Dilantin and threatened to suspend my driver's license.

I would see the doctor on a regular basis during our stay in Pottstown. I continued to take the Dilantin. I was a bit edgy about the situation after having the seizure and was a little worried that I might have another one. The Dr. told me to hurry up and find a house and get out of the hotel and get into a house where a more normal life could be restored. And so we did. We bought a very nice house on St. Peters Road just outside of Pottstown and moved our furniture, including the big barrel cactus, our old piano which I had found in Ralph Teamer's barn and which had now crossed the United States three times and had been moved in and out of storage six or eight times, and all of our belongings and other paraphernalia. We moved in and life seemed to return to normal. Cali lived in a little doggy house in the backyard.

The job went well, except that I was always aware that I was on Dilantin as a seizure preventive and that left me just a little uneasy at times. The job required that on occasions I had to be in high places that were still under construction and without adequate protective barriers and I was not always comfortable with that. Also, I did not want to be dependent on the drug Dilantin for the rest of my life. I wanted to take myself off of it but I was afraid to do so because of the increased risk of having another seizure where my safety, or the safety of others, was jeopardized. I developed a fear of being addicted to Dilantin along with the fear that I couldn't take myself off of it while still being required to be in risky places.

Also, I sensed for quite some time that Jean and Laura were not totally happy with our life style in Pennsylvania. Tricia was enrolled in college at a branch of Penn State and seemed to be doing totally fine. She had a boyfriend named Lance, who would bring us really good firewood for our fireplace and wood-burning stove. Jean didn't like the house because it was too dark. Actually it was dark but a lot of the darkness was due to the fact that we were in the East where it was less sun than we had gotten used to in California. Laura missed her softball friends and the swimming pool and she was unhappy with the school system. Since she was from California, the teachers assumed that she had received inferior studies so they insisted that she take lower math, for example, than other students.

One solution that would enable withdrawal from Dilantin while at the same time make the rest of the family happier was to quit the Limerick job and return to San Jose.

But returning to San Jose meant a real blow to my career, if I still had one, and it also meant that we would have to buy another house in San

Jose where real estate in the year that we were gone had skyrocketed. For example, to buy back the old Mojave Drive house would cost us at least 50 percent more than the price we received when we sold it just one year earlier. In spite of those significant negatives, we transferred back to San Jose. So, in the summer of 1977, we packed up once more and moved back to San Jose. This time we left the piano behind but we brought back the barrel cactus.

Chapter 11

Back to San Jose
1977

WHEN WE FIRST came back to San Jose, I resumed seeing a local neurosurgeon about my need or not for taking Dilantin. My memory is fuzzy on this but I think after a few brain scans and interviews, I think that he agreed that I could come off the drug slowly which I did with seemingly no ill effects. After about six months or so I was completely off Dilantin and had had no seizures, small or large.

Unlike the job situation when we first moved to San Jose in 1969 when the commercial nuclear industry was booming, it was clear that the industry when we arrived this time was on the decline. The number of new orders had practically vanished so that the San Jose work load was pretty much limited to working off a small backlog of orders which had not been canceled and servicing the plants that already existed. Consequently, opportunities for me when we returned to San Jose were also limited.

For about one year, I was a program manager (along with a plethora of other engineers). It was the program manager's job to assemble people as necessary to come up with solutions to customer problems. Sometimes the problem would require only a few other people and minimum effort, sometimes it would require a substantial effort with large groups of people and perhaps some equipment. One interesting problem that I had was to respond to a Utility Customer that had dropped a rubber boot into the open reactor vessel and they could not find it. They needed to know and be able to prove to the NRC that if they left the boot in the reactor it would not plug up the small spaces leading into the fuel bundles and result in a flow restriction which in turn could cause fuel overheating. My job was to set up a test in San Jose to prove that the rubber boot would disintegrate into very small pieces under conditions similar to the reactor. I was able to do this with only a few people and a test loop to simulate reactor flow conditions. I used our kitchen oven at home to heat chunks of a rubber boot to 500°F as part of the testing.

Another problem that I worked on required some of the best minds in GE. The job was to save the GE Test Reactor (GETR) located in Valecitos, California. This reactor was used for training operators, testing materials, and making radioactive isotopes for the medical industry. At that time, about half of the medical radioactive isotopes in the country came from GETR. But the NRC threatened to close it down because of a suspected earthquake fault that someone suggested existed near the site. The task for us was to prove that if an earthquake occurred and completely severed the main recirculation pipes, adequate cooling of the reactor core could be provided. Our group decided that the best way to do that was to provide a large container of water up on the hill above the reactor with a flow path to the reactor that would withstand any anticipated earthquake. The method that was chosen was to use a large flexible bladder, similar to a goat skinned bag, and a heavy duty fire hose. Both the bladder and the hose would flex in an earthquake and would not break. It was a very simple and logical solution. Only the combined efforts of some of the best minds could have come up with such a brilliant effort. However, I think our efforts were an exercise in futility because ultimately, GETR was shutdown and the Medical Isotope business went somewhere else. I was always a little annoyed and disappointed that this happened but it was enigmatic of the whole commercial nuclear industry at that time.

From the time we moved back from Limerick, I was less enthusiastic about my job and at times I was downright depressed. I was no longer on anything that looked like a career path and real honest to goodness success at anything that I was doing seemed to be missing from my life. These were the days when I was starting to think once again about moving or changing jobs.

CHAPTER 12

Side Trip to Italy
1978

Another Field Assignment:

WHILE SITTING AT my desk one day I overheard Paul Zimmerman saying that he needed a new Lead Test Engineer for Startup Testing at the Caorso nuclear power plant in Italy. Somewhat as a joke, I said, "why don't you send me?" The next thing I knew I was on a plane on my way to Italy with an expected stay of six months or more.

My assignment was to replace the current Lead Test Engineer who had requested a transfer because of rumors of Terrorist threats. This was during the days when members of the Red Brigade were shooting kneecaps of certain people, usually people of relatively high positions in the government. But Americans were also considered targets. The duration of the assignment was supposed to be about six months, but as just about all of the startup assignments went, the stay lasted well over one year. During that time, I came home about four or five times, Jean came to visit several times, and Tricia came over one time for a month. Otherwise I had no other family members with me the remainder of the time.

When I first went there, I lived for some time in the Hotel Roma in downtown Piacenza. I used a company car, a Fiat, to drive to and from work. Both the car and the hotel were temporary and I had to look for both an apartment and a car.

I spoke very little Italian when I first arrived. I spoke very little Italian when I left a year later. It was like when I had been in Spain eight years earlier. The job was in English so there was very little incentive to learn the language.

Temporary Stay in Apartment:

My experience of moving into my first apartment turned out to be a typical Italian ordeal. I took the day off from work and spent most of it waiting for my shipment which was supposed to arrive by truck. I was not given a phone number to call if there were problems so I just waited. Finally, in midafternoon the shipment hadn't arrived, so I gave up and went to work. The next day, I waited by the apartment as I had done the day before. This time it was supposed to be there for sure. But once again, it didn't arrive. The third day, started to look like a repeat of the first two days but finally around noon, my shipment arrived.

My shipment was very small. All I had was a stereo system, some clothing, a few books, and some personal items. So moving in was no problem. The place was furnished with what appeared to me to be early American antiques. The furniture was so ornate and fancy that I was afraid to use it. Also, the floors were all marble. It was cold and antiseptic. The bathroom looked like an add-on in a hallway. It was about 30 feet long and 3.5 feet wide.

In the living room was a table with a solid glass top. About one week after I moved in I decided to move the table. In the process, the glass top fell off and broke into a thousand pieces. I was in my bare feet at the time. There I was in the middle of the room with pieces of jagged glass all around me and some of the broken glass and the table still in my hands. It took some very careful maneuvering to get out of that mess. But that was the easy part. Getting the glass top replaced was the bigger challenge and getting it done without the owner knowing about it made it an even greater challenge.

I talked to Joe at work, who took care of such things, and he found someone who would do it but the price was several hundred dollars. I didn't like that so I went shopping on my own. I used a large piece of paper to draw the shape of the glass and then took along a sample of the glass to show the design that was built into the glass. I found a local shop that would make the new glass for under $100. I had some trouble communicating but I got the job done.

Life in Piacenza:

Shortly after that, I moved into another apartment which had a telephone. Those were hard to find in Piacenza at that time. Of course it wasn't hooked up when I moved in. Getting it hooked up of course took another month or more.

This place also had the marble floors but the furniture was less ornate so that I didn't feel any pressure not to use it. I would stay in this second apartment for almost a year. It had a kitchen with a small stove, very small refrigerator, a sink, cabinets and a small table. There was also a dining room with a large table and a hutch. Then there were two bedrooms and a bathroom with a bath tub but no shower. It was on a busy street so there was a lot of car and truck noise. And in Italy, cars don't always have good mufflers. And the exhaust was so bad that the balcony was unusable due to the black sooty dust that collected on everything.

The apartment also came with a pair of slippers which looked like dust mops. They were there for a long time and one day I told someone that there was a pair of slippers in my closet that looked like dust mops. They laughed and then told me that they were in fact dust mops. The idea was to put them on and then shuffle around the apartment and in so doing, the marble floors would get dusted.

A few weeks after I arrived in Italy, someone gave us a lecture on how to minimize the risk of getting harmed by the Red Brigade who, we were told, had the bad habit of shooting people like us in the kneecaps. They told us to try to avoid following the same schedule every day so that our locations could not be predicted. For example, it was suggested that we should not go to the bank every Monday morning at the same time using the same route, or walk through a dark alley to the same restaurant every Friday night at 7:00 p.m., or go jogging on a dyke in the fog down the road from the plant every night on the way home from work. He was looking at me when he mentioned the jogging habit. As a result of the lecture, I began looking for other places to run.

About two months after I moved in I bought an old rusty Fiat for traveling to and from work and for going to races on weekends. I bought it from a school teacher in Milan and it cost about $150 in American money. It ran pretty good but it had a real bad case of rust. Locals couldn't understand why I had bought such an old ugly car. They felt that a person of my status should be driving a better car. One day while at work one of the secretaries asked me if she could have a ride home with me. When she saw my car, she changed her mind.

During my early stay in Piacenza, before I had my own telephone hooked up, I sometimes had to call the plant site on weekends or after hours. To do so, I had to go down town to the telephone office with a fistful of *getanoes* (like slugs) to feed the telephone. I usually had to stand in line to get a phone and then if I was lucky, I would get through to the site after a few tries. The first couple of times I tried this, I would get cut off and would then have to call again and start over. After several tries I learned that I had to continually feed the phone more getanoes. If I stopped, or feed them too slowly, without warning, I would get cut off. So to be safe, I would just keep dropping them in the slot as I talked and hoped that I wouldn't get cut off.

Piacenza Fog:

In Piacenza there were times when it got so foggy that it was impossible to describe just how foggy it was. Someone at the plant came up with the idea of using the number of white line segments that run down the middle of the road that could be seen while you were driving with your head hanging out the window on the drivers side. Normally, on a clear day, you could see forever and there would be lots of white line segment visible. On a day when there would be some fog but not real bad, you might, for example, be able to see two lines. On a day when the fog was starting to really get thick, you might only see one line. That's when it was a good idea to slow down and drive with care. But when it got to be a half line or no lines at all that were visible, then you knew you were dealing with the dreaded "Piacenza Fog." In the chapter on Running, I talk about running on an elevated dyke surrounded by a sea of fog and being chased by a large dog dragging a chain. Here are a few examples of driving a car in the dense fog.

Several people at the plant decided to drive home in a really dense fog but they gave up and spent the night at the plant when they were having problems finding the front gate.

I left work with the intent of turning off the road at a special running place but I couldn't see the right side of the road to determine where to turn off. With my head out of the window on the drivers side I kept driving until I ended up in Piacenza near my apartment where I could see city lights which was several miles past my intended turn off. So I had to skip my daily run on this occasion.

Bob Lutman was at the site for special testing and Dick Baker invited he and I to his house for dinner and then to stay and listen to the World Series baseball game on the radio. It was broadcast live so we had to stay up late to hear it. We all fell asleep so we never really heard the outcome of the game. Bob and I had driven there separately so I left before Bob and I soon discovered that a heavy fog had rolled in and it was probably somewhere close to a half liner. We both had to take the same road back to town and at one point it went through a circle, similar to a roundabout that you often find in Europe. When I came to this place, I followed truck tracks which unfortunately went over a curb, or large bump, and then off the road to the left and came out on the wrong side of the road. Fortunately, it was late at night and there was no on-coming traffic. I managed to continue the rest of the way by driving very slow with my head out of the window most of the way. The next morning I went to work and didn't say anything to anyone since I felt embarrassed. Meanwhile, Bob Lutman didn't show up until later at which time he told this story about driving in the thick fog and running off the road to the left by the town circle and knocking a big hole in the oil pan of his rented car. At this point I 'fessed up and told him that I had done the same thing. He had come along only minutes after I had gone through the same place only he was not as fortunate as I had been.

Jean Visits:

When Jean came over to visit, she would stay about a month more or less. We would usually go for weekend trips when she came. One time we went with Dick Baker and his daughter to Rome for a long weekend. Before I left, I verified with the group that there would be adequate coverage in the test group. It was understood that Dieseldorf (that's what we called him and I forgot his real name) would be on call for Saturday. An old church was one of the first places that we visited on Saturday morning when we arrived in Rome. Coming out of the church as we were going in was, of all people, Dieseldorf. He explained to me that he had found someone else to cover for him.

On our way to Rome, Dick Baker had given us a lecture on how to hold on to our wallets and purses. He explained that there were thieves who rode mopeds who would drive by and snatch your purse before you knew what happened. Well, as it turns out, Dick carried a purse. Although he was an American, he had adopted the Italian custom of carrying a purse. As we were on our way to dinner our first night there, wouldn't you know, a moped came by with two young men, and one of them snatched Baker's purse. We started to run after them but another moped, an accomplice, came by and ran interference for the first. They got away with his money, his passport and his credit cards. He was real good about it though. He refused to let that incident ruin his and our weekend. I loaned him some money and we enjoyed the rest of the weekend as if nothing had happened.

We covered a lot of ground while we were in Rome. We visited many of the popular places where tourists go. My favorite place was the Coliseum and the old ruins. We saw a lot of naked statues. Dick and I took separate paths through a portion of the ruins and when we came back together he asked me if I saw anything interesting. I told him that I saw a lot of Mammary Maximums. We also visited Pompeii. I personally thought that was the most interesting place in Italy.

On another weekend, Jean and I and Dick and his wife Carol went to Germany for the Oktoberfest. On the way we stopped at a McDonald's just across the Italian border and had hamburgers. That was one of the highlights of our trip.

At the Oktoberfest, in case you don't know it, there was a lot of beer drinking and singing. They had Frauleins with healthy upper bodies who could carry up to six huge mugs of beer at once. I had so much beer the first night that I wasn't any good the next day. I was too hung over. I tried to run it off but it didn't work.

On that same trip, we were driving through the Austrian Alps in Bakers car and the muffler separated from the exhaust pipe. I crawled under the car and tried to fix it with a tin can and some wire. After I got back in the car, everyone started complaining about the smell. It seems that I had crawled into some cow manure while under the car.

During this same time period, we got caught in a major herd of cows that were being herded down the road by a very colorfully dressed cow herder. It seemed to take forever to weave our way through them and when we finally made it, I asked Baker to stop so I could get out and take some pictures. There were cows with the big bells and the cow herder with his colorful clothing looked so nice that I wanted some pictures. While I was taking the pictures, the herd went past us and as a result we had to weave our way through them a second time which drew a characteristic grumble from Baker.

My tin can and wire fix of the pipe to muffler break didn't hold and after several unsuccessful stops, we gave up on trying to fix it. We drove all the way back to Piacenza with no muffler. We drove in silence since it was too noisy to talk. The traffic noise outside our apartment after we got home was quiet by comparison.

Tricia Visit:

Before Tricia arrived, I went to the train station to get some travel information on traveling around Europe. I rehearsed what I needed to say in Italian and then approached the man at the window. I told him, in my best Italian, that my daughter and I would be taking a trip to Switzerland and I wanted to know what train to take, etc. He listened to me and then responded in perfect English. That's why I never learned Italian.

Tricia came and stayed for about one month. We took several trips in my rusty Fiat while she was there. One time we went to Pisa to see the city and the leaning tower. While there, our trusty car stalled in the middle of the street. We had to get out and push. How embarrassing.

We also went to Florence and spent a lot of time looking at art. On one occasion, we got separated and she saw me coming out of a room in one of the palaces that we visited. She asked me what was inside and I said, "Just a bunch of priceless art, let's get out of here and go get some pizza."

Tricia was a bit surprised at the modus operandi of the local prostitutes in Piacenza. To explain the situation, you have to understand that Houses of Prostitution were illegal in Italy at that time but prostitution itself was not. Therefore, there were prostitutes but they worked on corners and their "clients" picked them up in their cars. But in the wintertime it got cold so they needed something to keep themselves warm while they waited on their corner or at their place. In some cases, this was out in the country. For example, between Piacenza and the plant where I worked, there were about four places where prostitutes could be seen. All four of these places were in the country. So what they did to keep warm was sit by fires. There was a guy, the Pimp I suppose, that came by now and then and took care of the fires. But the most unusual thing about this whole technique was the fuel that they used for the fires. They burned old tires. That's right, old tires. When it was cold, you could spot these places for miles, unless it was foggy. Big black clouds of smoke marked the spot. They must have had to use a lot of perfume to overcome the aroma of burnt tires. But perhaps since fast cars are considered the in thing in Italy, the smell of burnt rubber may have been appropriate.

People coming from or returning to the states had standing orders to act as couriers. For example, anyone coming over to the site from San Jose, or from state side anyplace, would always be asked to bring a box of Dutch Masters cigars for Bob Tobin. There would sometimes be other requests for peanut butter for example, but for sure if you were coming to the site you had better bring the Dutch Master cigars. Can you picture my daughter bringing a box of Dutch Masters cigars through Italian Customs?

Similarly, if you were returning to San Jose, then the standing order was to bring back a bottle or two of Sambuca for Tom White. Tom had been to Italy and had acquired the taste for Sambuca. At that time, it wasn't available in the USA. Personally, I didn't really like the stuff that much because it was too sweet. Well, a little bit was okay, but just a little.

On the subject of Sambuca, when Tricia was staying with me, we took a train trip to Switzerland to visit Betty and Ken and their two kids Kevin and Tiffany. We got on the train in Piacenza and it was, if I remember right, a sleeper of sorts. But we shared it with others. As it turned out, it was Tricia and I and an English lady. There was also a French lady but I think she was next door and only showed up when the English lady opened a large bottle of Sambuca.

Tricia and I had packed several sandwiches for our trip but had not brought anything to drink. Conversely, the English lady had brought this large bottle of Sambuca but no sandwiches. She accepted a sandwich from Tricia but then I suppose felt obligated to open the bottle. The bottle, in fact, was supposed to be a present for someone back home in England. And it was the largest bottle I had ever seen. Well, once opened, it was a goner. We drank Sambuca all the way to Switzerland and all the English lady had left for a gift was an empty bottle. When we arrived in Geneva, Betty scolded me for setting a bad example for my daughter.

We went skiing the next day with Ken and Kevin. I had an awful time. I fell down a lot and I didn't really feel very good. Perhaps it was the Sambuca.

During the return trip from Geneva to Piacenza by train, Tricia and I decided to take a walk from our car to adjoining cars. We left our luggage and all our belongings, including our passports, by our seats. In the first car that we came to there was a woman passenger and no one else. We said hello to her and she talked back in perfect English. We soon discovered that she was a person of notoriety from Argentina. I forgot her name but after a short discussion we discovered that she knew a young lady named Sherry who at that time was actually my daughter in law. She was married to son Tom, but the marriage didn't last. But that's another story. She had lived in Argentina near Sherry and for a time period drove her to school. Sherry's dad owned a business in Argentina at that time. We spent some time talking to her when we suddenly realized that she was on a car that was going to be split off from the main train since she was not going to the same place as we were. We immediately exited the car and saw the rest of the train starting to take off. We ran and jumped on the trailing car just in time to avoid being stranded in some strange place without our luggage or passports. That was the first, last, and only time that either one of us ever hopped a train.

Three Mile Island:

I was living in the apartment at 42 Alberone, 29100 Piacenza, when the Three Mile Island accident occurred. I was in San Jose for business reasons at the time of the accident. Jean was in Connecticut with her mother who was terminally ill with cancer so I stopped by to see her and her mother on my way back to Italy. When I returned to Italy, I went to visit my favorite grocery store which was a Mom-and-Pop type place just around the corner from my apartment. I bought most of my fresh vegetables from them. The old man picked them up daily from the market and hauled them back to his store with a little old bicycle. When I returned and went into the store, the old woman scolded me because of Three Mile Island. She knew that I was a nuclear engineer at the Caorso site and I guess at that time, it was not a popular profession. She figured that I was partly to blame for the accident. I wasn't good enough in Italian to defend myself and discuss the situation with her.

How Not to Bargain in Italy:

When I was getting ready to leave Italy when the job was complete, I was worried about what to do with my old rust bucket car. Joe told me that the "Tractor Mechanic," that's what we called a local car mechanic and dealer, would take it. Joe and I took the car to see him to negotiate a sale. My bottom line was I was willing to pay him $50 just to take it off my hands. We drove in and Joe told him that I was interested in selling my car. It had a pretty new battery, the Tractor Mechanic had sold it to me, and the tires were pretty good also. He looked it over, kicked the tires, looked under the hood and scratched his head for a while and then offered me $25 American money. He was obviously making me a first offer and was ready for some negotiations. Of course you never buy or sell anything in Italy without some haggling, especially when you are dealing with a used car. Well, when he offered the $25 American money, there was only about a millisecond of silence before I responded in a very loud voice, "SOLD!" Well, I think that I ruined the guy's day. You just don't do things like that in Italy. He was probably completely upset for not offering me less. I told Baker what I had done so some short time later, he did the same thing with his old car when he left. Damn Americans don't know the first thing about bargaining.

Chapter 13

San Jose Finally Becomes Our Hometown
1979

Job and Career Becomes Secondary:

AFTER ITALY, I got more interested in hiking, fishing, a little hunting and more than anything else, serious running. The job became secondary. I was now almost fifty years old and was too old to think much about my career. I still had employment with GE and I was generally happy with what I was doing. My health was good and there had been no seizures, no entangled intestines, and no major anxiety attacks for quite some time.

When Did the Kids Grow Up:

When I came back from Italy, I realized that my kids weren't kids anymore. It was 1979 and Gary was now twenty-four, Tom was twenty-two, Tricia was twenty, and Laura was fifteen. Where did the years go? I remember when Laura was eleven years old and we had climbed Mt. Whitney, I though I should do this with each one of my kids. There were a lot of other things that I had planned to do with them. But where were those darn kids now when I was ready for them? They were gone. They had grown up.

Book of Names on the Mountain:

Bull Run Lake sits at about eight thousand feet above sea level in the Sierras off Route 4 about fifty miles east of Angels Camp, the city where they hold the annual frog jumping contest. Angels Camp is famous for other things, but most people will know it as the frog jumping city. Every year people come from all over to either watch or enter frogs in the contest. If you go to Angels Camp and keep going up the mountain on Route 4 past Bear Valley and Mt. Reba Ski Resort and then another four miles or so to Lake Alpine and then another couple of miles you come to a the Bull Run Trail Head. About three miles up the trail you will find a very pretty lake. This is Bull Run Lake.

For about seven or eight summers in a row, I went to Bull Run Lake, and sometimes more than once in a year. I liked it because it was a beautiful place and it wasn't crowded. Well, at least it wasn't crowded when I first went there. The last time or two, there were a dozen or so people there. The first couple of times that I went there, I was totally alone.

Gary and Marie tried to go there one time, based on my recommendation, but they went too early in the spring and the trail was still covered with snow and they couldn't make it.

Laura, Marie and I planned an overnight stay there one time but I was not feeling well at the time. So instead, we drove to Lake Alpine and stayed in a rustic cabin overnight and then the next day we took a day hike to the lake. Laura and I went there another time by ourselves.

I talked Jean into hiking in with me one time. I told her it was an easy hike. We took provisions for about two days. I carried most of the stuff and she had a light pack. The hike in is about three miles and it is almost all up hill on a well-marked trail which at places is pretty steep and rough. It turned out to be a lot harder for Jean than I had suggested it would be. We stayed at the lake two nights and we slept in sleeping bags inside a very small tent. We were sleeping essentially directly on the hard ground. It got cold during the night. We also heard some strange animal sounds. It was the first, last, and only time that Jean went with me. All the rest of my trips would be either alone or with Laura or Gary and Marie.

In the seven or so years, I estimate that I went there about a dozen times for an average stay of two nights during each stay. I would set up my tent by the lake and then I would do some fishing and would take day trips up the surrounding mountains.

On the way in to the lake, I always made it a habit of searching the creeks for fly larva. Usually I found some which I stored in pill boxes with air holes in the covers. I called them "Gadis Flies." I would use these to catch lake trout. It seems that if I had these larvae, I almost always caught fish. Without them, there was a much lower probability that I would have fish for dinner.

It was during my second trip to the lake when I met a couple on their way out. I told them that I planned to hike to the top of Bull Run Mountain during my stay at the lake. The woman told me that when I go to the top of the mountain to be sure to write my name in the log book. She said that everybody does so that there is a record of everyone who has climbed the mountain. She said that the book has been used for over twenty years and that it is interesting to look back and see the names of others who have been there. I told her that I would sign it if I could find the book. I had been there before and didn't see any book. I didn't know there was a book so I hadn't looked for one. She said that at the top of the mountain I would find a cross made out of rocks. At the very center of the cross I would find a flat rock. I should lift the rock and underneath would be an old can. Inside the can I would find the book and a pencil. I thanked her and said that I would be sure to log my name.

Next day I hiked to the top of Bull Run Mountain which peaks at about 9,500 feet. I looked for the cross of rocks but couldn't find it. But the mountain top was not clearly defined and it looked like it might have several peaks. So I commenced to search the top, including all the peaks. But I couldn't find the cross of rocks which would identify the location of the Book of Names. I spent a long time searching but never found the book. Next day I climbed the mountain again, but still didn't find the book.

From that first trip up the mountain looking for the Book of Names, I have been up and down that mountain a least a dozen times, probably more. I have never found the Book of Names. At one point I even considered that perhaps I was on the wrong mountain so I tried several of the adjacent mountains but still didn't find the book. The search had become like an obsession with me. To this day, I have never found the book.

As I write this, it has been many years since I have been on Bull Run Mountain. But I still wonder about that book. Perhaps the woman was pulling my leg. But I don't think so. It is very logical to have such a book. They do exist on many mountains. But if there is a Book of Names, it should have my name in it at least a dozen times.

So if you ever go to the top of Bull Run Mountain, find the Book of Names and enter your name, and notice that mine is absent.

Tom, Gary, Sir Pugsley, Fred, and the Party Rugs:

After they moved away from home, Gary and Tom lived for some time in a house in Campbell, which was another town right next to San

Jose. While they lived there, they were going to college and working part time (they had their own cleaning business for awhile). There was a shack in back of the house and their friend Fred lived in the shack. They also had a pet pig named Sir Pugsley who lived in the shack with Fred. The pig was friendly and more or less well behaved and would sometimes come in the main house to visit. When they first got Sir Pugsley, he was just a little thing but as time passed and much pig feed was consumed, Sir Pugsley got quite large.

The boys, acting as boys do, would occasionally have parties in their house and Fred and some other, probably rowdy friends, would attend. Sometimes Sir Pugsley, feeling otherwise rejected, would also join the party. Now since this was a rented house with reasonably nice furnishings including the carpets, the boys came up with an ingenious idea. They obtained old rugs which they used as party rugs. When they had a party, they put down the party rugs to preserve the landlord's best rugs and of course to protect their original deposit.

Eventually the owner discovered that a large pig was living on his rented property. So Sir Pugsley had to go. This called for another party. They invited all of their friends, including a friend who was a butcher, and they had their best party ever. Sir Pugsley was there as well only this time he was there as the main course.

Hawaii:

Did you know that in 1948 the tallest building in Honolulu was only two stories? That was the year that I thought I would be transferred to Pearl Harbor after I got out of submarine school but orders were changed after I got the mumps. I finally got to Honolulu and Pearl Harbor in 1984 a mere thirty-six years later when there were skyscrapers everywhere.

Jean and I went with Bill and Jan Barclay to Honolulu in December of 1984 and Bill and I did the Honolulu marathon. I had just spent two days in the hospital before the trip because of blockage in the small intestine. I was rushed to the hospital just a few days before our scheduled trip. They had to put a tube down through my nose into my stomach to draw out the gas. Nothing was moving in the normal direction. The pain was so severe that they gave me morphine. However, after a few hours of the stomach pump operation, the pain went away. When this happened, I remembered the words of the neighbor on Willow Lane in Schenetady in 1958 when he said my Meckel's diverticulum intestinal entanglement problem which required surgery then would be a problem later. I was hoping that he was wrong when he said it. Unfortunately, he wasn't. This same entanglement problem would reoccur again on at least six more occasions during the next twenty years and it would usually be at the most inopportune times.

We stayed in a hotel on Waikiki Beach. When we first arrived, we were carrying our luggage across the street in the direction of our hotel. A young "street" lady offered to carry Bill's luggage for him. He said he appreciated the offer but he could handle it. He suggested, however, that his wife Jan could use some help. The street lady declined.

While we were there, Jan hurt her arm and so we all went with her to the hospital. While there, we all had dinner in the hospital cafeteria and contrary to the normal comments on hospital food, we all agreed that the food at this hospital was pretty good. Especially me, I thought it was mighty fine. The following night when we were trying to decide where to eat, I suggested that we go to the hospital. I thought their food was the best.

We have returned a number of times to Hawaii but I think the first time was the best.

Taiwan Experience:

In 1989 at the age of fifty-nine, I semi retired from GE. I stayed on part time, essentially 50 percent of the time initially. Right after my semi retirement, I went to Taiwan to assist in a pipe replacement program on one of our nuclear power plants. They needed a lot of people because the job involved working part of the time in a radiation field and each worker was limited to a conservative amount of radiation which was well below safe limits.

When I got there, we went immediately to work after a long flight over. We had a long bus ride from our hotel to the site, we worked long hours, and I found it hard to sleep. After being there for only a few days, I had the misfortune of passing out one day while at work. They told me it was a seizure. They hauled me off to a hospital and my partner, poor Wally Shultz, went with me. I woke up on a hospital gurney in a long hall with what looked like wall to wall patients. Wally was using two chairs pushed together beside my gurney trying to get some sleep. I had no idea where I was. They found a female doctor who spoke English and she came to visit me. She gave me some pills and I understood her to say that the pills were Valium. I had heard real bad things about Valium so I refused to take them.

After a short stay at the hospital, they sent me back to the hotel to get some rest. When I got there, I was in a near panic state. I tried to work the next day but I couldn't handle it. I spent most of the day lying down in the nurses quarters. The following night I still couldn't sleep and I still felt panicked. The desk lady at the hotel, feeling sorry for me, sent me a large bowl of grapes and other fruit. But I was so sick, I couldn't eat any of it. After less than a week in Taiwan, and accomplishing nothing job wise, they made arrangement for me to fly home. The best flight they could find had me going from Taipei to Tokyo, then on to Seattle and from Seattle to San Jose. It was a long flight but flight attendants along the way had been instructed that I was defective baggage and to handle with care. They were real good to me but it was still by far the worst flight of my life. It was a near nightmare and I thought that any minute I was going to panic completely. I was on a 747 and was riding in the business class. I spent the entire flight from Tokyo to Seattle in the fetal position in my seat and barely moved. Occasionally a flight attendant would ask me if I was alright. I would grunt a muffled yes.

When I got home, I saw my doctor and he prescribed Zanax to calm my anxiety. His initial recommended dosage was not enough and he had to double it before it did any good. After I felt a little better we discovered that the medicine that they tried to give me in Taiwan was also Zanax. I could have minimized my problem then if I had not been so paranoid about the Taiwan hospital prescription.

As a result of the Taiwan experience, I was put back on Dilantin again. I also began carrying Zanax with me at all times just in case I got an anxiety attack. I found out later that some of my kids, grand kids, and my mother all had at one time or another some amount of panic disorder. I guess it is in the genes only in my case I think it is exacerbated by the fear of having seizures related to the head injury during the softball game in 1975 plus the fear of periodic small intestine entanglements related to the Meckel's diverticulum surgery in 1958.

About eight years after my nightmarish trip to Taiwan, I went back again with two other engineers for the purpose of presenting information to the operations personnel on ways to avoid unnecessary and unwanted plant shutdowns. This time it was a different situation for me. I felt good and our presentations went very well. However, there was one interesting lesson that I learned from this experience.

I had prepared presentations which were similar to ones that had been used for the same purpose domestically. They included slides which helped to support the words. I also liked to use jokes, and I found Gary Larson's humorous "Far Side" cartoons would often fit the bill for this purpose. I was advised to not use any jokes so I removed them from my slide package. However, during one of my presentations to about thirty site operators, one of the slides which I had failed to remove showed up on the screen. The Larson Carton that I had used depicted a time machine that had just landed among a herd of dinosaurs and the driver of the machine was seen walking away with an empty gas can. I had used it as an effective tool for showing the importance of being prepared for the unexpected. The driver of the time machine had not considered the consequences of going back to the time period before gas existed. It was one of my favorite Larson cartons. I started to skip by it but questions were asked so I had to explain it. Now these operators apparently looked at us like we were professors and the things we said and showed were treated as gospel. I think that they didn't expect any of us to make jokes. For the remainder of the meeting I noticed that operators were talking to each other which I gathered was their effort to understand the significance of the carton. They seemed to be worried that it would somehow be on a test to follow later. I tried several times, with minimal success, to emphasize that they should ignore the slide.

The Earthquake and the Pendulum Clock:

Jean says that this story isn't true. I say it is. Let's compromise and say it's more or less true.

The Loma Prieta Earthquake of October 17, 1989, which registered 7.1 on the Richter scale, hit as I was leaving work a few minutes early in order to watch the World Series base ball game. I was in my truck at the time and it felt like I had four flat tires. Although we were only about fifteen miles from the epicenter of the quake, we didn't have any visible damage to our house nor did any of our family members. However, it scared the living daylights out of us. There were a lot of aftershocks following the main quake so we didn't exactly sleep like babies that night. But sometime during the night I noticed that our old German pendulum clock down by the front door was gonging every hour just as you would expect. The funny thing is, the clock hadn't been running for several years. The quake had started it and it has been running ever since.

Jean thinks that I am exaggerating. I'm not really. The clock has always been a little temperamental. It insists on being wound every eight days or less, it is pretty picky about being level, and the working mechanism sometimes gets stuck for unknown reasons. I think that it was in one of those mysterious stuck situations. The jolt by the earthquake was all that it needed to give it a kick start.

As I write this, it is not running because I forgot to wind it.

Trips Back East:

After my tour of duty in Italy and even more so after semiretirement, I did some business trips that would take me back east. That would often give me the opportunity to visit family members in Pennsylvania. Additionally Jean and I would usually schedule a trip each year to both Connecticut to see her relatives and to Pennsylvania to see mine. On some of those trips, we would take my brother Merle and sisters Luella and Elaine to see Brother Floyd in Ohio. Those were fun trips for me. We were real country folks on some of those trips. Typically we would stop at some family restaurant on the way coming and going. We would be seated by the waitress and Merle would proceed to tell the waitress that we were all brothers and sisters and came from Garrett, Pennsylvania. He would go on to say that our dad was a farmer and timber man and he himself worked all his life on a farm and we were on our way to Ohio to see our other brother who used to work for Dow Chemical and was responsible for inventing Saran wrap and that I was currently living in California and on and on. In the meantime the waitress would be standing there taping her pencil on her order pad while other customers were getting restless.

Our brother Floyd had retired from Dow Chemical and was now living on a big farm in Ohio. When he first moved there, the farm house and out buildings were dilapidated and Floyd reminded us of a mythical farmer known as Peter Tumbledown. With a lot of help from his wife Shirley, they have fixed up the old house and cleaned up the landscape so it now looks like the kind of place many of us would like to have as a summer retreat if not to live there year around.

I loved those trips from Pennsylvania to Ohio and I wish I could live some of them over again. But Merle is dead now, Elaine has Alzheimer's disease and Luella walks with a walker after breaking both legs in an automobile accident. Yes, those days are gone but not forgotten.

Iva Fisher and the Butternut Acres Bed-and-Breakfast:

During our annual trips back east we would visit my relatives in Pennsylvania, and sometimes Ohio, and Jean's relatives in Connecticut. We usually made it a point to go to Vermont for a few days as well. On our last trip to Vermont in October 2002, we stayed overnight at the Butternut Acres Bed-and-Breakfast in Grafton. The previous year, we had stayed at the Grafton Inn, but Jean wanted to try someplace different because the beds at the Grafton Inn are so high she needed a ladder to get in and out of bed. So this time we decided to try the Butternut Acres B&B which is located just on the edge of Grafton and had just recently become a B&B. It turns out that this B&B had beds that were also quite high but we liked the place better. The place was originally a big old farm house. But the best part, and the real reason we stayed there, it was owned and operated by someone that we considered to be a very special person.

The owner and operator was a ninety-two-year-old woman named Iva Fisher. In prior years we usually made a point to stop at the farm house to purchase maple syrup. This time we decided to stay overnight.

If I was to make a list of the most memorable people that I have ever met, this lady would be at the top. I first met her when I went to Grafton to Nana and Grampy's cabin back in 1958. At that time she and her husband Theron and their son ran a large dairy farm. They had at one time approximately one hundred milk cows. It was a big operation for that part of the country. They also operated a maple sugar camp.

The first time I bought maple syrup from them was around 1960 at which time they operated on the honor system. They had an enclosed area on the side of their house with an unlocked door and inside they had syrup available in various sized containers. There was a price list and a box with money available for change. You selected the size you wanted and you put your money in the box, took change if you needed it, and that was it.

I have been going back to that place periodically since that first time in 1960 for over forty years and nothing has changed except they have had to increase the prices to keep up with inflation.

But there have been other very significant changes besides the fact that it is now a bed-and-breakfast. Some thirty years ago (I am not sure of the actual time period), their son died. Then some 10-15 years later, Iva's husband Theron died leaving just Iva alone on the big farm. She was forced to sell all the farm animals except the cat. When Jean and I were there in 2002, she and her very old cat lived there alone. But she still, with the help of a grandson, ran the sugar camp at the age of ninety-two. Of course, she also runs the bed-and-breakfast. She is an amazing woman.

Luella and Elaine Visits:

During the '90s, Luella and Elaine made several visits to California. At that time, Luella was close to eighty and Elaine was somewhere in her upper sixties. We took them to Yosemite, San Francisco, Alcatraz, the Winchester House and a few other standard tourist places. We would also drive up the coast first to Eureka to visit son Tom and then to Yelm, Washington to visit Helen. We also took them to Carmel and had lunch in

Clint Eastwood's Hogs Breath Inn. Seated at the table beside us was a new wave type guy with earrings, nose rings, tattoos, long hair, lots of jewelry and chains and other strange items of clothing. This was quite an education for them, especially Elaine who had never before been west of Columbus, Ohio.

Wherever we drove, we had a lot of trouble passing any gift shop without stopping for Luella to buy a souvenir. This was especially true when we drove through the Redwoods and the Big Foot Country on our way to Washington. At one store she bought a little piece of redwood cut in the form of a tree. When we got back to our place, I used her tree as a template and made another one for Elaine. Luella, good naturedly, gave me a hard time for letting Elaine get one free when she had to pay for hers.

On one of our trips north we stopped on the coast in Oregon and stayed in a hotel suite that was right on the beach. It had two rooms and one of the rooms, the best room, faced the ocean. It had a big window so you could see and hear the ocean. We gave them that room and Jean and I took the other room which faced nothing. In the morning I asked them how they slept. Elaine said that she hardly slept at all. I asked why and she said, "That darn ocean made so much noise I couldn't sleep."

We visited Helen in Yelm, Washington, and at that time Helen was not doing very well. They got a chance to see the depressing situation that existed with Helen before she moved back to Pennsylvania.

My Sister Helen:

Helen's life seemed to be filled with tragedies. The first big one came when in 1952 her husband died in an automobile accident and left her with two small daughters. Some years later she met, and planned to marry again but her husband to be died in a coal mining accident.

Still later, she, with the help of two brothers, built a day care center but this turned out to be another failure. The town of Somerset was not ready for a day care center.

Her oldest daughter Judy eventually married and moved to Yelm, Washington and Helen and her youngest daughter Patricia soon followed. They arrived in Washington just about the time Mt. St. Helens blew. Then they moved, it seemed like a good idea at the time but neither she nor Patricia were happy after they moved. After a few years in Yelm, Patricia died suddenly in her sleep due to a blood clot. After Patricia's death, Helen became more withdrawn and depressed. While in this depressed state, she apparently had a stroke.

Following the stroke, she was diagnosed as having dementia and she requested my help in moving her back to Pennsylvania. In her mind, I think she wanted to go back to her youth. We did help her move but the move was into an assisted living home and from there to a nursing home. Within a few years after the move, she died.

Her daughter Judy still lives in Yelm, Washington, with her daughter and one son. She had another son who, while on a camping trip, got up in the middle of the night in the dark and fell off a cliff. By the time the rescue team reached him, he was dead.

Unusual Sleepwear:

In the wintertime, and since I lost most of my hair, I sometimes wear a ski cap to bed to keep my bald head warm. We turn our heat down at nights and by morning the bedroom gets pretty cold. Also, all my life I have been plagued by very dry skin which causes my fingers and my feet, especially my heels, to crack. Sometimes the cracks are so bad on my heels that my feet look like the dry California earth that hasn't been watered for years. If I don't keep my feet greased with Bag Balm or equivalent, the cracks can get so bad that they keep me awake at nights. When this happens, I will sometimes put on a heavy layer of Bag Balm and then in order to keep from getting the sheets greasy, I will but small plastic bags over my feet. In order to keep the bags from falling off, I will put socks over the bags. Usually when the feet are cracked, so are my hands so while I'm at it, I put the Bag Balm on my hands and a pair of white gloves again to keep the grease off of the sheets.

One other thing, I sometimes sleep in the nude. I got in the habit of not wearing pajamas when it was real hot in the summer time. We rarely use the air conditioner when it's hot because by nightfall it usually cools down. Sometimes however it stays hot at night and I found that sleeping naked was more comfortable. After doing that for awhile, I got so I liked it. I am now less comfortable when I wear standard pajamas.

One time Jean woke me up saying that she heard a noise downstairs. She couldn't remember if we had locked all the doors. She asked me to go look. This was one of the times when I had the bags and socks on my feet, white gloves on my hands, a ski cap on my head, and nothing else.

I always keep a baseball bat by my side of the bed just in case. (In case of what, I am not so sure.) Jean keeps this big flashlight that Gary gave us by her side of the bed. So I picked up the baseball bat in one hand and the extra large flashlight in the other and went downstairs to check to see if there was a burglar. Jean wasn't worried about any harm befalling me. She figured that if there were an intruder, he would die laughing when he saw me. Fortunately I didn't see anything unusual and all the doors were in fact locked. We decided that the noise came from our new energy efficient refrigerator, which according to the salesman would make some strange noises during certain parts of its normal running cycle.

Discovering the Alaska Connection:

I only know five men in Alaska and they are all named John. I asked my nephew John if only men named John can live there.

In 2001, Tom and I went to Alaska to do a little fishing and just to get away. Tom had a lot of frequent flyer miles accumulated on Alaska air so it was a chance to use some of them. My nephew John Ogle, Luella's son, has property on the Kanai Peninsula plus his son (also named John) and daughter-in-law (named Denise and not named John) and three kids live there. We figured we would visit then while we were there. We first did some salmon fishing but only caught two. Those were caught by Tom. In the process, I broke his $300 fly rod and dropped my camera in the river while helping Tom land one of the salmons that he had caught. When this happened, one of the men fishing nearby asked me what I thought was the cost of the two fish that we had caught thus far. I said that it had to be at least several hundred dollars per pound.

My nephew has a big cabin at Anchor Point and his son John and John's wife Denise have several more cabins and they operated a fishing service called Bear paw Charters. After I broke Tom's $300 fly rod and ruined my camera, Tom and I went to visit them. Nephew John allowed us to stay in his big log cabin for several nights and young John took us fishing for halibut. When I saw old John, my nephew, it was the first time I had seen him in forty-eight years. Sometimes the years fly by when you're not looking. It was the first time that I had ever seen young John and Denise. They had three adorable kids named Corrine, Sophia and Leo. They also had a three legged dog. We got along great right from the beginning. I wondered why so many years had gone by before we made our first trip to Alaska.

By the way, Leo's real name is John. They call him Leo to avoid the confusion caused by having too many Johns.

We had a great visit at the big cabin. The cabin was built by the two Johns. Young John provided the talent according to old John. The cabin has a spiral staircase made out of logs.

The two Johns took us fishing and we caught our limit of halibut. Between Tom and I, we took home a nice batch of halibut fillets. I never knew halibut was so good. I determined that the best way to cook it is to cover it with mayonnaise on both sides and throw it in a hot frying pan with no oil or grease in the pan. Just the mayonnaise on the fish is all you need. Try it, you'll love it.

In 2002, Jean, Laura and I went back again and old John and Luella were also there. Laura and I ran the Midnight Sun marathon and the following weekend we also ran a 10k in Homer called the Spit run. We had a great time. I went fishing again and we took home some more halibut. We took a boat ride to a glacier and did some hiking and other fun stuff. Once again, I lamented that we had not met up with our Alaska connection sooner.

In 2003, just Laura and I went back to run the Midnight Sun marathon for the second time. I didn't have a very good run and ended up walking the last half of the marathon. We also did the Spit run again and little Leo did most of the 10k in a stroller until about fifty yards from the finish line. At that point he got off and ran across the finish line to the roar of the crowd. He was wearing a boot on one foot and a shoe on the other. It was priceless.

We also went kayaking and hiking and we played some lawn bocce ball. A moose came strolling through the yard and broke up the bocce ball game however. We also hiked to the beach and built a fire without matches. For us, anything we did in Alaska was fun. It was summer time and it was daylight all the time except for an hour or two and even then it wasn't totally dark.

The things we do in Alaska are pretty typical tourist type things. However, our Alaska relatives are, in my mind at least, real Alaskans. Each year they take trips to remote places to fish and hunt. One trip that John, Denise, all three kids, and the three legged dog have made takes them down the Yukon River to very remote regions where they fish, relax and hunt moose. They stay for three weeks. While gone, they live pretty much off the land by shooting water fowl, catching fish, and then possibly some moose meat on the way home. They eat a lot of moose meat and fish. In the wintertime, young John has a trap line and he has taught Sophia how to run it.

Betsy and John:

Betsy is a very special person. She is a good friend of Denise and we met her on our second and third trips to Alaska when Laura and I ran the Midnight Sun marathon. She was there both times with her dog Rowdy. We would see her and Rowdy at various points along the marathon route plus the finish line. She would greet us with camera and with an encouraging smile. Betsy, in typical Alaskan style, is always ready and willing to help others even though she herself is waging a personal battle with cancer.

Betsy and John live at some distance off the main highway between Soldotna and Anchor Point but nearer to Anchor Point. Their house sits on a river where the salmon run. They have their own electrical generator and a bank of batteries to provide their own electrical power. In some ways, their life style reminds me of my youth on the farm in Pennsylvania in that they catch, shoot, or produce much of their food. They catch fish, shoot moose, maybe a bear or mountain goat, have a garden, and they do a lot of canning and preserving. They have a large workshop attached to their house which is typical of the homes in Alaska. They burn wood to heat their house. Betsy can sit at her computer and view the outdoors including the river which is right below her window.

It's 3:00 AM and I can't sleep:

From the time I reached the sixties, I have had to get up at night to empty my bladder. First it was just occasionally and one trip to the bath room would do it. In my seventies, it was every night at least twice. For Jean, it was essentially the same story. In my case, it seems that one of those awakenings almost always occurred at about 3:00 in the morning and once I was awake, I often had trouble getting back to sleep. Usually during the day, I was happy and had for the most part happy thoughts. It seems that in the quiet of the night, I would often think of something disturbing that would keep me awake, sometimes until the sun came up.

Some common fears that would sometimes keep me awake:

- Not knowing whether to buy, sell, or hold.
- The fear of loosing my computer files, especially "My Book" file.
- Receiving disturbing information which can't be resolved outside of working hours which leaves me to stew over it until the next working day.
- Fear of seeing my name in the obituary column.
- Fear of missing a turn during a long distance race.
- Fear of being cheated, robbed or scammed.
- Fear of big government.
- Fear of the many forces that seem to be bent on doing damage to the America that I grew up in and learned to love.

A few examples of things that I find a little annoying or amusing but that generally don't keep me awake;

- People who are grossly overweight and don't exercise or eat properly and then expect someone else to eventually carry the above average medical burden that they are creating.
- Individuals, and especially their lawyers, who file frivolous lawsuits against people or companies with deep pockets as a get rich quick scheme.
- Individuals, and especially their lawyers, who contribute to high medical costs by filing frivolous malpractice lawsuits for outrageously high amounts of money most of which goes to the deep pockets of the lawyers.
- Drivers with no passengers in a super large gas guzzling suburban vehicle commuting to work when they could be taking light rail or bus.
- Physically fit people driving cars when they could be walking, running, biking, or using public transportation.
- Drivers waiting in line for a parking space close to the door when dozens of spaces are available at the other end of the parking lot.
- Drivers on cell phones.
- People who drink and then drive.
- Drivers who enter main streets or expressways without slowing down or even looking both ways before crossing the sidewalk which always exists along expressways or main streets. Are they not aware that a sidewalk is a pedestrian's expressway and are they not aware that per the driver's manual the pedestrian has the right of way?
- Those who put up signs along the bike trails in the city which warn us to be aware of the mountain lion danger. I have lived in California for over thirty-five years and I only know of two people who were killed by mountain lions and they were not killed in the city. In the same time period, thousands of pedestrians have been killed in California by people driving cars. Seems like the signs should be changed to warn us about the dangers of people in cars.
- Undisciplined kids, some of whom will end up on drugs, in gangs, jobless, or in jail. Or all of the above.

I'm sure with a little more effort that I could come up with more. Perhaps readers could add a few of their own.

Chapter 14

Running
1977-present

How It All Started:

I STARTED RUNNING for exercise in late 1977 at the age of forty-seven. If you were to ask me why I started, I would have to say that I was strongly influenced by John Kennedy and a man named Cooper. First John Kennedy had encouraged running or walking for health. If my memory is correct, there were fifty-mile walks or runs that were started in the sixties when he was president. Then Cooper wrote a book called "Aerobics" in which he said that in order to achieve and maintain good health, one should elevate the heart rate for twenty minutes at least four times a week. When I first looked at that, I told Jean that we should have sex at least four times a week for health reasons. She said it wouldn't work in my case because according to Cooper, I was supposed to keep it up for twenty minutes not just twenty seconds.

Since sex was out, I looked at the next best thing which appeared to be running. It was the simplest, the most foolproof, and cheapest (no costly club fees). It required no special equipment and could be done almost anywhere at a moment's notice.

So at the age of forty-seven, I embarked on a serious mission of becoming a runner. Before that, I hadn't done any real running for years so the first time I tried to run, I couldn't do more than a quarter of a mile without resting. It annoyed me that I was in such bad shape. Especially when I found out that my friend Bud Crockett could run eight miles. So I was determined to improve.

I started to run at least four times a week as Cooper recommended. Pretty soon it was six to seven times a week. Gradually, the miles built up. Before long, my pipe smoking had become unnecessary and without realizing it, I had stopped smoking. I started setting goals. My first goal was to run the seven mile "Bay to Breakers." So in 1977, or 1978, I can't remember which (it is the only race I never put in my log book) Gary and I did it. We started it together but he lost me on Hayes hill. That would be the only time that he would beat me in a race. Soon it became difficult, or impossible, for him to keep up with me.

Running in Italy:

In 1978 I went to Italy. That's where I really got into running. Shortly after getting there, I joined a running group which had members that went to running events every Sunday. They called them *Marcha Lungas* and they were held in a different small town in the region each week. The object of these events was to run the miles without emphasizing the time. There were no winners or losers. At the end of the run, there would be something to eat and plenty of wine. I benefited enormously from these runs by meeting people, seeing some beautiful country side and towns, becoming a better runner, and not to mention the fact that I got the opportunity to enjoy a lot of good Italian wine.

When I first arrived there, I did a run nearby with my boss Paul Zimmerman and Bill Selby and his wife. They put an article with our pictures in the local paper about it. One of the men at the Caorso plant commented to me that he had been running for years and never made the paper and those damn Americans run one time and make the headlines. He was putting me on a little bit but he was right. We made the papers just because we were from America. They did appreciate the fact that we participated in their activities.

That same thing happened other times. Once Tricia came to visit me and she ran in a local event with me and we were interviewed by a local TV station after. That night we went to a friend's house and waited for the news so we could see ourselves on Italian TV.

During many of these runs, I would often be given an award for being the best American. Of course, most of the time I was the only American. Unless Bill Selby showed up and if he did, he was the best American because he always beat me.

Once when I was doing a run of about twenty kilometers, I noticed a young woman running in front of me dressed in a skirt, tee shirt, and regular street shoes. I decided to catch up with her to get a closer look so I picked up the pace a little.

I chased her for nearly all of the twenty kilometers but never caught her. I guess she taught me that it takes more than good shoes and the right clothing to make a runner.

Aside from running in the Marcha Lungas on Sundays, I would do training runs on my own during my spare time. I found places to run near the plant where I could run during noontime or on the way home from work. One place I often stopped on the way home from work not far from the plant was on top of a long dyke along the river. One day while running there a thick fog rolled in while I was in the middle of my run. I estimated this fog to be in the one half to one line category. Or as I described in the chapter on Italy, it was a "Piacenza Fog." Heavy fog was common in the area and we had established categories based on how many of the broken white lines in the center of the road could be seen. A real heavy fog was one where less than one line could be seen. This was one of those. However, the fog was very close to the ground so the top of the dyke was above the fog. It was like running down a clear path surrounded on both sides by a sea of fog. When I was within about a half mile of my car I heard the bark of a very large dog coming toward me out of the fog. I could tell it was a very large dog because of the sound of the bark. As I ran past the location of the dog, I heard the bark and then I heard a large chain dragging and moving in my direction. I did my fastest run ever for a few hundred yards until I reached the approximate location of my car. The dog stopped chasing me after a few minutes perhaps because he was dragging a large chain. I may have set a personal sprinting record for a quarter of a mile or so.

During the noon lunch break, there was always a game of hearts in the office of Bob Tobin, who was the operations manager. I joined the game but never really enjoyed it that much. I was never able to shuffle cards very well and Bob Tobin would give me that impatient look every time it was my turn to deal. One day while shuffling the cards in my unique way, the cards slipped out of my hands and flew all over the desk and floor. At that point, I decided that I would start running at noon instead of playing cards. It was a good decision for me as well as the other card players.

Racing:

I ran my first marathon while in Italy. It was called the Laga De Garda. I went there with my friend Hans Krupe. We both finished the race but it took us well over four hours. Hans never made it to his work the next day. He was a basket case. His legs were too sore to get out of bed. I was only a little bit better but at least I made it to work.

When I came back from Italy I continued to run for exercise and fun but the running became much more competitive. I met Gene Silver and Bob Farrington and the three of us became a running threesome. When we first met, we were all getting pretty close to fifty years old. We may not have admitted it, but we were looking forward to reaching fifty so that we could compete in the fifty-year-old age bracket.

When the three of us did reach the age of fifty, it was not uncommon for use to finish first, second, and third in our age group in races. In the early eighties, we ran as many as thirty races in one year. Almost all of the races initially were 5Ks, 10Ks, half marathons, or full marathons.

In 1981, when I was just fifty, I joined the GE Track Team. The track events included a 5K and a 10K road race. When I joined the GE team, I was the oldest runner on the team. I ran most of the 5K and the 10K races for the GE team until 2003 when I was seventy-two and at that time I was still the oldest member of the team. I had been the oldest runner for about twenty-two years. No one had caught up to me. Some of the young runners in 2003 hadn't been born when I first joined the GE team.

Ultra Distance Racing:

Ultra distance racing, as used here, refers to any race that is greater than the marathon distance of 26.2 miles. Many runners, including myself, have found ultra distance running to be a rewarding experience perhaps because it embodies running, hiking, exploring and back country site seeing all in one. It is also appealing since the participant doesn't necessarily have to be a fast runner to participate. Most importantly however, it also gives the runner a feeling of accomplishment. Just completing a one hundred-mile run over difficult terrain, for example, regardless of how many other runners may have finished in a shorter time period, is still a significant accomplishment.

In the following pages, I write about some of my own personal ultra running experiences. I write about running, sometimes walking, in fifty-kilometer trail runs, fifty-mile trail runs, one hundred-mile trail runs, twelve- and twenty-four-hour track runs, a six-day race around a one-mile course, a 135-mile run through Death Valley in the summer time when the temperature was at it's highest, and other difficult events. Some of these events, especially completing four difficult one hundred-mile trail runs in a three month period, have given me a feeling of accomplishment.

Perhaps the most significant thing that I have obtained from participating in these ultra distance events is a deeper appreciation of the real hardships of those early explorers who did ultra distance traveling without the benefit of the crews, pacers, and aid stations that were provided for those of us who did the running. In some cases maybe the running was the easiest part. For example, we ran 135 miles starting at Badwater in Death Valley and ending on the side of Mt. Whitney. At no time were we ever more than a couple of miles from our private vehicle which contained a crew, food of all kinds, foot repair equipment, salt, pain pills, sun block, spare shoes, reflective clothes, lounge chairs, a bed, a shower, coolers full of ice and a large assortment of cold drinks, a garden sprayer to provide saturation cooling every mile or so, and enough water to float a small ship.

Compare this to what the early explorers had to endure A book titled *Death Valley '49ers* by Frank Latta describes the hardships of the first people to enter Death Valley in 1849. They traveled thousands of miles without the benefit of aid stations. What they endured makes our 135-mile Badwater race seem like a picnic. And when I ran it, they made a documentary about it and gave it the name *Running on the Sun*. Sounds pretty impressive. Too bad they couldn't have been there with their cameras when the '49ers came through.

Another amazing example of endurance under extreme hardships is that of Vitus Jonassen Bering, who was given the job by Peter the Great, Emperor of Russia, to go explore the region beyond Siberia which we now know as Alaska. Vitus packed his bags and took about three thousand helpers and proceeded to hike, without aid stations, across Siberia, about one third of the way around the earth. They paused at Kamchatka long enough to build two ships which he named *St. Peter* and *St. Paul* and then sailed out into the roughest seas on earth. Within a few days after they set sail they ended up in a fog bank and lost sight of each other so the two ships never saw each other again for two years. Meanwhile Bering in the ship *St. Peter* with a crew suffering from scurvy and other ailments encountered extremely rough seas and eventually crashed on an island (later named Bearing Island) where Bearing died. From the wreckage of the *St. Peter*, the crew built another smaller ship and eventually returned to Kamchatka. A good reference book on Bering's epic voyage is titled *Where the Sea Breaks Its Back* by Corey Ford.

Later in this chapter I talk about doing a training run with Gerry Simons when we had to do a stretch of eighteen miles over the Sierra in the heat of the day without water. I tell about eating dirty snow and make it sound like that was a hardship. How about the real life story of seven men who escaped from a Siberian Work Camp and hiked a mere four thousand miles to freedom. Their hike to freedom started just south of the Arctic Circle and went across the Siberian arctic, the Gobi Desert and then the Himalayas into India. They started with nothing but an ax, a knife, and a week's worth of food. With some help from friendly Mongolians, they somehow managed to finish this unbelievably long trek. I believe the hardest part had to be crossing the Gobi Desert without aid stations and without a single container to carry water. They survived by sucking water out of mud and eating snakes. This true story is described in the book titled *The Long Walk, The True Story of a Trek to Freedom* by Slavomir Rawicz.

So in the following stories about ultra running, if I speak of hardships, they should be taken with a grain of salt, whatever that means.

The Jed Smith Fifty-Miler:

In February, 1982 I ran my first ultra, the Jed Smith Fifty-Miler. Gene Silver also ran it. I had asked people for advice on how to approach a fifty-miler. The consensus was that it was best, especially for a first fifty-miler, to run some and walk some. When the gun went off I started running and I saw Gene Silver up ahead of me. I decided to follow him. I chased him for fifty miles and never caught him. We finished first and second masters. We were both over fifty and we had finished the race ahead of all the runners in the forty- to fifty-year age group. Gene's time was 6:19, and mine was 6:25, just six minutes behind him.

My Personal Records (PRs):

I have kept a record of all my races and all my total miles of running including racing and training since I started in 1977 until the end of 2004. My total miles that I have run/walked was over sixty-nine thousand miles. The total number of races that I have completed were 50 marathons, 112 ultra marathons, and 242 sub-marathons. I do not want to give the impression that these are unusually high numbers. They are not. They are typical for long distance runners but there are many runners who have much more impressive numbers. I only include them here since they represent part of my running experience.

I am now in my mid seventies and I still run only now I call it moseying. I run at a ten to twelve minute per mile pace and sometimes slower. When I was at my peak, I was running 10Ks at sub-six-minute miles.

Nearly all of my PRs came in the early eighties when I was fifty-one or fifty-two. Here are some of them:

One Mile	5 minutes and 8 seconds	May 1982
5K	18 minutes and 32 seconds	Nov 1981
10K	36 minutes and 6 seconds	July 1982
10 Mile	61 minutes	Aug 1982
½ Marathon	1 hour and 24 minutes	Feb 1984
Marathon	2 hours and 47 minutes	July 1982
50K (Hilly)	4 hours and 18 minutes	Aug 1982
50 Mile	6 hours and 14 minutes	Oct 1982
100 Mile	18 hours and 45 minutes	Mar 1986
12 Hour	71 Miles total distance	Oct 1990
24 Hour	114.5 Miles total distance	March 1988
6 Day	340 Miles total distance	Dec 1990

The Western States 100:

    Wendell Robie was the man responsible for creating a horse race that started at Squaw Valley and ended in Auburn. It followed the old trail that early immigrants took to get across the Sierra. The trail was know as the Western States trail which utilized some of the old trails that were first used by the Paiute Indians. The winner of the race was given a cup. The name of the horse race became "The Tevis."

    In 1977 Gordy Ainslie was entered in the Tevis but his horse had to be put on the disabled list. Gordy decided to try running it without his horse. He solicited the expertise of Dr. Lind to help ensure that he got the right amount of fluids, food, and electrolyte. With Dr. Lind's help, Gordy successfully completed the race. He finished about the same time as the average horse.

    The following year, the race became official. Only a few did it that first year but the word spread and soon there would be hundreds, and eventually thousands of runners applying for entries. They had to limit the runners so they were forced to have a lottery to get in. At the same time, other hundred-mile races were started. Now there are dozens of hundred-mile races in the United States and many more in other countries. Gordie Ainslie really started something.

    My first experience with the Western States 100 was in 1982. I crewed for my friend Fred Copeland and for Gene Silver. Prior to the race I went on training runs with them on the Western States trail and then during the race, I ran with Fred during most of the nighttime hours. During that time

I learned the importance of having good flash lights. Our batteries went dead and we had to buddy up with another runner to get through to the Route 49 crossing where we picked up a new flashlight. That same year my daughter Laura worked at the White Oak Flats aid station. She described it as looking like a Mash Medical Unit. We both got hooked on the run and I knew then that I wanted more than anything else, to run the WS-100.

For the next twenty-three years, I would be involved with the WS-100 either as a runner, crew member, or aid station helper. I would also go on many training runs even if I were not entered in the race. On these training runs, we did not have the benefit of aid stations so we were taking some risks if we suffered an injury or ran out of water. Here are just two examples of what I mean.

In one training run, Gerry Simmons and I ran out of water while trying to run the thirty-two-mile stretch over Emigrant Gap from Squaw Valley to Robinson Flat. I was so thirsty while traversing an eighteen-mile waterless portion of the run that I found and ate dirty snow. When we finally arrived at a river, we jumped into the cold mountain water clothes, shoes and all like the cowboys did in many of the movies we saw.

Another incident, also involving Gerry Simmons, nearly resulted in serious injury. We had decided to do a night run from the river crossing which was at the seventy-eight-mile point in the WS-100 race to the finish line. I had been down to the river crossing earlier in the day and noted that the water level was very low making it possible to cross on foot without the benefit of a steel cable or boat as was provided during the actual race. It was decided that late in the afternoon we would walk to the river and walk across and then start our run to the finish line. There were four other runners that decided to go with us. Gerry, his son and one other left ahead of us. Jerry Jackson, Steve Lorenz, and I followed some minutes later. When Jerry, Steve, and I got close to the river, we saw the three that had preceded us caught up in the current and were being washed downstream. We ran to help them but there wasn't much that we could do. They came out downstream with only a few bumps and bruises and with the loss of a few water bottles and items of clothing. But there was no serious harm done. What had happened? The water level when I saw it that morning was low because the flow was being restricted at a dam upstream. By the time the six of us got to the river, the flow was no longer restricted. The amazing thing was that Gerry Simmons and the other two tried to walk across when the water was clearly too high and the current was too strong. Just because I had told them earlier that the water was low enough to walk across, they apparently allowed that information to override their common sense. The three of us who had not yet crossed, went upstream where the water was calmer, but deeper, and swam across. Later when it got dark and we turned on our flashlights, I suddenly felt very strange. I told the others that something was wrong. The trail appeared to be waving in front of me and it was making me dizzy. One of the runners suggested that it might be vertigo. Another runner asked to see my flashlight. He pointed out that the part of the flashlight between the front glass and the dish shaped reflector and the bulb was half full of water. When we emptied it out and commenced running again, my problem went away. Later on during the night and while running on a narrow part of the trail, we encountered a skunk meandering along ahead of us. The six of us were lined up in back of it until it eventually wandered off of the trail.

To get into the WS-100 required being picked in a lottery. I didn't like that because that meant entry was being left to chance. When I ran the Western States the first time, I wanted to make getting in a sure thing. I had heard that those runners who held age records would get in automatically. I decided to look into the possibility of setting an age record. It was my understanding that Gene Silver's fifty-mile time of 6:19 at Jed Smith was an age record for a fifty-one-year-old. I was fifty-one and I was pretty sure I could beat that.

According to the running schedule, there was a flat fifty-miler scheduled for October in the state of Washington. Jean and I decided it was time to visit my sister Helen and her family and do the race while I was there.

On the way to Washington, we stopped to do some fishing in the Eel River south of Eureka and in the process we got our mini motor home stuck on a sandbar. Jean had advised me to stay off the sand with the truck but I told her I had wide tires and wouldn't get stuck. But I got stuck. We rocked the vehicle back and forth, we pushed, we dug, we hauled gravel, we cussed, we swore, but all without success. Finally, a big burly fellow on one of those huge front loaders with wheels that were bigger than our mini home came across the river to our rescue. He pulled up alongside and after attaching a big log chain, he pulled us out with ease. But in the process of all that effort, I hurt my back.

I visited a doctor in Eureka and got some prescribed treatments and medicine. At Helen's, I visited her doctor as well and the possibility of doing the race began to look slim.

On race morning, my back still hurt but I though I should at least start the race and see if the back would hold up. The race was laid out on a five-mile loop so we had to do ten loops to complete the fifty miles. There was an aid station at the start and another at the 2.5 mile point. Jean would stay at the start and be available every 5 miles. I had laid out a schedule that I needed to adhere to in order to complete the fifty miles in under 6:19. Jean would keep track of my time and let me know how I was doing relative to my target schedule. I had to maintain a 7:30 minute/mile pace which meant I had to make each five mile loop in about thirty-seven minutes.

After I got started the back pain essentially disappeared. I was able to hold the pace pretty close to my schedule for nine laps but according to Jean, I walked for several minutes at the start of the tenth and last lap. Also, on the last lap, as I was coming down the road near the finish line, some lady opened a car door just as I was passing the car. I ran into the door but fortunately no harm to me or the door was done. I was shooting for a total time of 6:10 to 6:15 and my actual time was 6:14. I think that I lost several minutes on the very last lap. The Ultra Runner magazine listed my time as an age record for a fifty-one-year-old and that assured my acceptance into the race for the Western States 100 in 1983.

I trained hard for the 1983 run and was probably in the best condition in my entire life. My expectations were to run the Western States 100 in under twenty hours and certainly in under twenty-four hours. But 1983 turned out to be the year of the big snow. The first twenty-four miles of the race were on snow. The goal of most runners is to finish under twenty-four hours and get the twenty-four-hour silver buckle. With the snow conditions, it looked like getting under twenty-four hours would be a lot more difficult. However, I wore my Adidas marathon trainer shoes which turned out to be perfect for the snow conditions. The bottom of the shoes looked like snow tires. They had big heels and they actually made running on the snow easier for me than running on the ground. When going down hill I emphasized my heel strikes so I wouldn't slip and I started to feel like I could almost fly down off the snow-covered mountain. I felt confident that this would be a good run for me. At sixteen miles into the race, the optimism would suddenly disappear.

I came into the Red Star aid station at 16 or so miles and I was not all that far behind the leaders. Due to the heavy snow, the aid station had only water which, along with the aid station individuals, had been flown in by helicopter. When I left the aid station I saw tracks and runners going in every direction. Some were going forward, some were coming back toward the aid station, and others were going sideways. Runners were lost. The ribbons that had been put up were either taken down by someone or the snow had melted around the stakes that held them and they fell down and somehow got hidden in the snow.

I saw Ron Kovacs and I decided to go with him since he had done the race before. He said if we just stay on this ridge we will be all right. I got separated from Ron but later ran in to Fred Copeland and two other runners. We were standing on top of a ridge, and one of the runners spotted a steady stream of runners, two ridges over. They were so far away I couldn't even see them. We decided that that was the place we had to go. Between us and them, were two ravines with streams at the bottom of each. The streams were covered with snow with the danger that if you walked across the snow, you could fall in. We took a chance and went down and up and down and up again before we came back on the right trail. Fred Copeland told me later that he actually feared for his life when we crossed the snow covered streams. He also spoke of feeling something tugging on his one leg when he was coming up out of one of the ravines. He looked back and noted that one of his socks had gotten caught on some brush and it was unraveling. There was a long white string behind him.

It cost us about 1.5 hours due to being lost. But much worse, it cost us energy and nearly broke our spirits. When I got back on the trail I felt that it was necessary to try to make up the lost time. I met my crew at Duncan Canyon which was the twenty-four-mile point and they gave me encouragement. Due to the heavy snow, the trail had to be changed when we went out of Duncan canyon so instead of going to Robinson Flat, the normal route, we took another route which kept us out of the snow. When I was an hour or so out of Duncan Canyon, I hit a low point and was moving slow and feeling really down. At this point Ron Kovacs who had also been lost saw that I was in a down mode and he told me something that I never forgot. He said, "Keep going, it won't get any worse." He wasn't necessarily 100 percent correct but the message was that since you are able to live with the pain level you are currently at, you can continue to live with it, so just keep moving forward and accept the pain as being part of the event.

In trying to make up for the time I lost, I passed about twenty-five people by the time I reached Michigan Bluff at the fifty-five-mile point. It was late afternoon and was about 80 degrees. I stopped at the aid station and after a few minutes, my body started to shake and I suddenly felt sick. Gordie Ainsley knew right away what was wrong and he brought me a cup of hot tea and within minutes I was fine. I was hypothermic and he recognized it. My core temperature had dropped even though the ambient temperature was over 80°F. I had to stay in the aid station for about an hour until they would let me go.

From Michigan Bluff, Kathy Hughes ran with me until we reached White Oaks Flat which was at about the seventy-five miles point. There I rested for a short period but once again I started to get hypothermic. They gave me something hot and I was okay. Bob Farrington ran with me from that point on. We agreed that I should keep going without any prolonged stops in order to avoid hypothermia again.

We walked most of the way and reached the finish line at 7:00 o'clock in the morning. My total time was twenty-six hours flat. The silver buckle would have to wait until another year.

Wendel Robie, who was in his eighties, was at the awards ceremony after the race. I asked him to read a poem that he had written. It made me misty eyed when he read it. I believe that he died shortly after. Here is that poem.

>"Worth marks the man
>There all the honor lies
>Not content with well or better
>He has raced 100 miles the winner"
>
>   Wendel Robie

I ran the Western States again in 1984 and completed it in 22:11 and got the silver belt buckle. I had only one really difficult stretch and that was in the canyons where I spent about a half hour lying on the ground resting and eating cookies trying to get my energy back.

After I completed the run that year, I wrote a poem. It was based on the original course which has since been changed. It was also written for the runner whose goal was to finish in 24 hours and receive the silver belt buckle. Purest runners will say that the original course was a little short. Here is my poem:

Auburn in the Morning

Three hundred and more in the morning chill
Together from Squaw Valley went up the hill
Following Paiute trails until
We reach Auburn by five the next morning.

Yellow ribbons hang in the still morning air
You follow them close with anxious care
One wrong turn and you won't know where
Lies the trail to Auburn in the morning.

Over Emigrant Gap the top of the run
About one hour from the sound of the gun
Your spirits are high with the rising sun.
At Lion's Ridge you're moving good
The adrenalin's working as it should.
Red Star Ridge in four hours you knew you could
You'll surely make Auburn by morning.

RUN, IT MIGHT BE SOMEBODY

At Duncan Canyon you're restored by your crew
And the San Jose Quicksilver aid station too
They provide the support to help you get through.
To Robinson Flat, the trail is long and its steep
And the schedule you set becomes hard to keep
But it's still too early to worry or weep
You'll still make Auburn in the morning.

Deep Canyon's next and the sun is bright
The trail is wide and the grade is right
For covering the miles before it gets night.
At Last Chance you're greeted by a friendly bunch
You take time out for a little Brunch
At this point you've more than just a hunch
You'll easily make Auburn in the morning.

Down into the Canyon you run all the way
You try to keep moving it's the hot part of the day
Up to Devils Thumb but walking's okay.
Eldorado's an oven and the trail is really rough
You're tired and you're aching, you've soon had enough
You walk and you stumble on up to Michigan Bluff
If you can just make Auburn in the morning.

After back-to-back canyons, they throw in one more,
They call it Volcano, I don't know what for
But before Bath road, your quads will be sore.
From Forest Hill through Todd Valley to White Oak Flat
You now have a pacer to help you do that
You feel at this point that your chances are fat
That you'll still make Auburn in the morning.

On down to Rucky Chucky this part is alright
Before you know it the River's in sight
The crossing's refreshing it's now nearly night.
From the river the trail becomes tough and depressing
You're pace has diminished to avoid over stressing
It is painfully hard to go without resting
But there's still hope you'll make Auburn in the morning.

At Auburn Lake Trails, there's repast and there's pity
On to the river down dreaded Quad City
When you turn from the river you're feeling quite giddy.
You come up out of Hell to the 49 crossing
Your crew urges you on trying not to be bossing
The cookies they gave you very soon you'll be tossing
Is there still hope you'll make Auburn in the morning.

When you reach No Hands Bridge, you feel barely alive
There's two miles uphill before you arrive
At the outskirts of Auburn on the Street Robie Drive.
From Robie you find from down deep in your soul
A strength unexpected and you go on a roll
Up Robie to the High School to accomplish your goal
You made Auburn by five in the morning.

Ephraim Romesberg, '84

There is a very special comradery that comes to exist between the runners, pacers, the crew and the aid station workers. I think that part of the reason for this is that a bond is formed between those who work hard for something and then succeed, or not succeed, but at least tried. Both the crew people and the runners share the finish. The runners cannot do it alone. Maybe Bernard DeVoto said it best when he wrote about the immigrants crossing the Sierras:

> "What they had done, what they had seen, heard, felt, feared—the places, the sounds, the colors, the cold, the darkness, the emptiness, the bleakness, the beauty. "Till they died, this stream of memory would set them apart, if imperceptible to anyone but themselves, from everyone else. For they had crossed the mountains"

When I ran the Western States in 1986 at the age of fifty-five, my good friend Dick Baker was part of my crew. He and his wife Carolyn and daughter Heather came all the way from Georgia to be part of my crew. With the temperature in the thirties, He stood by the trail at the forty-nine crossing dressed in a tee shirt and shorts from midnight to 0800 in the morning to run the last eight miles with me. I must have forgotten to tell him when to expect me. Perhaps he had a mind set that I would come through on the run and would not want to stop; somewhat like a pony express rider who would change horses on the fly without stopping. He didn't realize just how slow I was. I should have told him to put a light, or flag, on his car and I would find him.

I finished Western States a total of seven times. I dropped out at various places along the trail three times and on the last three times that I was entered, I never made it to the starting line. Although I finished seven times, I only get credit for six. In one of the seven, I missed the final cut off of thirty hours at the finish line. It was very hot during the last three miles and I felt like I was having a heat stroke. I lay down in a small brook for some time to cool off. When I crossed the finish line almost everyone had gone. There were no available cots to rest on so I lay down on the ground. Apparently the flies thought I was horse manure and they wouldn't leave me alone. Some nice young lady brought me something to drink and Helen Klein went off looking for my crew. They had gotten word that I had dropped out and so they had gone from the finish line. I found a ride to my hotel but when I got there, I was already checked out and my bags were in the lobby. The hotel lady allowed me to go back in my room to take a shower and get cleaned up. Some of my crew finally showed up while I was in the shower.

People who are accustomed to seeing track events where the runners cross the finish line within seconds of each other may not fully appreciate the enormous spread of the runners after one hundred miles of running/walking over rough terrain. The reality is that when the winner of a trail 100 race crosses the finish line, there are still runners on the trail as far back as forty miles. The time differential can be as great as fourteen hours between the winner and the last finisher. This can probably be best visualized by the following example. On one of my WS-100 finishes, I was coming down Finley Street at about 10:30 Sunday morning just before entering the track where the race ends when I noticed the Sunday morning paper lying in a driveway. On the front page of the paper was a picture of the winner of the race that I was finishing. The winner had finished, was interviewed by the local newspaper sports writer, gone to his hotel, showered, went out to dinner, had a good nights rest, had breakfast, and was back on the track when I finally came in.

The Six-Day Race:

Six-day racing had been popular way back in the 1800s but then went dormant until the late 1980s or '90s. Norm Klein set a first of a kind modern Multi-Day-Classic at Gibson's Ranch in Sacramento and scheduled it for December 29 through January 3, 1991. I had signed up for it during the previous summer without giving it much thought. The course for the race was a one mile loop on asphalt except for a short dog leg loop on cement that was included in order to make the loop exactly one mile. Rob Volkenand, an old time running friend from Bend, Oregon told me that he was planning to run it and he thought it would be fun. Fun, yeah right, Rob.

In preparation for the race, I loaded up my mini-motor home with a lot of clothes, mostly cold weather clothes since the forecast was for cold weather. I also took along lots of socks, foot cream, Vaseline, balm, lotions, Aspercream, Advil, Aspirin, Pepto Bismo, Tums, Band-Aids, ace bandages, foot pads, and you name it, I had it. I also took six pairs of shoes. As it came to pass, my feet were swollen after the first day running on the hard surface, so all six pairs were a little too tight for comfort.

The race was set up on a one mile loop inside of Gibson Ranch. It was entirely on hardtop roads. The loop went around a lake. Along the route were hundreds of ducks, sheep, horses, cows, and one donkey. During the course of the six days, we would all become very familiar with the birds and animals.

At the race starting point, Norm had set up two large army tents. One was set up with a front wall of glass windows. Inside were tables for the lap counters. There were several computers that were used for keeping track of laps. Each time a runner came around, the lap counters would record the lap on a sheet of paper and it was also recorded in the computer. The tent was equipped with a wood burning stove so it was pretty cozy for the cold weather.

The other tent was set up with food. As the runners, or walkers, came around each lap, they had available to them plenty of food and drink. Nearby were heated bunk houses that were available for the runners when they needed sleep.

At the end of the first day I had covered eighty-eight miles. I had stopped often to eat, go to the rest room, change clothes, change shoes, get my legs rubbed, take a shower, and to sleep about 1.5 hours. The first night, it was exceptionally cold. I wore tights and sweat pants and a long sleeve shirt plus a hooded sweat shirt and a jacket, plus a ski cap and gloves. Due to the cold weather, the bathrooms were out of order so outhouses without lights were provided in their place. So making pit stops was a little awkward. Also, my sweat pants had two draw strings which hung down in front of me. Also, my jacket had two more strings which also hung down in front. So every time that I went to the outhouse, when I finished and readjusted my clothing, almost every time, those four strings ended up inside my shorts tangled up with some of my body parts.

The second day I covered sixty-two miles for a total of 150 miles in two days. At the time I thought that was pretty good but later I discovered that the USA record at that time for forty-eight hours for over sixty-year-olds was 179 miles.

The third day I covered only fifty-seven miles and I was starting to feel the ravages of the run and was now doing a lot more walking. Also it was cold, real cold especially during the hours from about 3:00 a.m. to 7:00 a.m. On several occasions, I picked up a cold drink from the aid station tent only to find out as I was walking down the road that I couldn't drink it because it was frozen solid. I heard others report the same experience.

Sometime along about the third or fourth day, I began to feel a burning sensation inside my mouth especially on my tongue. I was concerned but had not yet mentioned it to anyone. During this time period, I was inside the lap counting tent when Richard Carp's wife approached Norm with the concern that Richard was experiencing a soreness inside his mouth which sounded very similar to my problem. I was both relieved and amused at Norm's response. He told her not to worry that it was just a reaction to the trauma that the body was being put through. Since I figured that I was having the same problem, I was relieved to hear that it was not serious but was quite amused to think that we were punishing our bodies in this race to the point where symptoms of trauma were showing up.

On the fourth day I managed to do another fifty-seven miles, but I was fading fast. My feet and my legs were beginning to rebel. I couldn't run anymore. As a result, I walked the last two days covering just thirty-eight miles on the fifth day and thirty-nine miles on the sixty day. My final mileage was 341 miles. The American record for men over sixty at that time was 387 miles which I think I could have beaten if the race had not been on such a hard surface and perhaps shoes that would have been more appropriate for the hard surface.

Late in the race several of us were walking around the one mile loop for the three hundredth or more time when a portly woman asked us what was going on. She wandered if we were having a walkathon. Barbara Eli told her that we were in a six-day race. She wanted to know why no one was running if we were in a race.

During the six-day period, I had a total of sixteen hours of sleep. The lack of sleep didn't seem to bother me. As it turned out, the six-day period was held in the middle of one of the coldest spells in California history. The temperature during night had fallen into the teens for each of the six nights during the race. Twice during the course of the race, I took a shower. The water was warm, but the shower room was not. It was a real challenge to get out of the shower and get dried and dressed without freezing something.

The winner of the event was Ian Javes from Australia who completed 460 miles. In second place was Silvia Andonie from Mexico who managed to do 450 miles.

There was also a runner from Japan, Tatsuya Muamatsu, who finished 318 miles. His wife, Meiko, was there helping him for the six-day period. She must have been really cold during those long cold night hours. I tried to speak to her several times but she was always silent because she was not fluent in English. Some weeks after the race, I was pleasantly surprised to receive a note with several excellent pictures from her. One of the pictures showed me walking through the flock of geese.

For nearly two weeks after the race, my legs and feet hurt so much that I couldn't sleep very well. I slept with a basin of cold water beside the bed so that every so often, I would swing my legs off to the side of the bed and soak my feet in the cool water. Also, I would wake up often in a panic thinking that I had to get up and log more miles by running around the lake among the geese.

Leadville Trail 100:

They call it "The Race Across the Sky." All of the race is above 9,200 feet, and about 90 percent of it is above ten-thousand-feet elevation. The race starts at 4:00 in the morning and the temperature is usually right around 32°F. During the day, the runner can expect that it will be hot during the day and cold at night. But the runner needs to be prepared for rain, sleet and even snow on the mountains. This requires careful planning for clothing in drop bags or a good crew available at every aid station. Starting in 1991, I ran the race seven times and finished just three. The first time was my best when I completed it in twenty-eight hours forty-four minutes. I failed to finish the next four times before I was able to go all the way for two in a row in 1996 and 1997. I have not tried it since then.

In 1995, one of those years when I started but didn't finish, I ran most of the first thirty miles with my running friend Shirley Church from Los Gatos. Shirley and I have had this friendly bickering thing going for years where we constantly give each other a hard time. But it is a friendly hard time and we do it because we are both from Pennsylvania and are really good friends. We often found ourselves running together because at that time we ran at a similar pace. Her husband Bob was one of my crew members at Leadville during one of my later runs.

This race started out okay with only a hint of rain on the first major climb up Sugar Loaf which peaks at around eleven thousand feet. On the way up, Shirley needed to make a pit stop so she asked me to carry her bottles. She uses those extra big bottles, not the twenty-ounce size that most runners use. After what seemed like at least a mile, I got tired of carrying the extra weight so I asked her why she wasn't stopping to do her thing so I could get her to carry her own bottles. She claimed that she couldn't find a bush big enough to do what she needed to do. Finally I moved on up ahead of her and sat her bottles down in the middle of the trail and told her to carry her own damn bottles. She reminded me of how mean I was many times since then.

Later as she and I left the aid station at approximately twenty-three miles or so, we got caught in a torrential downpour. I was wearing a water resistant coat with a hood, water resistant pants, and gloves so I thought I would do okay in the heavy rain. Shirley was in back of me when it started and I turned to see how she was doing. She was trying to put on this 69 cent poncho and she had her head in the place where one of the arms was supposed to go. I back tracked a short distance to help her. We got separated somewhere shortly after that. The rain continued for the next twelve miles more or less and the trail became a quagmire and the small mountain streams had become torrents. When I came into the Twin Lakes aid station at the forty-mile point, I was soaked and cold. My water resistant suit didn't even begin to keep me dry. I went in the corner by the heater and completely undressed and put on all dry clothes, including my underwear. The good news was that when I left the aid station it had stopped raining and I was wearing dry warm clothes for my trek up to Hope Pass which peaks at over twelve thousand feet. The bad news was that when I went to cross the river, which was higher than usual due to the rain, I fell head first into the river and got completely wet again. But that wasn't as bad as it was for at least one of the lead female runners who came through earlier. They had provided a rope that was stretched across the swollen river to provide a safe crossing for the runners but she was unable to hold on and she was washed downstream for some distance before she came ashore. She was okay and was able to continue the race. The other bad news for me was that with all the concern about what to wear, I had forgotten to bring anything for energy for my trek up the mountain. I had two bottles of water and nothing more. I did get over the mountain to the turn around at Winfield but it was too late for me to consider turning around and heading back. In the meantime, Shirley had somehow passed me and made it back to Twin Lakes on the return part of the run where she also dropped out. Neither one of us was able to finish the race.

Although my batting average there is not so good, it was my favorite race. It was not just the run that made it my favorite but rather I think it was the whole experience. I loved Leadville and the mountains in Colorado. Every time I went there I went to the top of Mount Elbert at least one time as part of my training. I think the mountains and the people were the draw for me even though I found Leadville 100 the toughest run for me to finish of all the others.

While in a favorite restaurant in Leadville during one of my visits, I found myself in the presence of a popular and fairly well-known female ultra distance runner. She was thirty-five years old at the time and I was sixty-five. She acted a bit insulted when I told her that I had forgotten her name. So I said to her, "Call me when you are sixty-five." She said, "but you'll be ninety-five." I said "I know, but call me anyway. Tell me about your memory." I would tell you her name but I forgot it.

After only one successful finish followed by four incompletes at Leadville, I really wanted to make it all the way during the 1996 run. As usual, I was at Leadville camped outside of Jay Jones' Clublead and as the race day was rapidly approaching, I still did not have a full crew. My old friend Keith Grimes had agreed to run with me the first sixty miles but I needed someone to drive my RV and meet me at various aid stations late in the run. I also needed someone to run with me the last forty miles. I had previously found a note in my RV from a twenty-two-year-old Victoria's Secret model offering to run with me, but I knew that was Raul Flores up to his usual tricks, so that didn't help. However, when time was about to run out, I met this young lady at the breakfast table in Clublead who agreed to help me. It was Alise Pittman from Virginia, and she said that she was meeting her twin sister Alexia the next day, and they would take my RV and crew for me during the night hours. What a stroke of good luck. During the race, they met me at, of all places, Twin Lakes, and followed me all through the night. They also found Robin and Sarah Lidstone from Canada who agreed to run with me during the night hours. Thanks to a tremendous crew, I was able to finish.

There was one other special memory that I have from this 1996 race. When I was leaving Leadville early Monday morning after the race, a man stopped me on the street on my way out of town. He introduced himself as Mike Devlin from southern California. He told me the following story. He was at the Hope Pass Aid station on his way back from Winfield and on his way to Twin Lakes. The aid station is near the top of Hope Pass and is at roughly the fifty-five-mile point in the race. He saw me come in to the aid station on my way back to Twin Lakes. He said he watched me as I went around the corner and threw up and then came back again to finish my soup. He also was there when I tried to talk Bruce Mauldin into not dropping out. He said he watched me go down the mountain with my soda crackers and he thought there was no way that I would be able to finish. He dropped out of the race at that point and he later saw me come across the finish line. He was amazed, after seeing me at Hope Pass, that I was able to finish. He told me that from that day on he would use me for inspiration whenever he felt like dropping out of a one-hundred-miler. I told him that I owed the successful finish to a good crew.

The Grand Slam of Ultra Running:

In 1986, give or take a year, someone must have decided that there were not enough ways to beat up the body, so they instigated the Grand Slam. I think it was Thomas Green, MD, age thirty-five. He was the first runner to do the so called Grand Slam when he did it that year. It grew in numbers each year and by 1997 I was the eighty-first runner to join the ranks of the finishers in this event. Since then there have been quite a few more. Helen Klein was one of the runners to do it in 1989 at the age of sixty-six, and she and I, along with one other sixty-six-year-old man, whose name I don't know, were the three oldest runners at the time to have completed the Grand Slam.

An ultra runner who simply completes four specific trail 100s in the same summer is considered to have completed the Grand Slam. The four races that make up the Slam are: Old Dominion 100 in Virginia in late May, Western States 100 in California in late June, Leadville Tail 100 in Colorado in August, and Wasatch Front 100 in Utah in September. They allow Vermont 100 in July to be substituted for Old Dominion. For an old man like me, it's a little hard to recover from one event in time for the next event

Failed First Grand Slam Attempt

In 1994, Tom O'Connell and Janice O'Grady and I signed up for the Grand Slam but both Janice and I dropped out during the first of the four, the Western States 100. We were planning to do Vermont as one of the four 100s instead of Old Dominion. Bill Sunderland was making a big deal out of what the three of us were trying to do so he wrote an article in the Mercury News after each event. So when Tom was successful with the first of the four events, He wrote a nice article about how Tom finished. Then he also made a point of mentioning that Janice and I who were attempting the same thing, went belly up. Later, when Tom successfully finished Vermont 100, he once again wrote a story about Tom's success and then he mentioned, of course, how Janice and Ephraim bit the dust at Western States. Still Later, Tom successfully finished Leadville Trail 100 and then Wasatch 100 and Bill in both cases casually reminded the readers that Janice and Ephraim went belly up during the first event while Tom went on to finish all of them. It was funny the way Janice and I got so much publicity when we really didn't want it.

Second Try

I didn't tell Bill Sunderland, nor did I tell anyone else when I set out to do the Grand Slam in 1997. I went to Pennsylvania to see my siblings and while there I took a side trip to Front Royal, Virginia to do the first of the four, Old Dominion. There I met up with Alise and Alexia Pittman who came up from Virginia Beach to crew for me. They were identical twins who I had originally met at Leadville, Colorado and they had crewed for me there.

Old Dominion (First of the Four)

Old Dominion was billed as being the easiest of the four 100s but they had a cutoff time of twenty-eight hours. I was bit concerned about being able to make the cut off. The race started on the flat and after a few miles it climbed up to higher elevation. When I came to the first aid station which was about six miles or so, they were out of water. This sometimes happens, especially for back of the pack runners like me. So I drank coke. The race was set up so that we ran in a five mile circle from that first aid station which brought us back to the same station so I was glad to hear them say that more water was on the way. I though I would be okay with just coke for five miles. However, when I got back to the same aid station the second time, they were out of water. They did get more but by the time I got there, it was gone again. But they still had coke. I had no choice but to drink coke again and this time I filled both bottles with coke as well. However, I found that running with coke instead of water does not work so well. To make matters worse, I missed a turnoff before I got to the next aid station because I was running on the left side of the road facing traffic and they had put the ribbons on the other side of the road. I found myself at an intersection with no ribbons so I had to back track and this time I did find the turnoff. As a result of my error, it lengthened the time it took me to get to a station where I could get water and I was beginning to be dehydrated. However, I started drinking a lot when I finally got to an aid station with water and Alise and Alexia provided me with food (they even had chicken drumsticks) and drink for the rest of the distance. Later during the run, Alise ran with me from dusk to daylight over a mountain on a narrow trail in a heavily wooded area. During the entire night, we were essentially alone. We would only see other runners occasionally. She told me later that it was an experience she would never forget. She could hear animals running in the dark woods that she could not see. I finished in just under twenty-seven hours so I made the cutoff by over one hour.

Western States 100 (Second of the Four)

The Western States 100 was the next event and I almost dropped out before I got to the start line. We stayed in our cabin near Soda Springs the night before the race and I got sick. It was most likely nerves but it got so bad that I announced that I would not go to the start. In the morning, Dale Fambrini woke me up and talked me into at least trying it. So I showed up at the start with little hope of ever finishing. Once I got started, I felt better but it turned out to be a long day and a long night. Cindy Howes ran as my pacer from Duncan Canyon (twenty-four miles) to Dusty Corners (forty miles). Then Doug Bailey took over to Forest Hills (sixty-two miles) where Toni Mounts took over and was with me for the last thirty-eight miles which included almost all of the nighttime running and the river crossing. Toni would relate to me and others later that the experience was memorable to say the least and one that evoked a flood of emotions. At the American River, the runners and pacers are given assistance in making the crossing by volunteers in wetsuits and a taut steel cable. Both runners and pacers, with their fanny packs around there necks to keep them dry, will walk across the river in water depths that will vary from above the knee to waist high while holding on to the cable. After making the crossing, Toni and I stopped at the aid station on the other side to change our shoes and socks and have a cup of coffee. We both sat down on lawn chairs on a slanted surface and in the process my chair upset and I and my coffee landed right into Toni's lap. Thank goodness the coffee wasn't real hot so that we could laugh about it then and later. Near the end of the race, I was listing to starboard, which I often do because of a back problem. Because of my tilt, I had a tendency to keep running/walking off the trail to the right and Toni had to encourage me to straighten up and stay on the trail. I finished in twenty-nine hours and forty-five minutes, with just fifteen minutes to spare. The day after the race Toni took her husband down to the river to look at the crossing in the daylight. Her experience in running the thirty-eight miles at night and crossing the river in the dark must have provided for her a very special memory.

Leadville Trail 100 (Third of the Four)

Leadville Tail 100 was the next of the four and was the one race that I thought was the toughest for me. Being a flatlander, the elevation and the weather would always be my worst fear. My crew for this event was Raul Flores from Kansas, Alise Pittman of the Pittman twins from Virginia Beach, Virginia, Colleen Barill from Breckenridge, Colorado, and Ann Stuart also from Breckenridge, Colorado. There's no way I could ever thank all these people for all the help they gave me. This is just another race that I could never have done without the crew people. They met me at aid stations and they ran with me and gave me encouragement when I was down. After the first fifty miles to the turn around at Winfield, I was already tired and ready to quit. They took turns pacing me for the last fifty miles and kept me going. I finished the race in twenty-nine hours and thirty-two minutes. I was one very tired, and grateful runner.

Wasatch Front 100 (Last of the Four)

Wasatch Front 100 was the last event that I needed to complete the Grand Slam. It is considered the most difficult so they allow a more generous cut off time of thirty-six hours to complete instead of the twenty-eight-hour cutoff at Old Dominion and thirty hours for Leadville and Western States. I think that because of the extended time limit, it actually becomes the easiest to finish. When I went to Salt Lake City to do it, Alise Pittman from Virginia Beach, Jay Jones from Leadville, Colorado, and Keith Grimes from Silver Springs, Colorado agreed to crew for me. This was no easy task for either of them. It meant traveling away from home just to help me. I was humbled. This would be the fourth one-hundred-miler where Alise crewed for me including three of the four grand slam events. I knew Keith Grimes when he lived in San Jose before he moved to Colorado and this would be the third time that he crewed for me. Jay Jones owned and operated Clublead which was a bed-and-breakfast place in Leadville. All three of them met me at certain places along the course and all three paced me part way. Keith walked with me during the last part of the run which was the most difficult for a pacer because at that point I was pretty tired and cranky. I was paranoid about getting lost and when I didn't see a ribbon for some time I would start worrying. For slow runners like me, I often run for miles without seeing another runner. I kept asking Keith if we were still on the trail since I hadn't seen a ribbon or a runner for a long time. Keith finally got tired of telling me we were on the trail so he got a ribbon and tied it to his backside. When I asked him if he had seen any ribbons after that he would wave the backside ribbon at me. I finished Wasatch in thirty-five hours and twenty-three minutes just thirty-seven minutes before the cutoff. I was told sometime after, that I set a record for the Grand Slam. When you added up the margin to cutoff for my four runs, it was a record low.

I think that of the running events that I have participated in, I am most proud of being able to have finished the Grand Slam especially at the age of sixty-six. Those who finish the Grand Slam get a nice trophy. It's one of the few trophies that I display. One of the reasons that I am most proud of completing the Grand Slam is that I am not really a very good runner beyond the fifty-mile mark. I always felt that the fifty-mile distance was my best. When I was in my early fifties, I could actually run, without walking, all of a flat fifty-miler. In my early sixties, I could run a high percentage of the fifty-miler. However, I could never run much, if any, of the last twenty-five or more miles of the one-hundred-miler. If I finished, it was by walking the last miles and many times, I did not finish. There are many runners who actually can run pretty much all of the one hundred-mile distance. There are also runners in their sixties who have demonstrated their ability to run four or more one-hundred-milers in the same season. The German runner Hans-Dieter Weisshaar completed eighteen difficult one-hundred-milers in the same year when he was sixty-two. At last count, and still counting, he has completed well over sixty one hundred-mile events.

Here are a few interesting facts (more or less) about the Grand Slam. The average runner, will take approximately one million steps, will drink approximately twenty gallons of fluid, will encounter over seventy thousand feet of elevation increase and decrease, and will consume between thirty thousand to fifty thousand calories.

Badwater:

The original run was the brainchild of Tom Crawford of Santa Rosa, California. It was the outcome of a bar room bet. The primary consideration was that the event had to be one that would inflict the maximum amount of punishment on the participants. They agreed that the run had to be in the hottest time of the year (July) and had to start in the morning at

Badwater, the lowest point in the Western Hemisphere, so as to have the runners cross the hottest part of Death Valley at the hottest part of the day. The run would go from Badwater to Stove Pipe Wells in Death Valley, then through Panamint Valley to Panamint Springs and on through the mountains and more desert to Lone Pine. At Lone Pine it would go to the top of Mt. Whitney, which is the highest point in the Continental United States. Then they would turn around and go back to Badwater. The total distance would be around three hundred miles. They actually did this and books have been written about it.

The current Badwater race is a little more civilized. It starts at Badwater and goes to the trail head of Whitney which is at eight thousand feet and ends. The total distance is 135 miles. Runners may go to the top of Whitney if they get a permit and they do it on their own and not as part of the Badwater race.

I finished Badwater twice, once in 1998 and again in 1999. My time was just over fifty-three hours in both races. That's pretty slow. They have a cut off of sixty hours. The vast majority of the runners finish in under 48 hours. They made a Documentary in the 1999 run but I think that the most interesting one for me was the 1998 one. Here are some highlights of that run:

I used the 1998 run as a fund-raiser for the American Cancer Society and was able to obtain $3,500 in pledges.

I used my RV as our race vehicle. At least one or two members of the crew would always be in the RV. They would drive it some distance, usually one to two miles, ahead and park. During almost all of the way, one member walked with me and sprayed me when it was hot. The RV was never far away if needed. I had a crew of five people. They were my daughter Laura, Cindy Howes, Dorsey Moore, and Dale and Bonnie Fambrini.

The night before the race, the hotel at Stove Pipe Wells misplaced my Crew (except for my daughter Laura). They put them in the wrong room. It was cause for concern for me just before the race. They had also failed to give the crew a letter from me, which contained some important instruction.

During the race, it was hot (No kidding). It was in the midnineties at the start. It peaked at about 130°F in the "Death Zone" between Furnace Creek and Stove Pipe Wells. It stayed hot at night. It was about 115°F up on the mountain out of Stove Pipe Wells. This was demoralizing for me. I expected cool nights. I was always told that it got cold in the desert at night. It was still hot the next day. It did finally cool down the second night but got hot again on the hike up to Whitney.

My crew kept my white reflective clothes sprayed with cold water and used ice around the neck. A crewmember traveled with me almost all the time and used a small spray bottle to keep me cool. It was a bit like walking in a car wash. I could have used wiper blades on my glasses. At Furnace Creek, I fully submerged in the creek and ate chicken while submerged. At Stove Pipe Wells, I went into the pool with all my clothes on. At Panamint Springs and at Lone Pine, I took a shower.

I used approximately twenty Succeed Caps by the time we reached Stove Pipe Wells and about fifty total for the race. The crewmembers each took one Capsule every two hours, more during the hottest part of the day. Also, based on the crew records, I consumed nearly four gallons of fluids by the time we reached Stove Pipe Wells. I probably used another six gallons during the rest of the run for a total of about ten gallons of fluids. That's about eighty pounds of fluid (I only weighed 135 pounds). Besides pure water, fluids consisted of clip, Gator Aid, Kerns nectar, Ginger ale, V8, Sprite, and soda.

We used several hundred pounds of ice and enough water to float a battleship. My daughter Laura bought water in Stove Pipe Wells at $4.00/gallon. Ice was only $1.50 to $2.00 per bag which equals almost one gallon of water. Gasoline was only $1.50 per gallon. I never quite understood why ice and gasoline were much cheaper than water? Must have had something to do with being in Death Valley.

Coming up out of Stove Pipe Wells and while taking a short fifteen-minute nap, I had a dream that I was in an oven and couldn't get out. Dale Fambrini told me that is was not a dream. During the first day, the liner in one of our coolers exploded in the heat. I got discouraged and had stomach problems from about 45 miles to about 80 miles. The problem was being stressed from pushing up hill in the heat. But it was also due to being in a low mental state due to the heat. I expected cooler weather at night. I did better in the daytime because I expected it to be hot.

Denise Jones fixed my blistered feet at Panamint Springs and showed Laura and Dorsey Moore how to do it. This turned out to be beneficial later in the race.

Power GEL worked the best for me during my sick stomach period. Baby food and pudding made me well and we wished that we had tried it sooner. Cindy said I actually looked happy eating baby food.

During the hot part of the second day, Cindy handed out popsicles. Best I ever had. She gave some to runners who happened to be close by. For them, and for me, it was like a gift from heaven.

My crew would make soup for me and keep it in a thermos bottle for later. During the second night, Laura made me some fresh soup and put it in the thermos. She didn't realize that there was some soup left over from the first night still in the thermos that had gone somewhat rancid. I ate some of this soup, which tasted pretty good, and then the crew realized that it smelled like vomit. Later I complained of a slight stomach ache. They didn't tell me about the "Vomit Soup" until later.

At about a hundred miles, Dale Fambrini suggested that I should change shoes. So I did. I ran the last thirty-five miles or so with no further shoe changes. The next day I realized that the shoes didn't match. The right shoe was from an old pair that I considered warn out.

To be more visible to cars, I used lights that resembled two "Bug Eyes" on my head during the night.

We flagged out at ninety-eight miles and went into the Motel at Lone Pine for foot repair, some rest and a shower. While there, we found out that eight feet of clearance was not enough for our RV. We took out one of our roof vents. Also, on the return to our flag to take up the race again, we had trouble finding the flag.

We did not use the RV refrigerator due to the inability to keep the RV level. We tried to keep all of our food in coolers. Eventually, most of our food spoiled. As a result, we had fewer choices of things to eat during the last part of the run.

Dorsey Moore sang to me while we walked together at night down the desolate road that runs through the desert. We also recited poetry to each other and looked at the stars, Milky Way, and shooting stars. At one point during the day he hid in the bushes and stalked us while dressed like a savage when we walked by.

On the second night of the run, my hallucinations seemed almost real. I could see perfect circles and other geometric objects. I continued to see rows of tall buildings beside the highway. I was seeing them all through the night. As we came through Keeler, I told someone about the buildings that I was seeing in my hallucinations. I told them that I was still seeing them. I was told that we were passing through Keeler and those buildings that I was seeing were real. I was to the point where I had trouble distinguishing the difference between hallucinations and real.

While walking by myself and looking at the stars, on several occasions, I heard and felt a change in footing as my feet hit the gravel to the side of the road. It was a lot like falling asleep while driving and the tires hit the gravel.

I avoided caffeine before and during the race except at night. I would take some surge when I felt sleepy and it seemed to work because it was loaded with caffeine. I had taken two of these during the second night and Cindy Howes, seeing how well it worked, decided to have one herself.

But she got the bottles mixed and gave the surge to me. It was my third one in a row. I drank it and didn't have any problem staying awake the rest of the night.

Laura had problems with an abscessed tooth all through the run. She also has problems with riding on steep curvy roads, so much so that she preferred walking with me on the up hills rather than riding in the RV. During the race, she covered about thirty miles, including the entire hike up from Lone Pine. She and Cindy hiked the last miles up to Whitney and sang and joked all the way. They kept me smiling.

Her tooth problem which all stemmed from the Crater Lake accident in 1971 required oral surgery shortly after the race. During the entire race period, she got very little sleep while taking penicillin and pain pills and did not complain even though many times she had a lot of pain.

Comradery among the different crews was great. One crew would wait for us and spray us and encourage us on, even though they were not our crew. Another crew found out we needed ice and they came to offer us some.

The following year I did Badwater again and finished in essentially the same time. In this event Mike Paradise and Fred Hornbruck crewed for me. Ron Nelson had planned to be part of the crew but after driving all the way to Death Valley he had to turn around and drive back to San Jose due to a family emergency so he was unable to be there during the race. This was the year that they did the documentary on the race which they called *Running on the Sun*.

Bill Barclay at Auburn Lakes Trail:

Bill Barclay was my pacer at Western States 100 during one of my successful runs. He ran with me during the nighttime hours from Forest Hills to the finish. We were on a really good pace as we came into Auburn Lakes Trail which had a cutoff of about 0630 in the morning. I think that we got there about 0300 so we had a lot of time to spare. However, I was tired and felt like a little shut eye would give me a lift. I asked if I could use a cot and a sleeping bag, and could they wake me at 0500 or sooner. The nice lady said that they could handle my request. Then I asked for the same thing for my pacer. They were agreeable to that request as well.

So I snuggled down in the borrowed sleeping bag and anticipated a good hour or so of restful sleep. However, it was a cold night probably in the forties and the sleeping bag that I was in was not warm enough for me. In the meantime, I was looking over at Bill sleeping like a baby. At that point, I noticed that his sleeping bag was real thick and apparently designed for use somewhere around the Arctic Circle. Mine on the other hand appeared to have been designed for the equator. As a result, I lay there shivering for about an hour while Bill slept like a baby.

Just before 0500, the lady brought us a nice hot cup of coffee. Even though I didn't sleep much, I did get some good rest. The aid station people were the best. They didn't realize that I was such a woos. By the way, I am probably exaggerating a little about my thin sleeping bag. All my life I have been complaining about inadequate sleeping bags so I think that maybe the problem is not the bag so much as it is the sleeper in the bag.

The Oscar Meyer Weiner Song:

Bill Eilers was going up the hill about halfway through the Quicksilver 50K when an opportunity for retaliation occurred. Up ahead moving at a pretty slow pace and clearly hurting was a runner who had on several occasions over the past two decades sang the Oscar Meyer Weiner song to him. This was a chance to return the humiliating favor. There was a young female runner near him at the time so he felt it necessary to explain to her what he was about to do. He explained to her that the runner they were about to overtake was this old geezer who had on a number of occasions in the past overtaken certain runners (including Bill himself) late in races in which they had gone out too fast and then hit the wall. When the old geezer would pass by, instead of talking he would sing the Oscar Meyer Weiner song and then keep going. It was meant to be entertaining and was not meant as an insult. So the young lady understood and they passed the old runner and Bill sang a few lines in passing. However, Bill made the mistake of singing the song too soon because it would provide too much time for the old geezer to recover.

When this happened, I (the old geezer) said in a very loud voice, "I'm gonna get you, Eilers. There's fifteen miles to go so there's plenty of time for me to catch you." For the next ten or so miles I chased him and when I could see him in the distance I would yell at him. As I was coming into the aid station manned by Sid and Peggy Melbourne for example I saw Eilers leaving and I yelled, "Eilers, I'm gonna get you, you can run but you can't hide." Sid heard me say that and he responded with, "that's interesting, I can hide but I can't run." Finally with only a few miles to go, I caught up with Bill and this time instead of singing the song, I suggested that we go in to the finish line together. Unfortunately, I saw Dick Lane, another of my running nemesis, up ahead so I had to go get Dick. I finished ahead of both Dick and Bill. Bill has been heard telling this story many times since. He sang the Weiner song too early.

Lee and Violet:

While leaving the aid station at the Fish Hatchery during my 1997 Leadville Trail 100 run I heard a muffled voice coming from a cot in the corner of the tent. This was at the approximate 77 mile point in the race. The voice was that of Lee Schmidt which surprised me because Lee was as tough as nails and one would not expect to see him in a cot. He said, "Can I get into your RV, I'm dropping out?" I responded by saying, "Get your fat behind out of that bunk and get on up the trail. I am instructing the twins to lock the door if they see you coming." I left the aid station and started up Sugarloaf not knowing if Lee dropped or not but I couldn't imagine that he did. About halfway up the mountain, Lee passed me. He went on to finish well ahead of me.

When Lee got to Leadville, as was his tradition, he put on a dress jacket and hat and ran across the finish line with Violet. He had been doing that routine for each of his Leadville Trail 100 finishes.

The following year I went to Leadville to visit and help others but not to run. I helped at the 100 mile bike race and then volunteered to crew for Ron Vetrees during the foot race. Ron had found two women who had agreed to meet him at Twin Lakes to assist him the rest of the way. I agree to be available with my RV. As it turned out, Ron missed the cutoff at Twin Lakes so I decided to help Lee instead.

I met Lee at the seventy-seven-mile mark, where he was in the cot the previous year which I spoke about above. I left my RV at the Fish Hatchery and ran with him the rest of the way. When we got to the aid station called May Queen, Lee stopped to pick up a back pack which contained a small box. I volunteered to carry it for him the rest of the way. When we got near the finish line, he asked me to give him the back pack which contained the small box. He hadn't told me, but I knew what was in the box. He wore the back pack with the small box containing Violet's ashes as he crossed the finish line. So Lee and Violet crossed the finish line together for the last time.

Lee and Violet had been regulars at Leadville for the 100 mile race for several years. Everyone knew both of them, especially Violet. They would both come to town early so that Lee could acclimate and do some training. They would stay at Clublead each year. When they would arrive, Lee would go to one of the bunk beds that had been reserved for him. Violet would come in and would go immediately to her assumed bed as well. Digger, Jay Jones's Dalmatian, would automatically give up his bed when Violet arrived. She would use Digger's bed for the duration of their stay.

After the 1998 finish, Lee went to the local Animal Shelter and found another dog. It was a dog that someone else had rejected. Whereas some people spend big bucks, like $1,000 for special breeds, this dog was of no special breed and was probably almost free.

Before I left Leadville during that trip, I heard the story that some anonymous donor had given $1,000 to the Animal Shelter. I wonder who that could have been.

Other Benefits from Running/Walking:

After I started running, I found that there were other benefits that come from running. For example, for several years I ran to and from work. I lived about seven miles from work so I would park my little RV in the parking lot at work from Monday morning until Friday afternoon. The rest of the week I would run to and from work while using the company shower facilities and the RV as my wardrobe.

On trips, business or pleasure, I would also manage to get in a run and sometimes it provided more opportunities than driving. Once on a trip to Rome, I got up early on a Saturday morning and I ran all around the Coliseum and the Vatican before the crowds arrived. I had a camera, a map, and cab fare if needed.

On vacation trips, I have used running to locate places to go. For example, when Jean and I would arrive at a hotel, or campsite if we are traveling with the RV, I would go for a run right after we arrived and look for a good restaurant or some other places of interests for that night or the next day.

When Jean and I went on a vacation trip with the RV, we would stay overnight at some campsite along the main route that we were traveling. Or we might in some cases just park along the road. In either case, I would often get up early in the morning and take off running along the road in the direction that we were heading and I would tell her to pick me up in two hours. Then when she picked me up, we would go on to the next town and have a big breakfast.

After I retired, it seemed like I was spending more time running in the city. For example, instead of driving to the Spa each time that I went, I would leave the car at home sometimes and I would run instead. The round trip was eight miles. Since I was going to the Spa in part for exercise, running seemed to make a lot of sense. They had a large parking lot there so when I did take the car, I would use one of the spaces at the far end of the parking lot and walk to the front door. I always found it amusing to see the young studs with the muscular upper bodies and their big classy cars competing for parking spaces near the door. Out where I usually park there are always plenty of empty spaces. Actually I think that many of the spaces had never been used.

Since I was generally not pressed for time, when the need for going someplace in town arose, I used the car only if running, walking, bike riding, light rail, bus, or train wouldn't work. If I needed to go to the post office, running was the way to go. If I needed something small at the hardware store, I would run or walk or take the bicycle. If Jean talked me into grocery shopping, I would use the three-wheeled bike with the basket in the back if it was not a big order. The three-wheeled bike is very heavy and provides an excellent leg workout. If I had to take the car, I would almost always pull into the first parking spot I saw and then walk to the front door. They have grocery carts so I figure why not use them.

I often thought that if everyone used this same philosophy of using the feet and legs more and the car less, we would go a long way toward solving our traffic congestion concerns. The extra walking would also help solve the overweight problem.

Legends:

Jesse Owens in my mind was a running legend because in 1936 he won four gold metals at the Berlin Olympics, and in so doing he did serious damage to Hitler's image of the Nazi Aryan superiority.

Although he was not a runner, I regard Joe Lewis as a legend, because like Jesse Owens he essentially destroyed the myth of Aryan superiority when he fought Max Schmeling in 1938.

For me, there is a lot more to this story than just the knockout. Joe Lewis and Max Schmeling first met in the ring in 1936. Lewis lost the bout in twelve rounds. My pop was a big boxing fan and he listened to that fight on the radio. I probably did too but I was only five or six at the time so I am not sure that I was there. I am quite sure that we all listened to the bout in 1938. The entire country listened to that fight. This was a fight of international importance. Before the fight took place, President Roosevelt spoke with Lewis. At that time, Roosevelt knew that Hitler was on the march with his insane plan of taking over the world. We can make a pretty good guess at what Roosevelt had to say during that conversation. Lewis came into the ring with the knowledge that the USA, including the President, was counting on him to win. And win he did. He knocked Schmeling out in just over two minutes of the first round.

Unfortunately, history had for a long time remembered Schmeling as a Nazi sympathizer. However, we now know that this was not the case. Schmeling actually put himself at great risk during the war by harboring Jews in his room which undoubtedly saved them from the Holocaust.

Also, when Joe Lewis died in 1981 he was not a wealthy man. Max Schmeling not only came to Lewis's funeral but he actually helped pay for it. Schmeling died in 2005 at the age of ninety-nine.

When speaking of Running Legends, one would be remiss if Emil Zatopek wasn't at the top of the list. I admired him long before I started running. He won Olympic gold for the 5K in 1948 but I am not sure that I knew that at the time. However, in 1952 he won gold for the 5K and gold for the 10K and then he decided he would run the marathon. It was his first marathon and he won that as well. Three gold metals in the same year. Can you imagine the enormity of what he did? Especially winning the marathon when it was his first one ever.

Zatopek's training routine was considered extreme and much of what runners do today was learned from him. He did interval training to the extreme. He was often found holding his breath to train his body to thrive on less oxygen (like training at high altitude). He worked during the day and would then run at nights in the snow wearing boots and carrying a flashlight. He believed that if you want to run fast in a race, you have to run fast when training. At one time, he held every world record from the 5K through the 30K. When he won the marathon in 1952, his time then was also a world record. When he raced, he would always put everything he could into the race. He was once quoted as saying, "If I'm standing at the finish line, I will be the winner."

In the late sixties, he spoke out against the communists and as a result, he was forced to work in a uranium mine and do other menial tasks such as cleaning toilets.

After he died in November 2000, he was named the "Czech Sporting Legend of the Century."

Special Memories From My Days of Running:

I have often been asked why I run and especially why I run the long distance runs. I usually have a different answer each time the question is asked but probably the best answer is that running makes memories. It takes less than thirty hours to run one of the one hundred-mile trail runs, but in that one thirty-hour period a flood of memories is generated for the runners and for the pacers and volunteers as well. Ross Waltzer once told me that when you get old, all you have are your memories. I hope that I am not that old yet but there is something in what he said.

One of my very best memories is of my second fifty-miler, the American River 50 in April of 1982. In that run alone, there would be at least three things that stand out in my memory.

Jean, Gary and Marie, and Laura were there and they met me at a number of aid stations along the way. When they saw me at the midpoint of the race, I was ahead of my nemesis Gene Silver but according to Gary there was another over fifty-year-old runner ahead of me. I asked Gary, "What is the color of his shirt?" "Yellow" was the reply. That question impressed Laura and she suddenly became a more active participant in the race. She told me later that she knew I wanted to finish ahead of Silver but my question regarding the man with the yellow shirt made her realize that I was also going for the fifty-year-old man ahead. I was going for the age group win. Several miles down the road I passed the man in the yellow shirt.

Later, with about ten miles to go, Gary joined me as a pacer. As we went down the trail with him as my pacer, he told me excitedly that I was just a short distance behind the leaders. As we passed non runners along the trail, Gary would call out "that's my dad, he's fifty-one years old," and the people would look puzzled like, "what's that all about?" His enthusiasm made me very proud.

I finished the race in seven hours and six minutes and was the first fifty-year-old to finish. The man with the yellow shirt was Roger Daniels who was actually not yet fifty. He and Gene Silver came in about a half hour later. I was the fourteenth runner overall. Wendel Robie presented me with a first place plaque for the fifty-year age group and he congratulated me and said "I wish I could have seen you run as a young man." I said, "I never ran as a young man, so what you see is all there ever was." The plaque was one of my favorite and I gave it to Gary.

Although I finished ahead of Roger Daniels and Gene Silver, in subsequent American River races they would both improve on my time by finishing in under seven hours.

Here are a few more of the flood of memories that I spoke of earlier:

- Tricia running a Marcha Lunga in Italy with me and then both of us appearing on TV after.
- Tricia and Laura trying to sleep on the bare ground at the river crossing at the Western States 100 in the middle of the night when the temperature was in the low forties.
- While Laura's friend Mike and Tricia's friend Leslie were sleeping together (in separate sleeping bags) in the car, Tricia and Laura were in one sleeping bag at the 49 crossing at WS-100 trying to get

some sleep but finding it necessary to sit up every time a runner came in to see if it was me.
- Having Dick Baker come all the way from Georgia to pace me from the 49 crossing to the finish line. He asked Jean when she thought I would be coming in to the 49 crossing aid station and she said that it would be sometime after 12:00. He stood by the trail in just shorts and tee shirt with the temperature dropping into the low forties from midnight until I came in at 8:00 in the morning. When I came in I asked him if he was enjoying the run so far.
- Going in the RV with Cindy Howes and Dale Fambrini all the way to Foresthill to do one of Norm Klein's night training runs only to find out that it had been cancelled due to snow. We ran anyway and nearly froze various body parts in doing so.
- Taking the bus ride to Robinson Flat or to the Green gate to the start of Norm Klein's WS-100 training runs. All the buses would be packed with runners who had made it a point to be hydrated prior to the start of the run. When the buses reached their destination, the runners would literally explode out of the bus to empty their kidneys. The boys would go on one side of the road and the girls on the other to pee in the bushes.
- Loading up on fluids after finishing the American River fifty-miler and then taking the bus from the finish line back to the start with a bladder ready to burst. On one of these events, I was just about to use Gene Weddle's water bottle when we finally reached the porta-potties.
- Camping out along the river near Arcadia and then running the Mad River fifty-miler. It was a "low-key" run with self serve aid stations. There were only eight people running the fifty-miler. Most runners quit at the 50K distance. I was there with Jean and son Tom. I ran the last nineteen miles without seeing a living person. When I came into the finish line, I had to wake the finish line attendant to tell him my finish time. Jean was asleep, or reading a book in the RV and Tom was fishing.
- Camping out in the RV in a rain storm in Washington State the night before the CleElum 50K run. There was an open space available to camp but the place was a sea of mud due to all the rain. There was only one other person camped besides Jean and I and He was in a small pup tent. We invited him in for a hot drink in the evening and then told him to come back in the morning for breakfast. It was Scott Jurak before he became famous by winning Western States seven times in a row and setting a course record during one of those finishes.

- My singing the Oscar Meyer wiener song to certain of my running friends late in races after they had gone out too fast and then faded so that I was able to catch up with them.
- Bill Eilers and I sharing a bed in a hotel in Sacramento the night before the California International Marathon. Bill was sharing a room with two beds with Greg Martin and while they were out to dinner, I managed to get into their room and was having a nap on Bill's bed when they returned. I didn't have a place to stay that night so Bill allowed me to sleep with him. For a long time afterward, every time that I would see Bill in a crowd, I would give him a big hug and kiss and would tell him how cute he was and how much I enjoyed sleeping in the same bed with him.
- Donna Allenbaugh showing me how to dress for the Colorado mountains by throwing all of the cotton shirts out of my drop bags and replacing them with shirts and jackets made from polypro or equivalent. She ran with me the last fifty miles the first time that I did Leadville 100 and helped me make it to the finish line in well under twenty-nine hours.
- Finding the Pittman twins, Alise and Alexia, to crew for me at Leadville and Old Dominion and then to have Alise come back to Leadville and Wasatch during my Grand Slam participation. They also found Sarah and Robin Lidstone from British Columbia to run in with me the last forty miles at Leadville.
- Having Keith Grimes, first from San Jose and later from Colorado, run the first sixty miles of Leadville with me and then to come to Wasatch and pace me with a ribbon hanging off of his rear end to ease my paranoia enabling me to finish the grand slam.
- Raul Flores toilet papering my RV outside of Club Lead in Leadville, Colorado. I cleaned up all of the toilet paper and put it in a bag and put it by my toilet in the RV to be used as toilet paper as it was meant to be used. Later when Alise and Alexia Pittman, whom I had just barely met, crewed for me using the RV they saw the bag of unfolded toilet paper by the toilet and though it was a strange way to keep toilet paper. The actual roll of toilet paper was out of sight inside of a door so they thought the unfolded paper in the bag was my normal way of keeping toilet paper.
- Finding a note in my RV from a twenty-two-year-old Victoria's Secret model offering to pace me in the race. Unfortunately, the handwriting was clearly that of Raul Flores.
- Raul Flores and Merilee O'Neal toilet papering my room and short sheeting my bed in the house where I was staying while there to

train and do the race. It had been a long time since I had been short sheeted so it took me some time to figure out why I couldn't get into bed after the party we had just had. I think that I ended up sleeping on top of the covers.
- Remembering my crew man Terry Clow eating both drumsticks from the chicken I had made available for one of the Leadville events. I told him earlier that I especially like the drumsticks and asked him to have them available later during the run.
- Bob Gilbert waking me at ten o'clock on the night before the run when I had to get up at 3:00 in the morning to tell me that he would see me in the morning.
- Cindy Howes and I running through Volcano Canyon in the dark without a flashlight during one of the Western States 100 events.
- Hearing Ken "Cowman" Shirk mooing on the way to Robinson Flat during one of the Western States 100 events.
- Finding Jay Jones lying in the fetal position halfway up Hope Pass. Keith Grimes, my pacer, helped him to get up and get going again. Jay had momentarily forgotten that he was on a tight schedule to make the Winfield cutoff.
- Seeing Lee Schmidt carrying the ashes of his dog Violet across the finish line at the Leadville Trail 100.
- Having Dale Fambrini go out shopping for chicken broth at midnight when I was not feeling well on the eve of the Western States 100. He did this for me even though he was also running in the race and it meant sacrificing some of his sleep time.
- Running with Gene Sliver in the Western States 100 and trying to drop out at the aid station known as California 2. Tom Crawford was the station Captain and he wouldn't let us drop out. We asked for a chair and he said they were all full. We asked for a blanket and he said they were all taken. We asked for a cot and he said they were all occupied. We said we wanted to drop out and he told us that it was a three hour ride out on horse back. I told Silver that it looks like it would be easier to keep going which is what we did.
- Having Dena Noble's daughter use me for show and tell in her first grade class room when the class was learning about the number 100. I was being presented as a person who ran 100 miles. The kids didn't seem to be very interested but the teacher was fascinated.
- A real special memory was when Tricia arranged for me to give a talk to Emily's second-grade class on running the "Grand Slam." I went there dressed in appropriate running garb, my fanny pack and

my head light. I also wore my Leadville shirt which had the words "there are no short cuts" on the front and an altitude profile on the back. The elevation of the mountains was somewhat to scale but the distance of one hundred miles was compressed down to twelve inches which made the mountains look extremely steep. The kids were very interested in what it was like running at night and over the tall mountains. They later sent me notes of appreciation with sketches which showed me looking like a stick man running up these almost vertical slopes with a light shining off of my head. Their sketches were priceless.

- Running with Emily's class in middle school when I was over seventy and having some of the boys trying, usually successfully, to stay ahead of me.
- Having Jean and other family members being at aid stations and the finish line during long runs just for the support.
- Having my daughter Laura run marathons and fifty-kilometer races with me during my declining years.

Winding Down:

When I reached the age of seventy, I usually had a pretty good chance to win my age group since as was the case most of the time, I was the only runner in the race over the age of seventy. When people commented on this, as did my nephew the Lawyer Ken Johnson, I would remind them that I beat all those over the age of seventy people who were absent because they were in nursing homes, or were at home on the couch watching football, or were too fat to run, or were dead.

As I approached seventy and eventually reached and went beyond seventy, I continued to enter long distance runs. I had completed the American River 50 about thirteen times and I always thought that I was good for one more time. The last time I was entered, I made it to the nineteen-mile mark and the trail sweep passed me.

At age seventy-three, I entered the Helen Klein 50 which is a flat run so I thought surely I can do that. I missed the cutoff time at the twenty-five-mile turn around.

The last three times that I was entered in the Western States 100, I never made it to the start line. On one of these attempts, Laura and I along with Karen and Larry Prowd went for a hike on the Pacific Crest Trail two days before the start of the race. We were hiking toward the Peter Grubb hut when my stomach started to hurt. I told them to go on without me and I would be waiting for them at the car. When they got back, I was curled up in the back seat in severe pain. They rushed me to the hospital where they gave me morphine and shoved a tube down into my stomach. It was the old Meckel's diverticulum problem popping up at the most inopportune time once again.

I have been asked at times why it is that I ran all these years and never had any problems with my knees. My response has been that I never played football, soccer, baseball, tennis or any sport that requires lateral movements which puts undue stress on the knees. I have always believed that the evolutionary process of man included long distance running in a straight line in order to catch food.

At the time of this writing, I am seventy-four and I still log about thirty-five miles a week. But the miles I log are a combination of walking and moseying. I can't honestly call what I do running anymore. Even so, I still like to do 50Ks on trails that have generous cut off times. It now takes me seven or eight hours or more to complete a 50K if I have a good run. During my so called training runs, I now try to maintain a twelve minute/mile pace at least when I first start. The pace usually drops closer to a fifteen minute/mile pace after an hour or so. When I was at my peak running condition, I would be embarrassed if I couldn't maintain a comfortable seven minute/mile pace or better for at least one hour.

Laura started to run with me a few years ago and has completed about five marathons and six 50Ks. She is now recuperating from knee surgery, and when she gets back to running, I look forward to running with her again.

I recently went to my doctor, and I said, "Doctor, I'm not feeling very well. When I try to run, I feel like an old man." My doctor looked at me in a humorous way and said, "You are an old man."

This sketch was by Emily's classmate in second grade after I talked to them about running the Grand Slam.

This photo shows my crew at Leadville during the 1996 Leadville Trail 100. In the back from left to right are: Robin Lidstone, Alise Pittman, Sarah Lidstone, Keith Grimes, and Alexia Pittman.

This is me coming back across Hope Pass during the 1996 run.

My Badwater crew during the 1998 event. From left to right in the photo are Dorsey Moore, Bonny Fambrini, Dale Fambrini, me, Laura, and Cindy Howes

Cooling down in an irrigation ditch while having lunch (chicken drumstick) at Furnace Creek which was seventeen miles into the Badwater run. The temperature was in the 120s.

Finishing WS-100 in 1997. Running on my right is Toni Mounts who ran with me for the last thirty-eight miles. On my left is Cindy Howes who was with me from twenty-four miles, to about forty. Doug Bailey also ran with me from mile 40 to 62. Notice that I am listing to starboard as is often the case with me due to lower back problems.

BVG